John Gay
and the
London Theatre

John Gay and the London Theatre

CALHOUN WINTON

THE UNIVERSITY PRESS OF KENTUCKY

Copyright © 1993 by The University Press of Kentucky

Scholarly publisher for the Commonwealth,
serving Bellarmine College, Berea College, Centre
College of Kentucky, Eastern Kentucky University,
The Filson Club, Georgetown College, Kentucky
Historical Society, Kentucky State University,
Morehead State University, Murray State University,
Northern Kentucky University, Transylvania University,
University of Kentucky, University of Louisville,
and Western Kentucky University.
Editorial and Sales Offices: Lexington, Kentucky 40508-4008

Library of Congress Cataloging-in-Publication Data

Winton, Calhoun.
    John Gay and the London theatre / Calhoun Winton.
        p.   cm.
    Includes bibliographical references and index.
    ISBN 0-8131-1832-8 (alk. paper)
    1. Gay, John, 1685-1732. Beggar's opera. 2. Gay, John,
1685-1732—Stage history—England—London.   3. Theater—
England—London—History—18th century.   I. Title.
PR3473.B6W56   1993
822'.5—dc20   92-39204

This book is printed on recycled acid-free paper meeting
the requirements of the American National Standard
for Permanence of Paper for Printed Library Materials.

Contents

For MONROE K. SPEARS
Friend and Mentor over Four Decades

Acknowledgments

My thanks are due to the institution where I teach, the University of Maryland at College Park. This book began with a semester research grant from what was then the Division (now the College) of Arts and Humanities and concluded with a sabbatical semester from the university itself. As Bob Scholes said about a book of his own, without which not. My department, English, has also given me support in various ways—not least the use of a fine laser printer—under the benevolent chairs Richard Cross, Deirdre David, and Eugene Hammond, whom I thank here individually. With the leadership of President William E. Kirwan and Provost Robert Dorfman, this campus has continued—in very adverse economic circumstances—to be a fine place to teach and pursue research.

I am grateful to the Folger Shakespeare Library and especially to its pleasant and knowledgeable staff. Most of the research for this book was done in the Folger's matchless collections. The Huntington Library was the site of the very beginning and the very end of research for this book, and I am grateful. Fellow scholars, and now friends, Yvonne Noble and Dianne Dugaw have given me important guidance at critical junctures. Shirley Strum Kenny, friend and colleague for more than thirty years, read the completed manuscript with the care of which only she is capable. My indebtedness to other scholars, important as it is, must be indicated by their presence in the endnotes. Remaining errors of omission and commission in the book, it goes without saying, are my own.

My gratitude, also, to His Grace the Duke of Buccleuch and Queensberry for permitting me to work in the manuscript collections at Drumlanrig Castle, with the expert guidance of Mr. A. Fisher, Archivist.

Two learned friends, Charlot Schaffner and Dorothy Bilik, have read parts of the manuscript and given me the benefit of their critical acumen. Martin and Ruthe Battestin, friends of very long standing, offered practical encouragement at a time when it was most needed. Sir Peter and Lady Thornton—Pete and Ros—have provided warm hospitality and friendship for so long now during my research trips to England that I am afraid they think I take such for granted, as I certainly do not.

To borrow George Garrett's words, I also want to thank a few close kin and a few close friends, who have kept the faith. They know who they are. George and Susan are of course among that select group. My continuing debt to Monroe Spears, and to Betty, is expressed in the dedication. My immediate family—Elizabeth, Jay, Peggy, and Will—pose a special problem when it comes to thanks. If I were to become sentimental here—as they deserve—my effusions would be greeted with that laughter which makes life with them so pleasant. I will, then, simply say love and thanks—they have been there when it counted, always.

Introduction

My guiding assumption in writing this book has been that most persons who know anything about the theatre in English know something about *The Beggar's Opera*—and that a great many of them cherish it as one of their favorite experiences in the drama. But as I have argued elsewhere, the very fame of John Gay's masterpiece has so dominated the landscape of his reputation that many of those same theatregoers are not aware he wrote anything else. The book, then, is intended as an introduction to John Gay in his role as dramatic author, and to the theatre for which he composed his plays, that is, the London stage between about 1705, when as a mercer's apprentice in the Strand he must have become conscious of the theatre world around him, and 1733, when his last plays were prepared for production after his death.

Gay was full of focused ambition for a career in the theatre, at least as early as his first adult days in London following his apprenticeship. He never lost that ambition: he left behind him three plays virtually ready to be acted, and one of them was produced soon after he died. For the last twenty years of his life there is scarcely a period as long as a year or two in which he was *not* working on something for the London theatre. *The Beggar's Opera*, far from being some kind of freak, produced more or less by accident on an occasion when Gay, "favorite of the wits," tore himself away from his fashionable friends, was instead a most successful experiment in a career devoted to dramatic experiment. The three plays he left at his death, for example, appear to have been designed

individually for different theatres: one for the legitimate
stage at Drury Lane, one for an experimental house such as
Little Haymarket, and one for the musical theatre at Covent
Garden. This was at a time when, in the closing years of a successful literary career, he could easily have chosen to live on
his winnings, to enjoy the financial rewards from production
and printing that *The Beggar's Opera* and its unproduced but
sensational sequel *Polly* had brought him. Instead he was
working on his plays to the very end: in the last letter of his
that has been preserved, written less than three weeks before
his death, Gay assured Swift that "I have not been [idle]
while I was in the country," referring to the plays he was then
trying to get in shape for rehearsal.

His earliest dramatic piece, *The Mohocks*, was itself a
bold experiment, a musical farce afterpiece set in London,
which looked ahead in a number of respects to the *Opera*, but
which was caught in the political turmoil of 1712 and never
reached the stage. It introduced Gay as a lyricist, however, if
only in the printed version, and started the career of associating words with music which would evoke his special artistic gifts. Working with and learning from Handel, the
greatest composer resident in Britain, provided him an opportunity unique in the history of English literature and, I
will argue, Gay took full advantage of that opportunity. The
association began probably with the production of Handel's
first opera in England, *Rinaldo*, in 1710, even before Gay ini-
tiated his own career in the drama.

The Wife of Bath, his second play, is an engaging contribution to the revival of interest in Chaucer and his works
which the young poets Pope, Gay, and Prior, following Dryden's lead, were helping to bring about during the reign of
Queen Anne, three centuries after their great predecessor's
death. Theirs was a poetic rather than a scholarly or antiquarian enthusiasm; Gay presents the poet in action, as it
were, including Chaucer as a principal character in his play.
It is, one might properly say, a literary play, with echoes of
Shakespeare as well as Chaucer, written when Gay was attempting to find his own poetic voice. *The Wife* also embodies

some of the country that John Gay brought with him from his native Devon: folklore, folk customs, and folk dialect. These country things would reappear in his comic pastoral, *The Shepherd's Week*, which he was working on while he was composing *The Wife of Bath*, and in his farce afterpiece, *The What D'Ye Call It*.

The What D'Ye Call It is a performance play, a play about putting on a play; its subtitle, *A Tragi-Comi-Pastoral Farce*, of course carries one back to Hamlet and his Players. The reflexivity of performance plays interested Gay throughout his career: *The Beggar's Opera* obviously represents the performance of an opera composed by the Beggar. One of his posthumous plays, *The Rehearsal at Goatham*, uses the performance motif for a satire on dramatic censorship. *The What D'Ye Call It* was Gay's first theatrical hit; after an excellent initial run it entered the standard London repertory as an afterpiece and remained there through the eighteenth century and into the nineteenth. Music was a prominent feature: one of the ballads with music by Handel became an enduring popular favorite.

The What D'Ye Call It was also the first of Gay's plays in which his fellow members of the Scriblerus Club, Alexander Pope and Dr. John Arbuthnot, had a hand. The extent of their contributions cannot now be determined, but the mock-learned preface with its straight-faced analysis of what goes into making a tragi-comi-pastoral farce could be included directly in the Club's *Memoirs of Martinus Scriblerus*. Into the afterpiece itself is woven a tissue of allusions to the tragic drama; Gay here demonstrates his mastery of literary burlesque which he had employed earlier, to a lesser extent, in both *The Mohocks* and *The Wife of Bath*.

Although Gay stayed away from topical references to politics in *The What D'Ye Call It*, the afterpiece gave form to a broad satire on the corruption of justice. In his next play, *Three Hours After Marriage*, Gay narrowed the scope of the satire and shifted the setting back to contemporary London. Full of verve and satiric venom, of all Gay's plays this full-length mainpiece shows most clearly the Scriblerian influence, and in fact Gay acknowledges in the preface to the printed play his indebtedness to Pope and Arbuthnot, though he does not name them. Two of the characters were transparently recognizable: Fossile as the eccentric physician and antiquary Dr. Robert Woodward and Sir Tremendous as the literary critic John Dennis, both longtime victims of Pope's satiric muse. The dialogue is racy and Gay's introduction of a mummy and a walking crocodile produced some memorable farce scenes. The play had a successful initial run in 1717 at the Drury Lane theatre but organized opposition, some of it by satiric targets of the farce, brought about its premature closing after seven performances to large, enthusiastic audiences.

Unlike his earlier plays *Three Hours* contains no music. About this time Gay was directing his energies as a librettist into a fruitful collaboration with Handel, composing the book for the pastoral comic masque or *serenata, Acis and Galatea.* This probably had its premiere in private performance at Canons, the seat of the Duke of Chandos. Handel seems to have written his setting to the libretto that Gay supplied him and demonstrated, by example and perhaps by direct instruction, the subtle relationships between text and music in dramatic presentations. Of its kind, *Acis and Galatea* is a small jewel, an authentic masterwork.

The ebullient comic pastoralism of *Acis and Galatea,* and of his own *The Shepherd's Week,* may have had the paradoxical effect of setting Gay's course in the wrong direction. Abandoning the comic where he had been successful, Gay wrote his next two dramatic works for the serious stage, as if to demonstrate that he could be serious, too. His next play, *Dione* is, significantly, a pastoral tragedy, in iambic pentameter couplets. Although the pastoral trappings are difficult to accept—they were roundly denounced by Samuel Johnson in his "Life of Gay"—*Dione's* story of feverish and thwarted sexuality has its own power and perhaps reflects Gay's admiration for the great French tragedians Corneille and Racine, whose works he had seen produced during visits to Paris. Gay drew on his influence at Court in 1720 to have the Lord Chamberlain order the Drury Lane company to produce *Dione* but the managers there ignored or evaded the order; *Dione* has never been staged.

His next dramatic work made it to the public theatre at Drury Lane and died there. *The Captives* is a tragedy in blank verse, set in "Media" sometime in the classical past and featuring court conspiracies, treacherous advisors, separated lovers, jealous queens—all the trappings of baroque tragedy. There was a continuing demand for such tragedies, at least among the literary critics of the time—Samuel Johnson began his own literary career writing one—but the public seemed reluctant to pay to see them, and very few had long runs. *The Captives* was no exception: opening in January 1724 at Drury Lane with a first-class cast, it played for seven nights and then closed forever, ending Gay's brief excursion into tragic drama. His own Scriblerian ear for literary burlesque might have warned him away.

It was, with appropriate irony, musical theatre that did in *The Captives*. Playing in competition at the other London patent theatre, Lincoln's Inn Fields, and playing around the performance of *The Captives* at Drury Lane itself, was a theatrical genre that was enjoying tremendous newfound popularity, the pantomime, a mixture of music, dance, and spectacle. With further irony, Gay contributed a ballad, "Newgate's Garland," which had a central position in one of those very pantomimes that were troubling serious drama, *Harlequin Sheppard*, produced at Drury Lane in 1724. Because this pantomime concerned the career and capture of a famous criminal, Jack Sheppard, Gay's association with it is of more than passing interest: some of the elements undoubtedly remained in his mind during the next few years when he was working on *The Beggar's Opera*, which was also about the career and capture of a criminal.

The Beggar's Opera enjoyed as everyone knows an initial run of unprecedented length and established itself in the repertory of the London theatres and in the provincial and colonial theatres of the English-speaking world: George Washington would ride horseback across Maryland or

Virginia to take in a performance of his favorite play at Annapolis or Williamsburg. The *Opera* became the most popular dramatic piece of the century, and perhaps the most influential. Its place in the partisan politics of Gay's own time has been told and retold, and is not emphasized in this book. My attention is on the musicality of the piece, the *Opera* as opera, though of course theatrical gossip cannot be excluded. Gossip about the *Opera* should be examined more skeptically than it ordinarily has been, however.

With the exception of an abortive rewriting of *The Wife of Bath*, the stage pieces of Gay's last years represent significant experimentation just when the enormous success of *The Beggar's Opera* was encouraging attempts at something new. This was the time when young Henry Fielding was finding his way in the London theatre world, and his and Gay's careers are interestingly linked for a few years. Fielding, for example, drew on *The Beggar's Opera* for theatrical ideas; Gay may have reciprocated, as argued here, in his posthumous plays *The Election at Goatham* and *The Distressed Wife*. His last two ballad operas, *Polly* and *Achilles*, may also be seen as Gay's attempts to extend the scope—and the musical sophistication—of the form, rather than, as has traditionally been the accepted version, failed attempts to reproduce his earlier success with the *Opera*. Both demand further study—and production!

As can be seen from this brief sketch, John Gay's associations with the drama and the stage were long-lasting, complex, and central to his literary career. It is surprising, therefore, that no book deals directly with John Gay and the theatre in which he worked. Patricia Meyer Spacks's *John Gay* is a critical study of Gay's poetry and treats the drama principally in its relationship to the poetic corpus. The standard biography by W.H. Irving, *John Gay: Favorite of the Wits*, includes discussions of his plays but does not focus on Gay as a dramatist. Irving, writing in the 1930s, was obviously not able to take advantage of the great efflorescence of theatre scholarship on this period during the past thirty years or so, symbolized by *The London Stage* and the *Biographical Dictio-*

nary and produced by such scholars as Philip Highfill, Leo Hughes, Robert D. Hume, Shirley Strum Kenny, Judith Milhous, Arthur H. Scouten, and, in recent years, many others. The appearance in 1983 of Gay's *Dramatic Works*, edited by John Fuller, ensures that the texts of Gay's plays are available for study, though as will be made clear later in the present work Fuller's edition has many problems, in terms of both theory and execution, and the texts must be approached with caution.

Because these scholarly resources are now available, this book is written to provide a fresh reading of Gay's dramatic canon, with special attention to the relationships between the author and the stage for which he wrote. It embodies both theatrical history and literary criticism, in varied proportions as appears appropriate for the individual works under discussion: the circumstances surrounding the production of *The Mohocks*, for example, are more significant than the structure of the afterpiece itself. Because the book is intended more or less as a guide, it could not include exhaustive critical examinations of any single work, though two chapters are devoted to *The Beggar's Opera*, his most important contribution to the theatre. Scholarly controversies are generally relegated to the appendices and endnotes, where most scholars begin a book anyway.

As I wrote years ago in another context and about another author, I hope this will be the starting point for further investigations by others. If I may introduce a special plea, it is for assistance from those competent in musicology and music history. This book is written by a music lover, not a musician, but after living with Gay and his works for a number of years I am convinced that he was possessed of a musical sophistication much greater than he has generally been given credit for. Demonstrating this will require working with the tunes and texts of his plays and ballad operas in a way that has simply not been done by literary scholars, to whom his memory has been entrusted.

Literary scholars have not treated that memory with respect. Gay has been almost overlooked in the modern renaissance of eighteenth-century studies. As I write this, I have at my elbow a late annual volume of *The Eighteenth Century: A Current Bibliography*, the standard bibliographical work on the period. Eight hundred and two pages of closely-printed entries, which include not a single essay, article, or monograph on John Gay and his works. His monument with the wonderful epitaph composed for himself ("Life's a jest") has been moved out of Poet's Corner in Westminster Abbey, we are told, and placed in a storage room somewhere.[1] Surely the creating founder of the modern musical theatre deserves better of a public that turns out in great numbers for performances of *The Beggar's Opera* at venues all over the globe. This book is intended for that public, and for Gay's memory.

ONE

Apprenticeship—A Prelude

It is a commonplace to refer to a playwright's early efforts in the drama as his apprenticeship. In the case of John Gay his apprenticeship was his apprenticeship. His service, that is to say, as apprentice to Mr. Willet, a mercer in London's Strand, selling neckcloths to fashionable customers, preceded his theatrical career and provided the Devon boy a view of the London stage from the gallery seats; he would never be inclined to idealize the drama or for that matter the London life around him from which that drama derived.[1] His poem *Trivia: or, the Art of Walking the Streets of London* (1716) warns the traveler against relying on an apprentice for directions:

> Seek not from Prentices to learn the Way,
> These fabling Boys will turn thy Steps astray;
> Ask the grave Tradesman to direct thee right,
> He ne'er deceives, but when he profits by't.[2]

An apprentice needed to learn London from the bottom up; others could find their own way.

On the other hand, a London apprentice could enjoy interesting angles of vision, if he were intelligent and observant enough to do so: a mercer's apprentice dealt every day with the gentlefolk, who were indiscreet in the presence of this boy who had not the status even of a servant; he was below a servant. An apprentice was provided "meat, drink, apparel, washing, lodging and all other things" by his bourgeois master.[3] Gay presumably lived over Willet's shop in the

Strand, an area near Charing Cross where Samuel Johnson a half-century later was to locate "the full tide of human existence."[4] This particular apprentice also brought with him to the metropolis memories of his rural origins, memories of folklore and folklife, the sights, sounds, and smells of his native Devon. These relationships, these mingled experiences must have struck the adolescent boy with peculiar force. None of those who would be his friends in later life—Swift, Pope, Arbuthnot—underwent anything remotely like Gay's growing up as a London apprentice. His later silence on the subject of his mercantile apprenticeship is highly significant: he was not proud of it later, he was probably ashamed of it all the rest of his life—his friend Pope was certainly ashamed of it—but apprenticeship provided the basis for much of his best work, for *Trivia*, for example, and preeminently for *The Beggar's Opera*. The music of his masterpiece is for the most part music in the London air when he was a boy; the dialogue is the speech he heard the gentry using in London shops and London streets, every day; the angle of vision is that of a young Londoner who sees the metropolis as it is, not as it might be.

The early years of the eighteenth century were interesting ones in the London theatres. Consider the situation in 1705, when Gay was still apprenticed to Willet.[5] Although Dryden had been dead these five years, many of his plays were securely in the repertory of the professional theatres; so were those of Congreve, who had stopped writing comedies after the cool initial reception of *The Way of the World* in 1700. Richard Steele, George Farquhar, and John Vanbrugh were young men in the process of changing careers, from the British army to the London stage; the comedies they were writing along with those of the theatre professional Colley Cibber would be staples of the London and provincial theatres for decades.[6] The musical theatre and music *in* the theatre were evolving rapidly: Vanbrugh and Congreve, sensing the evolution but misreading theatrical finance, had invested in a new playhouse in the Haymarket opening in 1705 which would be devoted exclusively to the musical theatre, or so it was planned.[7] Congreve and his collaborator the composer John Eccles were at work composing an opera, *Semele*, for production in the new house.[8] *Semele* would be sung in English, but on the horizon were operas in Italian, the *opera seria* in vogue on the Continent. Would the vogue spread to England?

Money could be made—and lost—in the theatre. Starring actors and actresses could make a reasonable living, particularly if they supplemented their earnings from the London theatres with performances at the street fairs. Good singers were in short supply and opera singers imported from abroad could demand and get salaries beyond the dreams of the ordinary player. Theatre managers, also, if they were shrewd, could do very well indeed.[9] With the turn of the century, periodicals of various kinds began appearing on the London streets; these could be used to advertise play performances or to advertise publication of the printed version of new plays. The practice was standard by 1705: plays were published to coincide with the initial production of a new play. The process could be mutually reinforcing; advertising sold plays to readers, who then paid to see the plays performed, or the other way around.[10] In that year, for example, Richard Steele saw his new comedy, *The Tender Husband*, produced in April at the theatre in Drury Lane. Jacob Tonson published the play sixteen days later in quarto format, advertising it in *The Daily Courant*. Steele received a copyright payment of unknown amount from Tonson and the author's customary benefit from the third night's performance.[11]

A widening realization of the fact that the stage was profitable is without doubt the principal reason the theatre companies were in almost constant turmoil during the first ten years of the eighteenth century. Two companies of actors had been authorized by patents granted by King Charles II in 1660 to Sir William Davenant and Thomas Killigrew. These patents, as Judith Milhous has observed, set up the theatres in "an absolutely unprecedented way."[12] The patents bestowed virtually unlimited authority on the managers, whose rights to exercise this authority were hereditable, hence could be bought or sold. The theatre companies, supervised theoretically and sometimes actually by the Lord Chamberlain or his deputies, were thus objects of value in themselves, quite apart from the buildings the performers played in. Financial and legal maneuvering to get, in the appropriate modern phrase, a piece of the action was virtually unceasing. By 1705 two companies were in operation, one under Christopher Rich at Drury Lane and a company at Vanbrugh and Congreve's new house in the Haymarket. Management arrangements would change, almost every year for the next eight years, with bewildering complexity. John Gay would be involved with the Rich family management later, in a famous relationship; Congreve would become a trusted friend. Could anything like this have been in an apprentice's dreams in 1705?

There were those who, far from wishing to see the theatres prosper, wanted to see them closed down. No one knows what Gay's master thought about the playhouses, but the areas around the theatres were notoriously places where susceptible apprentices could get into trouble. The theatre at Drury Lane was only a few hundred yards from the Strand; Vanbrugh's new theatre in the Haymarket a similar distance in the opposite direction; trouble was everywhere near for an apprentice. Daniel Defoe in his periodical *The Review* scoffed at the idea that the stage and drama could be beneficial to society; "to Reform the Stage, would be not to Build it up, but to pull it down." The prologue read at the opening of the new Haymarket theatre, which compared the work of the architect Vanbrugh to that of the Divine Architect, lodged right in Defoe's craw, and he offered his own prologue in reply, making use of the fact that the new theatre had been erected over the site of a stable yard and several privies (jakes):

> *Alay'st all this, Apollo* spoke the Word,
> And straight arose a *Playhouse* from a *T[urd]*.
> Here *Whores* in *Hogstyes*, vilely blended lay,
> Just as *in Boxes*, at our *Lewder Play*;
> The Stables have been Cleans'd, the Jakes made Clear,
> *Herculean Labours*, ne'r will Purge us here.[13]

Arthur Bedford, rector of St. Nicholas, Bristol, in a sermon delivered in January 1705 and later published for the edification of the public ascribed a recent destructive wind (the famous storm of 1703) as a premonitory judgment on a Drury Lane production of *The Tempest.* "*God* was pleased to shew us . . . that *he would not be mock'd* by visiting us with . . . a Storm of Wind." When the players revived the play in defiance of the warning, God answered "with another violent storm."[14] Defoe's and Bedford's attitudes were by no means exceptional. There were those, clergy and laity, who hoped to involve Queen Anne herself in the process of reforming, by getting rid of, the London stage.[15]

The London stage was in a state of flux in 1705, then, as it has often been, but money could be made there. Better still for a young man, literary and social reputations could be made there. Richard Steele, who as we have noted was just going through the process of becoming a celebrity, later observed that "nothing can make the Town so fond of a Man as a successful Play."[16] An easier way up the ladder than selling neckcloths to the gentry, John Gay, aged twenty, may have thought to himself. By the next year he had gained his release from his articles of apprenticeship, and, perhaps after a year or two in Devon, he was back in the metropolis.

By chance or fate he was then working for his old friend Aaron Hill, an individual as stagestruck as anyone in the entire eighteenth century. Gay and Hill had been classmates in the small and excellent Barnstaple Grammar School. Hill possessed or developed theories on almost every aspect of the theatre: on acting, on costuming, on historical accuracy.[17] He was, furthermore, always eager to put his theories into practice. Gay was serving as his secretary, an arrangement no doubt enabling Gay to keep body and soul together while he got started, on something. Being around Hill that something was likely to be the theatre. Hill had lived in Turkey as part of the entourage of his cousin, Lord Paget, Paget then serving as Ambassador to the Sublime Porte. By the time Gay returned to London, perhaps late 1707 or early 1708, Hill must have been working on his book about the Turks, *A Full and Just*

Account of the Present State of the Ottoman Empire, which appeared in 1709. Gay, as his secretary, may well have penned some of the manuscript. Although Hill later affected to be ashamed of this young man's book, it contains interesting eyewitness accounts of the Empire, including visits to Jerusalem and to Egypt.

Especially notable, because Hill later attempted to translate the spectacle to the London stage, are descriptions of the splendid pageantry associated with the Sultan's court and the reception of ambassadors there. The ceremonies were on a grand scale—Paget reported to the secretary of state that on a visit to the Grand Vizier—the Sultan's advisor—he was accompanied by "about 100 attendants."[18] And costuming was crucial: the garment given to the ambassador (the custom derived from Genesis 35:22: Joseph giving his brethren "Changes of Raiment") was indicative of the esteem the ambassador and his government enjoyed in the eyes of the Sultan. The ambassador, of course, had to reciprocate. Since the recipient would keep it as his personal possession the garment was also a source of income and, it hardly needs saying, an accepted medium of bribery on the part of the embassies: they were a regular part of the Ambassador's accounts, where they were always referred to as "vests." Paget bestowed a vest, woven with silver, gold, and jewels, which cost £660 on the new Grand Vizier, who was, his clerk assured the auditors in London, "a friend to his Excy & the [British] nation."[19] For comparison, the annual stipend of the Lord Bishop of Oxford was then £500. Here was spectacle on a scale undreamed of in London. Yet.

Hill had returned with Paget's entourage, to Vienna and through western Europe, where he no doubt encountered the Italian style *opera seria,* then sweeping the continent. It is also possible that he met, or at least heard of, the young German musical prodigy, George Friedrich Händel. Back in London, Hill volunteered himself for the literary scene, publishing poems and translations, working on his *Ottoman Empire* (for which he secured as a subscriber Queen Anne herself—Hill had his connections), and directing from 1708 *The British Apollo,* a question-and-answer weekly.

Gay, in the literary world by association as it were, wrote copy for the *Apollo.* Questions came in from every direction and on any subject, and were answered, so the masthead said, "by a Society of GENTLEMEN." Some of the questions no doubt originated with the staff, pressed to fill column inches. Was it a correspondent or John Gay who inquired in the spring of 1708, "Pray what is the reason that feeding a Monkey with Meat will make him eat his Tail?" The Gentleman gravely replied that the monkey probably gets used to having meat for his meals and does "endeavour to satisfy his Longing Appetite, by chewing his Tail."[20]

In May 1708 Gay saw his first poem published, *Wine.* This celebration of vinous conviviality was advertised in the *Apollo* and enjoyed the minor flattery of being pirated immediately by the well-known literary scavenger "Pirate" Henry Hills.[21] Aaron Hill's heart, however, was always in the theatre. His efforts, and presumably those of his secretary, would soon be turning in that direction.

Late in 1709, to the surprise of almost everyone except perhaps Hill himself, he was named manager of the company at Drury Lane by William Collier, a Tory Member of Parliament. Collier had wangled a license from the Lord Chamberlain and had seized control of the theatre by a *coup de main:* as Judith Milhous and Robert D. Hume have put it, "by the simple expedient of breaking into the theatre and seizing it."[22] These actions should be seen as part of that unceasing turmoil, noted earlier, in which the theatres were involved. Hill was not interested in making money in the theatre, however, except perhaps incidentally; with breathtaking ambition, he wanted to remold the entire London stage nearer to his heart's desire. He was twenty-four years old. Gay, who was also twenty-four, presumably watched the manager attempt to impose his will on a glum and unwilling troupe of veteran actors and actresses. In June 1710 the players borrowed a leaf from Collier's book, rioted, and threw Hill and his entourage out of the theatre at swordpoint.

Before his ejection, however, Hill had managed to get produced a tragedy and two farces written by himself. That, of course, was a prime advantage, or perquisite, of being a theatre manager. One of the farces, *The Walking Statue*, was an afterpiece, a very early and enduring example of this new form, which the theatres were just then introducing as audience come-ons, to supplement the mainpiece offering.[23] It seems anomalous that Hill displayed this early talent for farce and then moved away from the form forever. He was never known except on this one occasion to display any talent for or disposition to boisterous humor, or indeed humor of any variety. Hill was a serious man. It may well be that his secretary, who would soon give evidence of a keen ear and eye for farce, was helping him with his work.[24] Gay would start his own dramatic career with an afterpiece farce.

In the autumn of 1710, implausible as it may have seemed for someone who had been thrown out the stage door a year earlier by his own actors, Hill found himself for a second opportunity a theatre manager, this time of what had become once again the opera house, the Queen's Theatre in the Haymarket. This was the grand building into which Vanbrugh and Congreve had sunk their own money, in 1705. Their dreams of opera had not materialized in the harsh financial weather of the London theatre world. Hill would give it another try; against all the odds he succeeded.

He had impressive resources, in some ways. Musicians and singers were hard to find in London, and Hill's company, with a virtual monopoly on musical theatre, had access to the best ones around. For example, Nicolini, Nicoló Grimaldi, the great male soprano from Italy, was on contract at the astonishing annual figure of 800 guineas (that is, £840).[25] Hill had good theatre musicians. At some point, he secured the young cynosure of European music, Handel. (In England Handel lost the umlaut but of course retained the German pronunciation of his surname, so that his contemporaries often referred to him as "Mr. Hendel.") Just how Handel and Hill came together is still uncertain.[26] What is certain is that together they brought about the first, remarkable performance of Handel's earliest opera produced in Britain, *Rinaldo*. What is probable is that this was the school where John Gay began learning about opera, from the inside, as it were.

Hill selected the topic, sketched the scenario, perhaps wrote the entire opera in English, from a familiar episode in Tasso's *Jerusalem Delivered* that relates the victory there of the Christians under Godfrey of Boulogne over the pagans led by Argante, King of Jerusalem. Handel's librettist, Giacomo Rossi, put it into Italian. A bilingual libretto was published, in which Rossi averred that Handel had composed the opera in two weeks.[27] The opera was produced on 24 February 1711. Exactly one week later Hill was out of a job again; in one of those strong-arm excursions that were becoming almost commonplace, Collier with his minions had taken possession of the theatre and, as Hill complained later, "set himselfe up for the sole Master and director of the Theatre Royal."[28]

Hill was justified in some vexation, for his and Handel's production was on the way to becoming a great success. Although Addison and Steele satirized *Rinaldo* unmercifully in the pages of *The Spectator*, it was Handel's most popular opera during his lifetime.[29] With or without Hill in charge, *Rinaldo* played an extraordinary fifteen performances in that first season. Audiences liked the spectacular staging, with dragons puffing smoke and a cast, if not of thousands, of many. Visual aspects of the production were drawn from Hill's own remembered experience. Argante, for example, is described in the libretto as entering Jerusalem "drawn through the Gate in a Triumphal Charriot, the Horses white and led in by arm'd Blackamores. He comes forward attended by a great Number of Horse and Foot Guards." The white horses, the armed "Blackamores," the horse and foot guards are all precise details from the Sultan's processions Hill had witnessed in Turkey—the horse and foot guards are the famous spahis and janizaries, as the contemporaneous painting now in the British Embassy in Ankara vividly illustrates.[30] Unlike anyone else involved, Aaron Hill had also actually been to Jerusalem, where he had copied the inscription from Godfrey's grave.[31]

Although performed in Italian and though its success encouraged the further production of such "foreign" works,[32] *Rinaldo* sparked Hill's ambition to invigorate opera written in English. Years later he wrote Handel, proposing that the conductor, by then easy with his English librettists, return to opera via one in English, "deliver us from our *Italian bondage,* and demonstrate that *English* is soft enough for Opera."[33] Gay's experience with *Rinaldo* may have persuaded him to learn, or teach himself, Italian. Perhaps he had acquired the knowledge earlier, when and if he was assisting Hill on the Italianate *The Walking Statue.* By 1720 he was skillful enough in Italian to prepare his own translations of Ariosto.[34] His eventual contributions to the operatic tradition would, however, be in English, but they would be powerfully influenced by his association with Handel and Handel's musical world. After *Rinaldo* Gay was ready to try his own talents in dramatic writing, and in music.

TWO

The Mohocks

In 1711, Aaron Hill was out of a job in the theatre. His secretary appears to have been examining his options that year, all of them, to his mind, literary. Gay provided a survey of the current periodicals, which were proliferating in London as literacy rose and authors and the printing establishment hastened to supply the demand for reading matter.[1] Many of these were conceived as imitations of Addison and Steele's papers, *The Tatler* and *The Spectator*. In his survey published in May 1711, which he entitled *The Present State of Wit, in a Letter to a Friend in the Country*, Gay paid a handsome compliment to the supposedly anonymous *Spectator*, which was "writ in so excellent a Stile, with so nice a Judgment, and such a noble profusion of Wit and Humour, that it was not difficult to determine it could come from no other hands but those which had penn'd [the *Tatler*]."[2] If Gay was smarting from the *Spectator*'s satiric jabs at the production of *Rinaldo* he did not show it; he probably left the agonizing to Hill. The *Present State* demonstrates that Gay recognized, earlier than most, what a powerful medium the new essay periodical in its various guises had become.

Steele especially was using his periodicals to advance the cause of the drama and theatre; he had virtually invented theatrical criticism in *The Tatler*, and his papers regularly contained material about what was happening on the London stage. The famous editor was a useful young man to know, not yet forty years old. Gay was directing his favorable comments in *The Present State of Wit* to the notice of Richard Steele.

When Steele started his next paper, *The Guardian*, Gay would write for him. In the meantime, as will be seen, Steele would be involved in the preparation for the stage of Gay's first play—and in its sudden demise.

The Present State is dated May 3, 1711. In the second half of that year, Gay turned his attention from prose to poetry and to a young poet, Alexander Pope. He met Pope through their friend in common, Henry Cromwell, who aspired somewhat languidly to the literary life. Gay was full of juice: he followed up his introduction and sent a translation from Ovid's *Metamorphoses* for inclusion in the bookseller Bernard Lintott's next *Miscellany*, which Pope was editing. Also in the *Miscellany* when it appeared in 1712 was another poem by Gay, "On a Miscellany of Poems. To Bernard Lintott," which is a sort of commentary on contemporary poetry, as *The Present State* had been on periodical prose, and which features a glowing tribute to "*Pope*'s harmonious Muse," as displayed in his *Pastorals*.

> His various Numbers charm our ravish'd Ears,
> His steady Judgment far out-shoots his Years,
> And early in the Youth the God appears.[3]

This is the way to catch an author's attention. In December 1711 Pope, who presumably had seen "On a Miscellany" in manuscript and who evidently was well enough acquainted with Gay by then to know of his dramatic aspirations, wrote Cromwell, "I hop'd, when I heard a new Comedy had met with success upon the Stag[e], that it had been his, to which I really wish no less; and, (had it been [any] way in my power) shoud have been very glad to have contributed to its [in]troduction into the World."[4] By the beginning of 1712, then, Gay had made his plans in the drama known to Pope and, I shall argue, to Steele as well; he had been cultivating the good regard of both. His play would be a comedy and it would be called *The Mohocks*. His association with the bookseller, or as we should say, publisher Lintott also marks a milestone in his career: Lintott was a first-class literary bookseller, and Gay would be on his list for some time.[5]

The Mohocks, though it was not produced in Gay's life-time—nor, as far as I know, since—deserves more attention than it has received. It *is* apprentice work, but the apprentice knows his craft surprisingly well, the knowledge coming from his immersion in London and, with Aaron Hill, in the London theatrical world. Dramatic practices that found their triumphant fulfillment years later in *The Beggar's Opera* are delineated in *The Mohocks*. And the circumstances of the play's aborted production are interesting, too: as drama sometimes does, this brief farce reflects the turbulent political climate of London in 1712, both in the subject matter of the piece and in the manner it was received, or not received, by the managers at Drury Lane who were expected to produce it. It involves peripherally well-known literary figures: Alexander Pope, Richard Steele, and that shadow of early eighteenth-century English literature, Daniel Defoe. The chances are that Gay's first play was caught at the intersection of politics and theatrical warfare, and lost its opportunity for production not because it was a bad play but because it appeared at a bad time. Finally, *The Mohocks* helped give reality to an imaginary London club, the Mohocks of the title, which has entered history and indeed the *Oxford English Dictionary* in spite of its nonexistence.

In April 1712, Aaron Hill's sometime partner and recent antagonist William Collier became—that is, bought his way into becoming—one of the partners in the management of the Drury Lane theatre.[6] This company since 1710 had a monopoly on the production of plays, while its rival possessed a monopoly on staging operas. Whether Collier's arrival drove the final nail into *The Mohocks'* coffin we do not know; perhaps it did, but Gay by that time faced other obstacles in the way of his play's production, which may have seemed so easy when he was describing his plans to Pope the previous autumn. Collier's partners, the actual working managers, were hard-bitten professional actors: Colley Cibber, Robert Wilks, and Thomas Doggett, who were disposed to play it safe in repertory choice, to go for the tried and true. This of course made it difficult for new plays to find production. Playwrights would bleat about this right through the century—the note is still sounded today—but the fact is that actors are conservative in their professional lives and distrustful of innovations, if only because they have to memorize new lines and stage business for a new play. Furthermore, since Drury Lane had competition from the musical stage at the Haymarket but from nowhere else, the managers were reinforced in their conservativism by the monopoly. Much the same sort of managerial conservatism would confront Gay and other dramatic authors ten years later. Underlying all these considerations in 1712, however, was a very tense political situation, which will be described. As a result, the managers played it most cautiously, offering only three new plays in the entire season 1711–1712. Even so, they encountered political backlash from one of those, Susannah Centlivre's *The Perplex'd Lovers*.

The script Gay brought to the Drury Lane partners was not on its face a loser, however, and all evidence indicates that Gay expected it to be produced. It was a one-act farce in three short scenes, an afterpiece with topical relevance. The managers were beginning to sense audience demand for afterpieces: Aaron Hill's *The Walking Statue*, which perhaps benefited from Gay's assistance, had entered the repertory and recently been paired with *Othello*. This mingling of theatrical styles—tragic and farcical—did not seem to offend eighteenth-century audiences; in fact, they appear to have demanded it.

The Mohocks concerns a group of London toughs, the Mohocks of the title, who are ruled over, significantly, by an Emperor. The Mohocks capture members of the watch, exchange clothes with them, and thus disguised bring the watch before the justices of the peace. There they charge the watch with being the street toughs. At the end the truth, or a version of it, emerges and all join in a concluding dance.

Here, clearly, is the transvaluation of values to be seen again in the *Opera*. What sort of a world is it where a criminal can be taken for a police officer, a rogue for a gentleman? Our sort of world, says Gay. Patricia Meyer Spacks has complained of *The Mohocks* that there is not "any definite focus of mockery."[7] The same charge could be leveled at *The Beggar's Opera*, and Spacks recognizes that the attitude toward the law portrayed in *The Mohocks* suggests "some of the complexities of feeling that were to make *The Beggar's Opera* perplexing" (p. 131). Exactly so; perplexing and aesthetically satisfying.

The reader, or playgoer if *The Mohocks* should ever find its way to production, will observe that the focus of mockery shifts, as it does in the *Opera;* that each group becomes the satiric victim in its turn. In the opening scene the Mohocks use Miltonic blank verse to describe their trivial pursuits, blank verse of the sort much employed in contemporary tragedies.[8] A candidate for membership, Cannibal (the name, again, is significant), is introduced to the Emperor of the Mohocks by his sponsor, Mirmidon:

> I'll answer for him, for I've known him long,
> Know him a Subject worthy of such a Prince;
> Sashes and Casements felt his early Rage,
> H'has twisted Knockers, broken Drawers Heads,
> And never flinch'd his Glass, or baulk'd his Wench.[9]

After the Mohocks swear allegiance to the Emperor and their calling ("Villainy and all outragious Crimes"), the Emperor invites them to have a drink:

> Now bring the generous Bowl—Come—pledge me all—
> Rouse up your Souls with this Celestial Nectar.
> What gain'd the *Macedonian* Youth the World?
> 'Twas Wine. What rais'd the Soul of *Catiline*
> To such brave, unparallell'd Ambition?
> Wine, Potent, heav'nly Juice, Immortal Wine. (i.60-66)

The faintly Miltonic verse and most un-Miltonic sentiment look back to Gay's first published poem, *Wine*, which appeared during his time with Aaron Hill, in 1708:

> Of Happiness Terrestrial, and the Source
> Whence human pleasures flow, sing *Heavenly* Muse,

> Of sparkling juices, of th'enliv'ning Grape,
> Whose *quickning* tast adds *vigour* to the Soul.[10]

The scene itself looks forward to the assembly of Macheath and his gang of highwaymen in the second act of the *Opera*.

The incidental music for *The Mohocks* has not been found, so we cannot tell whether Gay intended to use a ballad tune for the Mohocks' drinking song, but the verse reveals a gifted librettist at work, in his first attempt:

> Come fill up the Glass,
> Round, round, let it pass,
> 'Till our Reason be lost in our Wine:
>> Leave Conscience's Rules
>> To Women and Fools,
> This only can make us divine. (i.69-74, original in italics)

Note that the lilting anapestic form is precisely that of Captain Plume's song in Farquhar's *The Recruiting Officer* ("Come, fair one, be kind"),[11] the music of which by Richard Leveridge was borrowed by Gay for Macheath's famous Air XV, "My Heart was so free," in the *Opera*. He may have borrowed it for the first time here in *The Mohocks*. Here is Macheath in the *Opera:*

> My Heart was so free
> It rov'd like the Bee,
> 'Till *Polly* my passion requited;
>> I sipt each Flower,
>> I chang'd ev'ry Hour,
> But here ev'ry Flower is united. (I.xiii.18-23)[12]

Gay deflates the pretensions of the Mohocks in this mock-heroic first scene in blank verse and then, as Peter Lewis has pointed out, shifts to prose varied by song lyrics for the remainder of the piece.[13]

In Scene Two the constable and his watchmen, supposed guardians of law and order, are depicted as poltroons who, trembling when they hear the Mohocks approach, push one another to the fore: "Hold, hold, Gentlemen," cries the Con-

stable, "let us do all things in order—Do you advance, Gentlemen, d'ye see, and while you advance I'll lead up the Rear"
(ii.l29-30). Gay is here building sight comedy into the
promptbook, the good farceur's first requirement, already in-
stinctive with him. John Fuller points out that the parts of
the feeble watchmen are tailored for Drury Lane's great
knockabout comedians, "Pinky" Penkethman and "Jubilee
Dicky" Norris, both masters of farce.[14]

In portraying the fop Gentle who is seized by the Mohocks
(posing as the watch), Gay devotes special care. As with the
watchmen, he almost certainly had a specific actor in mind.
The Emperor, supposedly the Constable, asks Gentle what his
business is:

> *Gentle.* I am a Gentleman, Sir.
> *Emperor.* A doubtful, a shuffling Answer! we need no further
> proof that he is a *Mohock*—commit him.
> *Gentle.* 'Tis a strange thing that the vulgar cannot distinguish
> the Gentleman—pray Sir, may I ask you one Question—have you
> ever seen a *Mohock*? has he that softness in his Look? that sweetness
> of delivery in his Discourse? believe me, Sir, there is a certain *Je ne
> scay quoi* in my manner that shows my Conversation to have lain al-
> together among the politer part of the World.
> *Emperor.* Look, ye, Sir, your Manners in talking *Latin* before Her
> Majesty's Officer, show you to be an ill-designing Person. (ii. 223-34)

Here surely Gay envisioned Colley Cibber, co-manager
and comedian, as playing Gentle the fop, leering at the audience, milking his lines as he had done to great acclaim with
Sir Fopling Flutter in *The Man of Mode* and Lord Foppington
in his own *The Careless Husband.* Cibber's aspirations to gentility were one of the Town's favorite jokes for a quarter-
century or more, apotheosized in *The Dunciad* and here, it
may be, finding one of its earliest literary expressions. It was
a joke carefully nurtured by Cibber, however ambiguous his
own inmost feelings might have been. Jokes, Cibber found,
paid well.

The final satiric victims are the justices, discovered at the
opening of Scene Three *en banc*, holding court in a tavern.
Justice Scruple informs his colleagues Wiseman and Kindle
that there were Mohocks in Queen Elizabeth's time and that

precedents could be found for taking action against them. Kindle argues that no precedents are necessary; Mohocks are "disturbers of Her Majesty's Peace, and as such . . . may and ought to be committed." Wiseman, as his name denotes, is the closest approximation to a *raisonneur* that Gay can bring himself to employ. Wiseman suggests to his fellow justices that they "be guided by Reason." The response to this quix-otic advice is immediate:

> *Kindle.* What has Reason to do with Law, Brother *Wiseman*? if we follow the Law, we must judge according to the Letter of the Law.
> *Scruple.* You are in the Right, Brother *Kindle*—Reason and Law have been at variance in our Courts these many Years—a mis-spelled Word, or a Quibble will baffle the most convincing Argu-ment in the World; and therefore if we are guided—Mr. Justice *Wiseman*, my hearty respects to you—if we are guided, I say, in any measure by the Law, 'tis my Opinion, that we must keep strictly to the Letter of the Law. (iii.21-31)

Swaggering toughs, quivering watchmen, obtuse justices: how is the drama to be resolved? It is resolved by a dance. Justice Wiseman decrees to all assembled on the stage—Mohocks, watchmen, wives, fop, whores, and magistrates—that justice will be done tomorrow at ten. Of course it will. Meanwhile the watchmen dance and the Constable sings:

> This is the Day—the joyful Night indeed
> In which *Great Britain*'s Sons from the *Mohocks* are freed.
> Our Wives and Daughters they may walk the Street,
> Nor *Mohock* now, Nor *Hawkubite* shall meet.
> *Mohock* and *Hawkubite*, both one and all,
> Shall from this very Night date their Down-fall.
> (iii.185–90. Italics reversed.)

Gay had picked up some affection for spectacle from Aaron Hill. Having the entire cast on stage at the curtain would make for good dramatic effect (compare the curtain scene in the *Opera*) but under the circumstances it is a dram-aturgical flaw because it prevents doubling. There are

twenty-two speaking roles in *The Mohocks,* and this is probably more than the attenuated Drury Lane company could
cover comfortably in 1712. Hill, for example, got along with
just five in *The Walking Statue,* which Drury Lane produced in
May as an afterpiece to Dryden's *The Spanish Fryar.*

Still, the managers might have given it a try with some
cuts, one would think: it was lively, full of good sight comedy,
and it was larded with music, a song in every scene. Opera at
the Haymarket was Drury Lane's only competition, so a play
with attractive music might have seemed a worthwhile risk.
Drury Lane had actors who could sing and dance. It was,
however, principally the world outside the playhouse, to
which the Constable's reference to Mohock and Hawkubite
pointed, that, I would argue, kept Gay's play off the stage. If
Gay chose his subject for its topical value he probably succeeded all too well.

Was there a club of young toughs like those in the play,
who called themselves Mohocks and made life miserable for
the law-abiding inhabitants of London and Westminster? The
Oxford English Dictionary returns an unequivocal answer:
Mohocks, sense 1: "One of a class of aristocratic ruffians who
infested the streets of London at night in the early years of the
18th century," followed by citations of Swift's *Journal to Stella*
and Thomas Hearne's *Collections.* The Mohock Club, in sense
3, attributive and adjective, draws on Steele's *Spectator* No.
324, significantly, for its supporting evidence. Modern scholars have almost unanimously followed the *OED:* Robert J.
Allen in his influential *The Clubs of Augustan London,* assumes the case is closed: there were Mohocks roaming the
streets, and they constituted a club by his definition.[15]

The name of the supposed club, and of Gay's play, is derived from memories of the visit of a group of American Indian chiefs to London in 1710. Some of them were Mohawks;
Richmond Bond has decribed their visit, which was referred
to in Steele's *Tatler,* where significantly, Steele described their
leader as an "Emperor," and later in *The Spectator.*[16] It is important to understand that Steele, editor of these papers,
knew exactly who the Mohawks or Mohocks were. In the late

winter of 1711–1712, word circulated in London that a number of young men wearing disguises were assaulting passersby in the streets. As Gay's Justice Scruple observed, there was a long history of such behavior in London, the term "scowrers" was in general usage, and it is fair to say that Londoners were prepared to believe the rumor. Swift certainly did: he reported to Stella in March 1712 that Henry Davenant's sedan chair had been run through with a sword.[17] In *The Spectator* No.324 for 12 March, already mentioned, Steele printed a letter from "Philanthropos" which affirmed that a "Set of Men . . . have lately erected themselves into a nocturnal Fraternity, under the Title of *The Mohock Club;* a Name borrowed it seems from a sort of *Cannibals* in *India,* who subsist by plundering and devouring all the Nations about them. The President is stiled *Emperor of the Mohocks.*" These "Misanthropes" practice various specialties: some "tip the Lion," that is, squeeze the victim's nose flat and gouge out his eyes; others are dancing masters who "teach their Scholars to cut Capers by running Swords thro' their legs."[18] Philanthropos calls upon Mr. Spectator to take a stand and save the younger Mohocks, who "will probably stand corrected by your Reproofs."

Knowing good copy when he saw it—he may have written it himself—Steele followed Philanthropos's letter with one from "Jack Lightfoot" on 21 March: Lightfoot reports that he had been set upon by Mohocks in Fleet Street but had made his escape in "a handsome and orderly Retreat." When Sir Roger de Coverley proposes going to see Ambrose Philips's redaction of Racine, *The Distrest Mother,* then the season's only hit at Drury Lane, he asks Mr. Spectator "if there would not be some danger in coming home late, in case the *Mohocks* should not be abroad." The party agree to take Captain Sentry along with them as escort when they go to the theatre.

It will be observed that Steele and his collaborators do not treat the Mohocks with the same seriousness as Swift does. In fact they treat them with no seriousness at all: the bantering tone is much like that of Gay's in his play. Mr. Spectator does not take up Philanthropos's call for a rebuke to the younger Mohocks, nor does he correct his ethnography. Steele knew quite well that the Mohawks did not come from India and were not cannibals. Sir Roger's outing to Drury Lane comes off without a tumbler or a dancing master in sight. How may one account for this? Why were Swift and Thomas Hearne in March of 1712 suddenly so exercised?

What had happened is that the Mohocks, like almost everything else in early 1712, had become politicized. So Daniel Defoe, to his annoyance, was to discover. It will be necessary to undertake some historical backtracking to clarify the circumstances under which Gay's lighthearted farce became identified with sinister political machinations and assisted in the creation of a fictitious club.

In late 1711 Robert Harley, now the Earl of Oxford, was consolidating the hold on power that he and Henry St. John, Viscount Bolingbroke, had achieved at the expense of the Junto Whigs and their ally, the Duke of Marlborough. That December the Whigs brought Marlborough's military colleague Prince Eugene of Savoy to London, to shore up support for their side. Oxford struck back: by having the Crown appoint new peers, Oxford acquired in 1712 a firm hold on the House of Lords (he already possessed a working majority in the Commons). He proceeded to attack Marlborough indirectly by seeing that Robert Walpole, Junto Secretary-at-War, was accused of corruption on trumped-up charges and in January sent to the Tower.[19] Were you for or against the Duke of Marlborough? This was for several months in early 1712 a fairly reliable litmus test of one's political orientation. Susannah Centlivre's *The Perplex'd Lovers*, mentioned earlier, premiered in January but the epilogue she had designed for the play did not receive a license from the Vice Chamberlain in time for opening night. The epilogue complimented Marlborough and Eugene. Anne Oldfield, the actress who was slated to read it, received letters advising her to forbear, "for that there were Parties forming against it."[20]

In this period of crisis the Mohocks appeared. Or did they? Swift, as we have seen, believed in Mohocks and assured Stella on 9 March that "they are all Whigs." Years later he was still convinced that the Mohocks were Whigs, seeing their depradations as a kind of micro-plot that was designed to serve as a screen for the macro-plot, instigated by Prince Eugene, to bring about Oxford's assassination.[21] The crusty arch-Tory Thomas Hearne, surveying the London scene from Oxford, was also sure that the Mohocks existed and that they were "all of the Whiggish Gang."[22]

In 1712 a plot was in the eye of the beholder. Mohocks were around every corner. Early in March Defoe, then secretly on Oxford's payroll, drew a parallel in his *Review* between the plight of the Huguenots in France and the Dissenters in Britain, the French Protestants, he wrote, having been abandoned by their former guardians, "the *Juncto* or *Whig-Lords* of those Days."[23] Just as the Junto Whigs were now abandoning the Dissenters—and Oxford, by implication, was assuming the role of their protector. Clear enough. Too clear by half for one anonymous controversialist, who issued a broadside the title of which makes up in fullness of exposition what it lacks in succinctness: *England's Delivery, or the Fanaticks discover'd. Being a Full and true Account of a most Notorious Plot against the Queen and Parliament, contriv'd by Daniel D'F—e, and carried on by the Presbyterians under the Name of the Mohocks; together with the apprehending and taking several of 'em, and their Commitment to Prison by the Worshipful Bench of Justices, who sat Yesterday at the back of St. Clements Church.*[24] According to this observer, Defoe is attempting in his recent *Review* essay to incite the Dissenters to rebellion and at the same time is using the Mohocks to spread general panic in the streets. The Mohock leader, one Nehemiah Newcomb, is alleged to have quoted the *Review* in order to stir the crowd to a frenzy. Other conspirators apprehended include Sir Richard Tonson [sic]; John Adams, Knight; Father Nery, an Irish priest; and so on. A crude woodblock, two columns wide, shows the Mohocks at their dirty work, slitting noses and stabbing servant girls.

The broadside, in form and content, strikes one immediately as purest moonshine but Defoe seems to have taken it seriously. In the *Review* of 15 March he had recommended the use of Protestant flails on the Mohocks, with right-minded persons taking the law in their hands. "*I would be a Volunteer under their Command at any time."* Now he finds himself accused of planning the Mohock conspiracy. On the twentieth of March he replies to the broadside: "But is it not strange, that while I am proposing to you the readiest way to Root [the Mohocks] out, I should be Printed and cryed about the Streets as one Concerned in such a Villainous Practice? . . . This indeed is *Mohawking* me a New-fashion'd way, like Crying out a *Mad-Dog,* and setting the Parish upon him, but *it will not do*— I am ready to shew myself to Mob or Magistrates, in spight of these, or any other kind of *Mohawks* in the Nation."

Defoe's lifelong resentment toward Gay may stem from the events and publications concerning the Mohocks in early 1712; he may have suspected that Gay had written the offending broadside and Gay just possibly may have done so. The "Sir" Richard Tonson is a suspiciously literary reference. Gay had written and seen published an anonymous broadside, *An Argument Proving from History, Reason, and Scripture, that the Present Mohocks and Hawkubites are the Gog and Magog mention'd in the Revelations.*[25] Gay burlesques the style of the French Prophets, Protestant refugees from the Cévennes region, who had made a stir in London a few years earlier with their apocalyptic preaching.[26] He provides a jocular political twist in this fevered political time with a reference to the Junto Whigs: "If you look into the History of *Philo Judaeus,* you will find the following Words. The Day shall come, when the *Junto* shall be overthrown, then shall GOG and MAGOG arise, and the MOHOCKS and HAWKUBITES shall possess the Streets, and dwell in their Quarters, they shall come from far at the Sound of the Cat-call—Yea, they shall come from the furthermost Part of *America.*"[27] The broadside also parodies the sort of activity Gay had been engaged in on Hill's question-and-answer periodical, *The British Apollo:* this might almost have been an office-parody of an answer to the question, What do Gog and Magog, mentioned in the Book of Revelation, mean?

Most important for our purposes is the association of Mohocks and Hawkubites. The two groups, it will be remembered, appear in the Constable's curtain song in the play

("Nor *Mohock* now, nor *Hawkubite* shall meet"). Gay in the play is thus echoing his own broadside. As far as I am aware Gay and no one else this early associated Mohocks and Hawkubites. I suggest that the broadside and Steele's references to Mohocks in *The Spectator* constitute preproduction publicity, or puffs, for Gay's play. The correspondent "Philanthropos," who describes the nefarious doings of the Mohocks, with their Emperor and cannibals, may be John Gay himself. He could have shown the play to Steele in manuscript; for Gay's next play Steele would in fact be invited to rehearsal at Drury Lane. Gay perhaps envisioned adding to the hullabaloo about the Mohocks as an incentive for the Drury Lane managers to produce his play.

The script he gave them was itself scrupulously nonpolitical; other plays had been written recently on political themes, and they conspicuously had not been produced. For example, the anonymous *The General Cashier'd*, printed, the manuscript note in the Folger copy avers, "as designed for the stage."[28] Set in some unspecified European court, the play concerns the machinations of a sycophantic villain Cosmo who misleads the sovereign into cashiering his favorite general. Dedicated to Prince Eugene of Savoy, *The General Cashier'd* is a transparent Whig allegory of Queen Anne, Oxford, and Marlborough, but it is a genuine play and the author no doubt hoped that its topicality would persuade the managers to risk producing it. Not a chance. The Drury Lane managers were nervous about Vice Chamberlain Coke's interference in their operations anyway, and they were pursuing a conservative course in choice of repertory that season, with an eye on both Coke and their operatic competition at the Haymarket.[29] When the opera company produced Apostolo Zeno's *Ambleto* (*Hamlet*) in April, Drury Lane came back with Shakespeare's version, Robert Wilks playing his famous Hamlet. No new plays at all were produced in the months of April, May, and June: nothing but standards from the repertory.

Innocuous as it may seem today, *The Mohocks* probably struck Cibber, Wilks, and Doggett as somewhat too sensational; after all, it treated the Mohocks lightly, and many people were convinced that Mohocks were Whig, or Tory, plotters. And it satirized the forces of law and order in the persons of the Constable and his watch, and the justices of the peace. Besides, the big cast made it uneconomical for an afterpiece. Tell the young fellow no, but to bring us his next one when he writes it, the managers might have said. Has talent, no doubt about that.

Bernard Lintott paid Gay two pounds six shillings for the copyright and published the play in April, in a modest octavo.[30]

The published version contained a mock-dedication "To Mr. *D****." That is, John Dennis, written by one "W.B." and dated April 1. "I am not at all concern'd at this *Tragedy*'s being rejected by the Players, when I consider how many of your immortal Compositions have met with no better Reception." Dennis had attacked—and been attacked in—Pope's *Essay on Criticism* the previous year.[31] This dedication is probably by Pope, that promised introduction to Gay's first play that he had mentioned to Henry Cromwell.

The brief Prologue, on the other hand, is Gay's, though it is to be "Spoken by the Publisher." The Publisher mentions Norris and Penkethman in their roles as watchmen, and the "Mighty Emperor."

> As matters stand; there's but this only way,
> T'applaud our disappointed Author's Play:
> Let all those Hands that would have clapp'd, combine
> To take the whole Impression off from mine.
> That's a sure way to raise the Poet's Name:
> A New Edition gains immortal Fame.[32]

Gay could spend his two pounds six shillings copy money as he pleased, and postpone to the next theatre season his quest for immortal fame. He would have another play ready for the managers by then.

THREE

Chaucer in Augustan England

The hopes of Gay and his bookseller Lintott for a second edition of *The Mohocks* did not materialize. At some point Gay, who naturally had more faith in his play than Lintott did, bought the copyright back for what Lintott had paid him.[1] The Drury Lane managers continued on their extremely conservative choice of repertory during the spring of 1712—not a single new play after Ambrose Philips's *The Distrest Mother* in March and only three all season. And the Mohocks suddenly stopped harrying pedestrians in Fleet Street, if they had ever been around there in the first place. Gay's total return was whatever he had learned about the Drury Lane troupe that he had not known earlier, and Lintott's two pounds six shillings. Knowledge of the Drury Lane company, of whom more later, was an important asset for a playwright who wanted to see his work produced. He had written *The Mohocks* with big roles for a number of the principal actors, male and female, at Drury Lane and he would do so the next time, too. This gave him a talking point when he approached the managers with a script, for the managers were actors themselves and relished big roles.

Gay needed more than Lintott's two pound six to live on. At some point he had come into a small inheritance, possibly on the death of his brother Jonathan,[2] and late in 1712 became domestic steward to the widowed Duchess of Monmouth. This appointment was to provide Gay a comfortable berth at the Duchess's residence in Chelsea for the next two years, during which time he was to further his friendship

with Pope and to become acquainted with Swift and Arbuthnot. The Duchess, Anne Scott, who was also Duchess of Buccleuch in her own right,[3] provided Gay an entree into, or at
least an acquaintanceship with, the circle of Scottish peers
where he was later to find his ultimate patrons, the Duke and
Duchess of Queensberry. As the widow of Dryden's Absalom,
who had lived through the whole tempest of Monmouth's rebellion and its fatal aftermath, she must also have been a rare
source of gossip if she had felt inclined to chat with her steward. Gay was of course hired help, in spite of Alexander Pope's
later anguished instruction to Gay's biographer that he state
he was "*Secretary* not *Servant, to the Duchess of Monmouth.*"[4]

Gay's duties as domestic steward or secretary were presumably not taxing; he was able to finish a considerable
amount of poetry during the next two years and to see his second play produced. Now that he was established in the metropolis, his thoughts seem to have returned to the country.
Perhaps this was a natural reaction, but it is interesting that
both the poem *Rural Sports*, which he published in 1713, and
The Shepherd's Week, on which he was working that year, obviously draw on his Devon origins. So, in special ways, does
his play *The Wife of Bath*. It is as if the West Country was
echoing in his memory, now that he had made the final, de-
cisive move to London.

John Gay's second play, *The Wife of Bath*, has, as Howard
Erskine-Hill complains, "been regularly dismissed."[5] Like
Erskine-Hill, I would argue the dismissers mistaken and call
for a second opinion. Investigators would find a work of originality, both in conception and execution, by a playwright
who has continued to learn his craft. In his second attempt he
moves from a one-act to a five-act format, testing his skills at
the standard length. Perhaps burned by his brush with the
heat of national politics in *The Mohocks*, Gay makes his next
play apolitical: it is a domestic intrigue comedy, offset in
time from Whig-Tory realities by some three centuries, and
placed in the peaceful English countryside to boot. That
peaceful English countryside had its own brand of politics, as
he knew, and he would introduce rural politics in his third

work for the stage, *The What D'Ye Call It*, but satire in *The Wife of Bath* is wholly social satire, without any sort of political reference.

The play also sheds significant light on what Gay and his contemporaries, most especially Pope, knew and thought about Chaucer. The careless answer is, of course, not much; Chaucer had been dead for more than three hundred years and the formal scholarly Chaucer revival was still in the future.[6] Furthermore, the Chaucer Pope and Gay knew was by way of a black-letter reprint of Speght's 1612 edition, a most forbidding example of the "art of the book."[7] It is a fascinating fact, however, that around 1712 Pope, Gay, and Matthew Prior were each engaged in writing about, or in the manner of, Chaucer. Gay, it will be recalled, had hailed Prior in "On a Miscellany of Poems," saying he wrote "With *Chaucer's* Humour, and with *Spencer's* Strains." Pope had published his early "translations" of Chaucer in 1709 and was working on his imitation of *The House of Fame, The Temple of Fame*.[8] The three youthful wits, early in their literary careers, were thinking about the great poet.

Dryden's decision to include modernizations of Chaucer in his *Fables* (1700), along with translations from Boccaccio, Homer, and Ovid, demonstrates that Dryden and his bookseller Jacob Tonson regarded Chaucer's language as being virtually unintelligible to the average reader.[9] Dryden said as much in his famous preface: "I grant that something must be lost in . . . all Translations; but the Sense will remain, which would otherwise be lost, or at least be maim'd, when it is scarce intelligible; and that but to a few. How few are there who can read *Chaucer*, so as to understand him perfectly? And if imperfectly, then with less Profit and no Pleasure."[10] This worried Alexander Pope, too, who admired Chaucer and who also admired Dryden. It is perhaps not straining the evidence too much to guess that Pope's worry brought about Gay's play.

In his *Essay on Criticism*, Pope presented the fate of Chaucer's poetry as emblematic of that awaiting anyone who chooses to write in the vernacular rather than in one of the classical languages:

Our Sons their Fathers' *failing Language* see,
And such as *Chaucer* is, shall *Dryden* be.[11]

Pope had by that time (1712 or so) been preoccupied with
Chaucer, via Dryden, for a long time. Many years later, in
1736, he recalled approaching Chaucer as a youthful exercise—very youthful if we are to believe him. "Mr. *Dryden's Fables,*" Pope wrote, "came out about that time, which
occasion'd the Translations [i.e., Pope's] from *Chaucer.*"[12]
Pope would have been eleven years old when the *Fables* appeared. Be Pope's recollection of precocity as it may, he certainly had Chaucer much on his mind during his early career,
as the quotation from the *Essay on Criticism* attests—a very
melancholy quotation when one thinks about it, because it of
course applies with greatest force to *him,* Alexander Pope.
"And such as Dryden is, shall Pope be." Leopold Damrosch
has recently shown how Pope approached Chaucer by way of
Dryden, mastering "Dryden's epigrammatic mode, which
does not actually condense the thought, but rather expands it
in clearly charted dimensions."[13]

In some respects, then, Pope's early translations of Chaucer and his imitation, *The Temple of Fame,* may be seen as attempts to shore up Chaucer's reputation, to rescue his
language from the failure that the young poet in a gloomy
mood foresees as somehow inevitable. Pope was working on
The Temple in 1712: he sent a version to Steele in that year. For
aught anyone knows Pope may have introduced Gay to Chaucer about this time; both Pope and Gay were essentially au-
todidacts, with Pope enjoying the role of tutor in Gay's case:
he was not displeased when someone referred to Gay as his
élève.[14] The Franklyn, who is a character in the play, describes
the Canterbury pilgrims as "certainly the most diverting
Company that ever travell'd the Road."[15] This could be taken
as Gay's own delighted first reaction to Chaucer's band of pilgrims. Almost anyone would need encouragement before trying Chaucer in Speght's daunting black-letter edition;
perhaps Pope steered Gay in Chaucer's direction to take his
mind off *The Mohocks* fiasco.

Pope in 1712 was modernizing Chaucer's poetry to the
standards of verse he had set forth in the *Essay on Criticism;*

John Gay was at the same time trying to dramatize a version of the poet himself. It is as if the two young writers sat down and discussed ways of presenting to the public the old-fashioned author whom they admired. Perhaps they did just that. At any rate, in 1713 Pope was still working on *The Temple of Fame* (not published until 1715) and in May of that year Gay's play had its premiere at Drury Lane.

This involved negotiations with the prickly managers, the "Triumvirs" Thomas Doggett, Colley Cibber, and Robert Wilks, and rehearsals with the company. The negotiations were successful. The managers accepted the play on its merits. Gay had no shadow of noble patronage, not that these managers would have paid much attention to pressuring from the nobility in any case. The fact that Gay published *The Wife of Bath* without a dedication may be an indication of how little support from the political establishment, Whig *or* Tory, he enjoyed; it may also be an indication of his desire for literary independence. He was not above soliciting publicity for his play, however. When the play went into rehearsal, Richard Steele, now editing his new paper, *The Guardian*, attended a rehearsal, presumably at Gay's invitation. Gay received his anticipated puff in *Guardian* No. 50, of which more later.

The Drury Lane company had gone through the turmoil of theatrical ownership and competition described earlier and was settling into a period of stability which would last for almost twenty years, at the acting if not at the management level. It was a remarkably able and varied company, with strengths in several areas. Their long suit was the theatrical standards: tragedy, especially Shakespearean, and domestic comedy, but they also had people who could dance or sing or throw a pratfall or sport a funny hat if the play demanded it. The managers assigned an excellent cast to Gay's play: one of their own number, Robert Wilks, taking the role of Chaucer himself, and first-line male comedians and female actresses for the remainder of the roles. This no doubt had to do with the fact that the company was also playing Addison's

Cato in repertory. *Cato* has little need for females and none at all for comedians; the best in both categories could be spared for Gay's new play.

Wilks was the matinee idol of Drury Lane, though the term had not been invented: he played the male romantic leads (such as the Numidian Prince Juba in *Cato*). Margaret Bicknell, who was to play Alison, the eponymous Wife, had made her way as a dancer and singer but she was also becoming known as a skillful comedian; "an agreeable girlish Person," Steele in *The Spectator* had called her the year before.[16] Gay evidently liked her style because he wrote two more big parts for her in his next two plays. Mary Porter, who was to play Myrtilla in *The Wife of Bath*, was on the other hand developing tragic roles—by 1720 she had become the leading tragedienne in London. Benjamin Victor said that she had "a *plain Person* and a *bad Voice*" but admitted that she was a great performer.[17] Samuel Johnson befriended her in later life. Gay wrote no more for her until he himself turned toward tragedy, when she starred in his ill-fated classical tragedy, *The Captives*. Henry Norris and William Penkethman, wildly successful knockabout comedians whom as we have seen Gay expected to act in *The Mohocks*, were cast here in differing ways: Norris, as so often, a servant but Penkethman as an important character, the Franklyn. "Jubilee Dicky" Norris, so-called from his stellar performance in Farquhar's *Trip to the Jubilee*, was fondly remembered by Victor for his "little formal Figure, and his singular, squeaking Tone of Voice."[18] Pinky Penkethman was the bane of living dramatic authors because of his predilection for ad-libbing, often risqué ad-libbing. Dead authors could not complain, and audiences certainly loved it and him. If the evening seemed to drag, patrons in the cheap gallery rows were known to begin beating on their seats until the performance was interrupted, and Pinky came downstage to sing the Black Joke for them.

William Bullock, an experienced comedian, played Doublechin the Monk, and his son Christopher created the role of Merit. The Bullocks exemplified the acting family, which would be increasingly important as the theatre became more professional in both Britain and America: the Baddeleys, the Booths, the Barrymores. So did the actress who played the ingenue Florinda, Susanna or Susan Mountfort, whose parents were both performers and in whose honor, theatre gossip had it, Gay wrote his most enduringly popular ballad, "Sweet William's Farewell to Black-Ey'd Susan."[19] Americans may be surprised to learn that Gay's compliment is entirely to Susan's black, i.e. brown, eyes and has nothing to do metaphorically with flowers of the genus Rudbeckia. The flower took its name from the popular ballad and not the other way around.[20] Just about this time Susan exercised her considerable charms on Barton Booth, the leading tragic actor of the company, and became his mistress. It was a small and interesting world with which Gay was acquainting himself, the Drury Lane company.

All seemed to be going well for an April premiere. Then Addison's *Cato* opened, with an enthusiastic prologue by Pope. Applauded by both Whig and Tory for its presentation of Roman virtue, *Cato* became the hit of the season. My "play comes on, on the 5th of May," Gay wrote a friend in the country; "it was put off upon account of Cato; so that you may easily imagine I by this time begin to be a little sensible of the approaching Danger."[21]

Gay's apprehensions were well-founded. After playing *Cato* all of April and into May, the Drury Lane company presented a repertory favorite, Steele's *The Funeral* on Monday, 11 May and the premiere of *The Wife of Bath* on 12 May. *Venice Preserv'd* followed on Wednesday and *The Wife* was advertised but not acted, for reasons unknown, on Thursday. Then on Friday, 15 May, *The Wife* was given its second and final performance, "Benefit the Author." This is distinctly odd. It suggests that Gay may have fallen victim to some kind of backstage machinations. Possibly the free-floating hostility toward Pope, even at this early date, may have rubbed off in some way on Gay—two years later this would certainly be the case. A simple conclusion, however, may be that the great financial rewards of *Cato* worked against Gay's play getting a fair chance at success. Why, the managers could have asked themselves as they were counting the bulging receipts from *Cato*, should they bother? They were an iota less conservative in repertory selection that season: six new plays produced versus three the preceding season, but only relatively less conservative. No contemporary reports of those two early, isolated performances of *The Wife of Bath* are known to exist, so all this must be speculative.

In any case, and significantly, Bernard Lintott, the bookseller and a hardened veteran of the publishing world, thought enough of the play to pay Gay twenty-five pounds for the copyright, a tenfold increase over that for *The Mohocks*.[22] The payment represents a substantial vote of confidence by Lintott for this playwright who was virtually unknown: he had paid Farquhar only 16 pounds 2 shillings sixpence for the highly successful *The Recruiting Officer* in 1705.[23]

For his own purposes of plot, Gay sets his play on 21 January, the Eve of St. Agnes, three months before that Aprille with his shoures soote. Chaucer and his band are on the road to Canterbury, spring or no spring however, and the play takes place in an inn on the road between the cathedral city and London. The Franklyn proposes to marry off his daughter Florinda to a pretentious young poet Doggrell, and to invite all the pilgrims to the wedding the next day. The play opens with Chaucer, the heroine of the play Alison, and a Lady Myrtilla, all separated from the band for reasons unspecified. Present in the inn also are assorted servants, Doublechin the Monk, and Merit, a worthy young man, as his name certifies, who is in love with Florinda. As all readers of Keats know, on the Eve of St. Agnes one sees one's intended spouse. Various mistakes of the night ensue, deriving from this folk motif. On this night for apparitions, Chaucer, disguised as an astrologer, engineers apparitions in some excellent farce scenes. Florinda refuses to marry Doggrell but gives her hand to Merit; Chaucer vows to marry the Lady Myrtilla, thereby saving her from entering a convent, and the Wife of Bath tricks Doggrell into a marriage with Busie the maid.

Gay has rather more plot than he knows what to do with, but there are many good things here. A number of the characters, such as Doublechin the Monk and Doggrell the poet, are conceived in the Jonson/Shadwell tradition of humors comedy, in which some psychological characteristic, as the twentieth century would put it, is emphasized for comic effect. Steele liked the play in rehearsal and as a professional playwright himself recognized its ancestry in humors comedy; he always included humors characters in his own comedies. Writing in *Guardian* No. 50 about Margaret Bicknell as Alison, Steele observed, "If the rest of the Actors enter into their several Parts with the same Spirit, the humourous Characters of the Play cannot but appear excellent [in] the Theatre."[24]

Gay's Chaucer is represented to be an affable, resourceful man, much given to bursting into spontaneous poetry. Played as noted earlier by the romantic lead Robert Wilks, Chaucer exemplifies the power of good poetry: his singing proposal to Lady Myrtilla in the last act represents this power:

> *Daphne*, a coy and foolish Dame,
>   Flew from *Apollo*'s Charms,
> Had he confess'd in Verse his Flame,
>   She had flown into his Arms.
>
> Whenever *Orpheus* touch'd the Lyre,
>   Or sung melodious Airs,
> He made the very Stones admire,
>   And tam'd the fiercest Bears.
>
> Are Ladies Hearts more hard than Stone,
>   And Wolves and Bears less fierce?
> Then, prithee, Nymph, no longer frown,
>   But own the Pow'r of Verse. (V.71-82)

When the Lady Myrtilla agrees to marry him, Chaucer responds in another song:

> Marriage, the chiefest Good that Mortals know,
> Doubles our Joy, while it divides our Woe:

What anxious Cares can then our Bliss controul,
When Heav'n assents, and Love unites our Soul?

(V. 103-106)

A minor oddity of Gay's characterization with some historical interest is that he represents Chaucer as being fat. The
saucy servant Busie declares to Chaucer: "that Body of yours
will scarce be able to enter a Chink or pass through a Key-
hole." What has been taken to be the earliest reference to
Chaucer's embonpoint is Urry's edition of 1721.[25] Perhaps
Urry had seen or read Gay's play. Gay himself waged a battle
all his adult life with his expanding waistline.

Contrasted with Chaucer, who is in charge of the action
throughout, is Doggrell, the would-be poet. Like Daniel Foe
(Defoe) and Thomas Durfey he traces his lineage to France:
"My name is originally of *French* Extraction, and is written
with a D, and an Apostrophe—as much as to say, *De Ogrelle*,
which was the antique Residence of my Ancestors" (I.i.26-
28). Doggrell is a literary trifler; some of Gay's animosity toward the type shows through in the characterization. The
Franklyn, a countryman innocent of these things, says of him,
"Mr. *Doggrell*, they tell me, writes only for his Diversion, nay,
he pays the Bookseller for printing his Works,—and writes
the most like a Gentleman of any Man on this side *Parnassus*"
(I.387-90). Sure enough, the kind of poetry he writes is in that
high heroic vein which Pope and Fielding were later to burlesque, with much invocation of the heavenly powers:

Ye Gods! did *love* e'er tast such Charms,
When prest in fair *Alcmena*'s Arms
O ye Immortal Pow'rs!

"Mark the Harmony, Sir," Doggrell advises Chaucer, "—and
the easie Cadence that falls through the whole Stanza. . . . I
defie the *Italian* to run more soft." Gay's penchant for literary
burlesque, which flowered in *The Beggar's Opera*, is working
well here, too.

It will be discerned that Gay, like Pope in the *Temple*,
does not attempt to reproduce Chaucerian language, though

he was capable of doing so, as he demonstrated in his "An Answer to the Sompner's Prologue of Chaucer" (1717). This begins

> The Sompner leudly hath his Prologue told,
> And saine on the Freers his Tale japing and bold;
> How that in Hell they searchen near and wide,
> And ne one Freer in all thilke place espyde,
> But lo! the Devil turned his erse about,
> And twenty thousand Freers wend in and out.[26]

Gay's ear was always finely tuned. To the Franklyn's servant Antony, played by "Jubilee Dicky," he gives dialect but it is English country dialect, of the sort Gay was accustomed to hearing in his native Devon. Antony and his colleague William contemplate rescuing Florinda from Doggrell:

> *Antony.* Look-ye there,—yonder she is, i'faith—softly, softly *William,*—swop upon en at once, knack en dawn, and I will secure young Mistress. (II.i.41-43)

The pair tackle and bind the protesting poet. Gay is letting the diminutive Norris exercise to the full his talent for farce and command of the audience, and introducing by him some taste of country speech.

Country superstitions, which Gay's prologue alleges run "through all the Kind," that is, all the human species, are everywhere in the play. Some of them are given a Shakespearean ring, no doubt quite intentionally by the young poet, who was reading that master as well as Chaucer. The spell Chaucer casts for Alison in Act IV is, for example, reminiscent of *The Tempest* or *A Midsummer Night's Dream:*

> Thrice I wave my Wand around,
> And consecrate this Spot of Ground.
> *Zutphin*, and *Zephin,*—ye that Reign
> Far beyond the Norther Main.
>
> Quickly, quickly take your Flight,
> And leave the dark Abyss of Night;

> Hither, hither, gently fly,
> Ye milder Spirits of the Sky,
> Let now my Science be your Care,
> And bring her Lover to the Fair.
>   (IV. 187-96, italics reversed.)

Most of the superstitions, like this one, appropriately, have to do with love and marriage, and they are often given a racy turn by Gay, like those in his *Shepherd's Week*, which he was also working on at exactly this period.[27] Alison, for example, guides Busie in the search for and interpretation of moles on her body.

> *Busie.* Ay—this must be one here—with two little things branching out; for that is an infallible Mark of a Husband.
> *Alison.* You search in the wrong Place, Child. (I.152–54)

The title role of Alison was played by Margaret Bicknell, about whose acting in rehearsal Steele waxed enthusiastic in *The Guardian*. The Wife of Bath—a much younger and less cynical character than Chaucer's—exudes proverbs and folk wisdom. "What is bred in the Bone," she soliloquizes, "I find, will never out of the Flesh" (III.301-2). Bicknell was also a good singer, and, as we have seen, Gay in this play continued his experiments with song lyrics, which he had begun somewhat tentatively in *The Mohocks*. In the third-act drinking song he gives to Alison, he casts the first stanza in iambic and the second in anapestic, as if to demonstrate his virtuosity:

> The Maiden and the Batchelor,
>   Pardie—are simple Elves,
> And 'till they grow to Man and Wife,
>   Know nothing of themselves.
>
> Then since we're each others by Nature design'd
>   Let's unite, and our Knowledge improve;
> Here's a Health to the Lass that is passively kind,
>   And the Youth that is active in Love. (III.i.105-12)

Twentieth-century audiences might wonder about lasses who are passively kind, but in fact Gay is evenhanded in his

treatment of gender in the play, portraying Alison sympathet-
ically and awarding her the rich Franklyn at the curtain. Florinda the daughter is given dialogue that strikes a feminist
note. Told by the Monk Doublechin that her father's wish that
she marry Doggrell amounts to a command, a daughter not
being a free agent, she exclaims, "Not a free Agent! How, Father, what, compliment the Sex with Slavery?—marry a
Woman to her Aversion, and give her a Mortification for
Life?" (V.ii.160-62). Gay was to return to this question of children versus parents several times, though of course so did
many other dramatists—and novelists.

It was a burning question, one without any apparent so-
lution. Florinda escapes her father's edict because Doggrell
mistakenly marries the maid Busie; even so, the Franklyn is
furious at her recalcitrance, avowing that "I will marry on
purpose to get Heirs to disinherit thee, Gipsie." At the curtain
Chaucer promises that we "will all turn Mediators, and rec-
oncile Differences at a more convenient Opportunity," then
calls for the customary concluding dance.

The continuing hostility between Florinda and her father
does not invalidate the play's comic premise, however; audiences at stage comedy in those days were used to inconclusive
conclusions, closed with a dance. Except, possibly, for
costuming[28] and for the presence of Doublechin the Monk,
the play presents little or nothing in a mode of archaizing:
the issues dramatized are contemporary social issues, not
those of Chaucer's era. Perhaps gun-shy after the fate of *The
Mohocks*, though, Gay excludes anything that could even remotely be interpreted as partisan in the overheated atmosphere of London, 1713. This play was intended to please the
public and in one respect at least it did: Alison's ballad in the
final act, "There was a Swain full fair," was published in
broadside form with music by John Barrett, a leading composer of incidental theatre music, and became a standard
popular-music hit, the earliest of Gay's ballads to achieve enduring success.[29] With an excellent cast, good music, and
publicity from Steele in *The Guardian*, *The Wife of Bath*'s dis-
mal fate remains a mystery.

Pope almost certainly contributed the Epilogue to *The Wife of Bath*[30] and in the winter of 1713–1714 both he and Gay went publicly over to the Tory side, associating themselves with Swift, Dr. John Arbuthnot, and the Earl of Oxford in the Scriblerus Club. In spite of its subsequent fame, the Club accomplished little in the way of literary productions at the time, but the association was undoubtedly energizing for each member. Their principal project, the *Memoirs* (1741) of the pedant Martin Scriblerus, was perhaps substantially the work of Dr. Arbuthnot, the learned and respectable physician to the Queen. Arbuthnot had a vein of facetiousness, as displayed in his *John Bull* pamphlets of 1712, and a facetious tone runs through the *Memoirs*. The *Memoirs* singles out too many satiric victims to be easily categorized, but primary attacks are made on what the Scriblerians took to be antiquarian and scientific pedantry. Arbuthnot knew more about both science and antiquarian pursuits than any of the other Scriblerians, and he probably led the way, with the others happily following.[31] Much of the *Memoirs'* power derives from its successful burlesquing of scientific and antiquarian language, the sort sometimes employed in the *Transactions* of the Royal Society or in the treatises of historical philologists or textual critics. Swift had earlier sounded this burlesquing note, of course, in *A Tale of a Tub* (1704), and Gay's next two plays were to make much use of the technique.

So did his long poem *The Shepherd's Week*, which appeared in April 1714. This work was in part a burlesque of Ambrose Philips's verse pastorals.[32] More interesting for our purposes than the burlesque, however, is Gay's extensive use of folklore, folk dialect, and folk customs, which he had employed as we have seen to some extent the year before in *The Wife of Bath*. *The Shepherd's Week* secured Gay the literary acclaim he had not so far won with his plays. By that spring of 1714 he was feeling confident enough of his status to seek and find employment as a diplomat. He accompanied the Earl of Clarendon to Germany as his private secretary. Clarendon was sent by the Tory ministry to ingratiate the ministry with the House of Hanover. Queen Anne's health continued to decline. Unfortunately for the Tories and for Gay personally, the queen died soon after the mission arrived in Hanover; the reins of government slipped away from the divided Tories, and Gay was without formal employment again.

He had met some persons in Hanover, however, who would figure prominently in his life: Princess Caroline, wife of the future Prince of Wales, a vivacious and intelligent woman, had asked him for a copy of *The Shepherd's Week* and subscribed to Pope's translation of Homer on Gay's recommendation.[33] This was heady stuff. A young Englishwoman was in Hanover with her husband at the same time, like Gay hoping for future employment. The couple's prospects, however, were far better than Gay's. Henrietta Howard was of impeccable gentry background: she was born a Hobart of Blickling Hall, Norfolk, and her husband, Charles Howard, was the third son of the Earl of Suffolk. Unfortunately he was also, according to Lord Hervey, "wrong-headed, ill-tempered, obstinate, drunken, extravagant, [and] brutal." Henrietta received unusual praise from the waspish Hervey, "Good sense, good breeding, and good nature were qualities which even her enemies could not deny her."[34] Gay's sanguine temperament must have provided a welcome contrast to that of her husband: he and Henrietta became and remained close friends. On her return to England she was named Woman of the Bedchamber to Princess Caroline: she would be helpful to Gay.

Back in London himself, Gay found the Scriblerus Club effectively dispersed as a club but Arbuthnot and Pope still available for literary companionship. Looking for a patron or for regular employment, Gay drifted into Pope's orbit and remained there in outward circumstances for much of the rest of his life. His intellectual independence, however, he retained to the end, as his friend Pope came to recognize.

The Tories were out of office, apparently for a long time, and employment with the government was not now a possibility. Gay would need to continue as a literary man. By the end of 1714 he was at work on a new play.

FOUR

Words and Music

The next several years after the death of Queen Anne in 1714 would be those in which Gay moved into his mature style as a farceur, paradoxical as the application of the term "maturity" to farce may seem. They would also be the years in which he received his final lessons as a librettist from the great master of the musical stage, Handel. By 1718 Gay was ready in all essentials to write *The Beggar's Opera:* he had mined an apprentice's knowledge of London lowlife for *The Mohocks,* he had learned how to put together a full-length comedy, and a good one, in *The Wife of Bath,* he had tuned his ear for burlesque and adjusted his eye for farce in *The What D'Ye Call It* and *Three Hours After Marriage,* and he had watched Handel put music to the words he himself had written for *Acis and Galatea.* Gay had been working on *The Mohocks* in 1711; the seven-year period ending in 1718 constitutes an apprenticeship for the stage of appropriate length— and extraordinary quality.

Although Gay's political friends were among the outs after the death of the queen—Oxford, Bolingbroke, and Prior as architects of the Tory peace were targeted for prosecution by the newly dominant Whigs—the situation in the London theatres was now much better than it had been for an aspiring dramatic author. Richard Steele, on the winning Whig side after the Queen's death, was offered and accepted the governorship of the Theatre Royal in Drury Lane. This was only partly, and not principally, a political reward: as a practicing playwright and working journalist who knew personally all the theatrical professionals, Steele was widely judged to be the man for the job. A playwright would be sympathetic to new work by other dramatists. Day-to-day management would remain in the hands of the veteran actor-managers Barton Booth (who had forced his way into the partnership at Doggett's expense), Robert Wilks and Colley Cibber, but Steele's influence would be great, both with respect to what was produced and who came to see it. As Cibber later put it, "many Days had our House been particularly fill'd, by the Influence, and Credit of his Pen."[1]

Swift and Steele had parted ways, irrevocably, in 1713 because of partisan differences, but Pope and Gay continued to write for Steele's *Guardian* through the autumn of that year and in any case Steele was the sort to let bygones now be bygones. Besides, Drury Lane needed plays. In December 1714 the brothers John and Christopher Rich reopened the theatre at Lincoln's Inn Fields and persuaded several of the Drury Lane actors to join their troupe, including Robert Pack, who had created Doggrell for Gay in *The Wife of Bath*. Unable to produce some of their plays because of the actors' defection, the Drury Lane managers were watching their profits carefully.[2] It was time to try something different.

Gay had a new afterpiece ready for them by early 1715. This was *The What D'Ye Call It*, a farce burlesque, or as its subtitle runs, echoing Hamlet's players, "A Tragi-Comi-Pastoral Farce." In two short acts with introductory and closing framing scenes, the play is set in the country, Gay once again drawing on the knowledge of folklore and folklife he had shown earlier, in *The Wife of Bath* and *The Shepherd's Week*. A long mock-learned preface to the printed version, in which the author discusses, with owlish seriousness, objections to his play's being termed a comedy, a tragedy, or a pastoral, stems directly from the lucubrations of the Scriblerus Club, and Pope and Arbuthnot may well have had a hand in it. "The Judicious Reader will easily perceive," the Author observes complacently, "that the Unities are kept as in the most perfect Pieces, that the Scenes are unbroken, and Poetical

Justice strictly observ'd."[3] "Pinky" Penkethman, who played the comic lead Peascod, took a different line in the Prologue:

> Criticks, we know, by antient rules may maul it;
> But sure gallants must like—the *What d'ye call it.*[4]

The play's setting is the hall of a country justice of the peace, where the host, Sir Roger, and his fellow justices are overseeing the production of a Christmas play, a tragedy in blank verse to be put on by the members of their households. The steward's daughter, Kitty, reveals in an aside that she is pregnant by Sir Roger's son, Squire Thomas. The character she portrays in the tragedy is in the same delicate condition by her love, Thomas Filbert, who is of course played by Squire Thomas, art faithfully reflecting life, or the reverse. Filbert is apparently hauled off to war by a sergeant and his press gang, who also prepare to shoot Filbert's companion Thomas Peascod for desertion. Five ghosts arise to condemn the justices for sending Peascod to his death, and one of them sings a song; "dismally," orders Gay in his stage direction. A last-minute reprieve and the sergeant's arrest for stealing Gaffer Gap's gray mare, a mad scene and attempted suicide by Kitty lead to a final wedding between Filbert and Kitty, which turns out in the framing drama to be the real thing, too: Squire Thomas makes an honest woman of the steward's daughter. The parish clerk pronounces perhaps the shortest epilogue in eighteenth-century drama, and perhaps the best: "Our stage play has a moral—and no doubt / You all have sense enough to find it out" (1716 ed., p. 41).

The What D'Ye Call It demonstrates that Gay was by now the perfect master of stage farce and, as Leo Hughes has judged, the most important voice in dramatic burlesque of the two decades before burlesque reached its high point with Fielding in the 1730s.[5] It is a burlesque not only of blank-verse tragedy but of all tragedy, indeed of the very spirit of tragedy. A published *Key*, prepared by someone who knew a fair amount about Gay and Pope,[6] demonstrates that every

scene, almost every line, burlesques some motif or some passage in stage tragedy. For example, Pierre's famous remon-
stration to Jaffeir in *Venice Preserv'd*, when he is facing
execution:

> Is't fit a Souldier, who has liv'd with Honour,
> Fought Nations Quarrels, and bin Crown'd with Conquest,
> Be expos'd a common Carcass on a Wheel?[7]

The rhetorical question and the situation are echoed in
Peascod's lament, as he also faces execution, for desertion:

> Say, is it fitting in this very field,
> Where I so oft have reap'd, so oft have till'd;
> This field, where from my youth I've been a carter,
> I, in this field, should die for a deserter? (p. 27)

This particular echo draws criticism from the author of the
Key, who calls it "an unpardonable Burlesque from one of the
finest strokes of Pitty that perhaps ever was drawn."[8] But that
of course is what burlesque is all about. It will be observed
that Gay casts his burlesque of blank verse tragedy in couplets, allowing the delicious rime of carter/deserter.

No tragic writer is exempt from burlesquing: if there is a
ghost in *Macbeth*, there are five of them here, one singing "Ye
goblins and fairys,/With frisks and vagarys." Shakespeare,
Jonson, Dryden, Otway, Addison, Rowe, each is laid under
contribution, but no one needs a *Key* to enjoy *The What D'Ye
Call It:* it is self-contained and self-explanatory, as the best
farce must be. For example, the convention of verse tragedy
that calls for the filling-out of a pentameter line no matter
how many speakers may be involved is ludicrous enough as it
appears on the printed page. But Gay builds comedy into the
lines themselves even as he follows and burlesques the convention; no printed page is necessary. Kitty and Filbert bid
each other farewell, completing an iambic pentameter line in
four lame attempts, as it were:

> *Kitty.* To part is death——
> *Filbert.*   'tis death to part.

Kitty.	—Ah!
Filbert.	—Oh! (p. 15)

Reasonably competent actors can make a good thing of this scene, and in the first production the Drury Lane managers cast the old comedy hand Benjamin Johnson as Filbert, and Margaret Bicknell, the Wife of Bath, as Kitty. Bicknell was an excellent singer and Gay provided her a lyric with music by Handel that became one of the most popular songs of the century, " 'Twas when the seas were roaring."[9]

Because this is one of the earliest of Gay's lyrics that indisputably became a popular success, it is perhaps a suitable one to focus on in attempting to establish what constitutes a good song lyric and how Gay became a superior lyricist. Nothing definitive can be achieved on the printed page in such an inquiry because, as Gay had learned from Handel's example, words must play against music and the reverse. Still, some generalizations can be made in shorthand form. The successful lyric must be clear; that is to say, it must be intelligible to the listener on first hearing. Yet it also must possess some metrical and poetic virtuosity in its own right, qualities of art and wit that make it memorable with or without its music. The two qualities of clarity and poetic virtuosity are of course potentially in opposition, clarity becoming banality and virtuosity merging into auditory obscurity.

Gay's ballad sets out its pathetic situation in the opening two stanzas:

> 'TWAS when the seas were roaring
>   With hollow blasts of wind;
> A damsel lay deploring,
>   All on a rock reclin'd.
> Wide o'er the rolling billows
>   She cast a wistful look;
> Her head was crown'd with willows
>   That tremble o'er the brook.
>
> Twelve months are gone and over,
>   And nine long tedious days.

> Why didst thou, vent'rous lover,
>   Why didst thou trust the seas?
> Cease, cease, thou cruel ocean,
>   And let my lover rest;
> Ah! what's thy troubled motion
>   To that within my breast?

"Deploring" and "reclin'd" are just right: this is burlesque, not tragedy; Kitty the Steward's Daughter, alias Kitty Carrot, not Ophelia, sings.

> The merchant rob'd of pleasure,
>   Sees tempests in despair;
> But what's the loss of treasure
>   To losing of my dear?
> Should you some coast be laid on
>   Where gold and di'monds grow,
> You'd find a richer maiden,
>   But none that loves you so.

Gay was to echo the image of love on a foreign strand—no doubt deliberately—in the *Beggar's Opera's* famous duet between Macheath and Polly, "Were I laid on Greenland's Coast." The merchant's vexation also of course reappears there with Peachum and his double-entry bookkeeping: over here in one column money, over there love.

> How can they say that nature
>   Has nothing made in vain;
> Why then beneath the water
>   Should hideous rocks remain?
> No eyes the rocks discover,
>   That lurk beneath the deep,
> To wreck the wand'ring lover,
>   And leave the maid to weep.

C. F. Burgess has noted that the weeping Maid is here echoing the complaint of Dorigen in Chaucer's "Franklin's Tale."[10] She is also setting up the tragic outcome, with its gentle burlesque of *Hamlet*. Gay is very consciously associating the popular ballad here with "formal" literature, a process that, as Dianne Dugaw has shown, long preceded the ballad "revival" later in the century.[11]

> All melancholy lying;
>   Thus wail'd she for her dear;
> Repay'd each blast with sighing,
>   Each billow with a tear;
> When o'er the white wave stooping
>   His floating corpse she spy'd;
> Then like a lilly drooping,
>   She bow'd her head and dy'd.

Gay's ballad with Handel's music was on the street soon, in a song sheet that was collected as early as the following year, and Gay's editor, John Fuller, has identified fourteen other editions that appeared before the end of the century.[12] This ballad's success would have convinced Gay of the power of popular music, if he had required any convincing.

Fuller has observed that in *The What D'Ye Call It* Gay "has lodged as much criticism of social injustice as one's belief in the characters can bear."[13] This adds up to a considerable amount. The setting is the English country as in *The Wife of Bath*, but that setting is no longer benign. The pregnant Kitty, in both roles, is a victimized female. The justices are revealed to be brutal or corrupt or both, by the ghosts of those whom they have condemned:

> 4th GHOST.
> I was begot before my mother married,
> Who whipt by you, of me poor child miscarried.
>   *another woman's ghost rises*
> 5th GHOST.
> Its mother I, whom you whipt black and blue;
> Both owe our deaths to you, to you, to you.
>   *[all the ghosts shake their heads.]*
> SIR ROGER
> Why do you shake your mealy heads at me?
> You cannot say I did it—

BOTH JUSTICES
no—nor we.
　　　　　lst GHOST.
All three——
　　　　　2d GHOST.
——all three——
　　　　　3rd GHOST.
——all three——
　　　　　4th GHOST.
——all three——
　　　　　5th GHOST.
——all three.
　　　　　(p. 17)

The last-minute wedding of Kitty and Squire Thomas is an example of the "Poetical Justice strictly observ'd" that the "Author" pointed out in the Preface, like the ending-but-one of *The Beggar's Opera*. The wedding also provides for a splendid bit of visual farce at the close, in the manner of the assembly of wives and babies at the end of the *Opera*. The parson refuses to lend the company of players a gown for the wedding, calling it "a Profanation," so the wedding is held just off-stage—like the bloodshed in classical tragedy—and described to one and all by Sir Roger, the young Squire's father, "*at the door, pointing.*"

So natural! d'ye see now, neighbours? the ring, i'faith. to have and to hold! right again—well play'd, doctor; well play'd, son *Thomas*, come, come, I'm satisfy'd—now for the fiddles and dances. (p. 39)

The implied moral of the epilogue, for those who have the sense to find it out, might well be seen as the same one the Beggar pronounces for his *Opera*: "that the lower Sort of People have their Vices in a degree as well as the Rich: And that they are punish'd for them." *The What D'Ye Call It* dramatizes this subversive theme but it does so in Gay's rural mode: the country people, the country setting, the country ballads are those of *The Wife of Bath* and *The Shepherd's Week*. Gay is back in Devon, where he came from.

The What D'Ye Call It opened at Drury Lane on 23 February 1715 as an afterpiece, surely the ideal afterpiece, to Nicholas Rowe's tragedy *Jane Shore*, and won an audience immediately. It was played again the following day, a command performance for the Prince of Wales. Henrietta Howard, Woman of the Bedchamber to the Princess, must have been working hard on Gay's behalf. Rich countered that day at Lincoln's Inn Fields with a perfect match to Drury Lane's offering, Farquhar's *The Recruiting Officer* and Aaron Hill's *The Walking Statue* as afterpiece. The third night, 25 February, was Gay's first benefit and by the following week Pope could report to his friend John Caryll that though there were "still some grave sober men" who did not like the play "the laughers are so much the majority, that Mr. Dennis and one or two more seem determined to undeceive the town at their proper cost, by writing some critical dissertations against it."[14] By the end of the season *The What D'Ye Call It* had been played seventeen times, and Gay received sixteen pounds two shillings sixpence from Lintott for the copyright.[15] Penkethman took it to his booth at the Southwark fair the following summer. These booths were a sort of temporary theatre, in vogue since the turn of the century and much deplored by the authorities as cesspools of vice, which though temporary could however accommodate two hundred or more spectators.[16] *The What D'Ye Call It* remained in the London repertory for a half-century and more, and in the twentieth century it has twice been adapted as a one-act opera.[17] After *The Beggar's Opera* it has been Gay's most frequently performed dramatic work.

It also, in its printed version, occupies a small but interesting place in British printing history. David Foxon and James McLaverty have pointed out that in the so-called third edition of 1716 the printing custom of capitalizing initial letters of nouns is abandoned. This new edition was prepared by a different printer from that of the first (and "second," which is the first with a new title page). One "must assume," Foxon and McLaverty state, "that change was made on [Gay's] instructions."[18] They propose that this was the first, perhaps experimental, attempt on the part of Gay and Pope to alter certain obtrusive printing practices.

In the letter to Caryll, Pope spoke of a preface to be "pre-fixt to the farce in the vindication of the nature and dignity of this new way of writing." The Preface, as noted earlier, is pure Scriblerian mockery, of a high order. Pope and Arbuthnot both undoubtedly had a great deal to do with writing it, as the small London world immediately recognized. From this point rumors began circulating that the play itself was in part, or even principally, by Pope and Arbuthnot. There is lit-tle or no evidence that the play was by anyone other than Gay; his friends presumably made a suggestion here and there, and some of it at one time was in Pope's handwriting.[19] The fact that Pope and Gay were rumored to be co-authors, however, could have serious consequences for Gay. By this time Pope was being stalked by Addison's followers who gath-ered at Button's coffeehouse: Addison's "Little Senate," as Pope was to describe the group later. Though the attacks had their origin in rival translations of Homer, of which Pope was preparing one and Addison's protegé Tickell another, to a cer-tain extent they were on party lines: the Scriblerians were identified as Tories, and Addison and his flock were Whigs. But Gay continued to maintain friendships with Court Whigs, especially those around the Prince and Princess of Wales, and he still longed for patronage from some friendly quarter, somewhere. When *The What D'Ye Call It* was ready for the stage, Gay had written Parnell, "after this is play'd, I fully design, to pursue the Street Walking with Vigour, & let nothing interfere but a place, which at present, I have but lit-tle Prospects of."[20] No place materialized; the place-seeker pursued his street walking.

Gay's next major publication was the poem to which he referred in his letter to Parnell, *Trivia: Or, the Art of Walking the Streets of London*. Published in January 1716, the poem was an immediate success. Arbuthnot reported to Parnell that "Gay has gott so much money by his art of walking the streets, that he is ready to sett up his equipage [i.e., buy a carriage]. he is just going to the bank to negotiate some exchequer Bills."[21]

The poem that rescued Gay from his pedestrian habits may be experienced in different ways. Martin Battestin has seen it as typical of the Augustan poetic mode's concern for form and artifice as a defense "in a world too often hostile and unmanageable."[22] In terms of his dramatic practice, the poem is appropriately symbolic: Gay turns from the country settings and preoccupations of *The Shepherd's Week* and *The What D'Ye Call It* to the metropolis, for his poem and for his next play. Among its other qualities, *Trivia* has dramatic values, that is, it is an embodiment of London in action. For example, the walker—approximately Gay—sees the London apprentices in a pickup football game; a film camera could do justice to the former apprentice here watching himself. It is a scene from a comedy.

> from far,
> I spy the Furies of the Foot-ball War:
> The 'Prentice quits his Shop, to join the Crew,
> Encreasing Crouds the flying Game pursue.
> Thus, as you roll the Ball o'er snowy Ground,
> The gath'ring Globe augments with ev'ry Round;
> But whither shall I run? the Throng draws nigh,
> The Ball now Skims the Street, now soars on high;
> The dext'rous Glazier strong returns the Bound,
> And gingling Sashes on the Pent-house sound.[23]

If *Trivia* presents the poet alone, the observer walking the streets of London, Gay's next play, *Three Hours After Marriage*, is the poet as collaborator. It is the most Scriblerian of all Gay's plays, and no doubt the one most embodying the advice of Arbuthnot and Pope. The position here argued, however, is that it is essentially Gay's work, in conception and execution. *Three Hours After Marriage* shares several of the satiric targets of *The Memoirs of Martinus Scriblerus*, especially in its attack on the physician and antiquary Dr. John Woodward. It is reasonable to suppose that Gay, Pope, and Arbuthnot were once

more at work on the *Memoirs*.[24] In an advertisement to the
printed version of the play, published during its initial run,
Gay acknowledges "the Assistance I have receiv'd in this
Piece from two of my Friends;" these two friends were immediately recognized as being Pope and Arbuthnot.[25] This association no doubt provided good things for the play, but it also
provoked a severe reaction from Pope's enemies and in the
long run damaged the reception of the play and Gay's reputation for originality.

Three Hours After Marriage presents another version of the
December and May theme, already ancient in European literature by Chaucer's time. In this case Dr. Fossile, physician
and antiquary, has just married Mrs. Towneley but has not
yet consummated the marriage. Mrs. Towneley has apparently distributed her favors to half the male members of the
London smart set (as her name suggests), and the play con-
sists of Fossile's bungling attempts to prove her infidelities,
countered by her machinations to subvert this proof. She is
aided by two of her lovers, Plotwell and Underplot; in a famous scene they appear disguised as a mummy and a crocodile. A female poet, Phoebe Clinket, and a literary critic, Sir
Tremendous, add comic effects. Phoebe is so enamored of the
muse that she employs a maid with a desk strapped to her
back, ready to receive Phoebe's latest inspiration. Gay was
writing for the Drury Lane company. Margaret Bicknell, who
had demonstrated her abilities in both *The Wife of Bath* and
The What D'Ye Call It, was called on to play Clinket, and Cibber himself created Plotwell. Clinket introduces Plotwell to
Mrs. Townley (played by Anne Oldfield, still the leading lady
of Drury Lane):

> This, Madam, is Mr. *Plotwell*, a Gentleman who is so infinitely
> obliging, as to introduce my Play on the Theatre, by fathering the
> unworthy Issue of my Muse, at the reading it this Morning.
> *Plotwell.* I should be proud, Madam, to be a real Father to any of
> your Productions.

We may imagine Cibber's foppish leer at this point, sweeping
the two women and then the audience.

Sir Tremendous, played by John Boman, agrees to examine Clinket's opus. A splendid farce scene follows:

> *Sir* Tremendous *reads in a muttering Tone.*
> Sir *Tremendous.* Absurd to the last Degree [*strikes out.*] palpable Nonsense! [*strikes out.*]
> *Clinket.* What all those Lines! spare those for a Lady's Sake, for those indeed, I gave him.
> Sir *Tremendous.* Such Stuff! [*strikes out.*] abominable! [*strikes out.*] most execrable!
> *1st Player.* This Thought must out.
> *2nd Player.* Madam, with Submission, this Metaphor.
> *1st Player.* This whole Speech.
> Sir *Tremendous.* The Fable!
> *Clinket.* To you I answer— Sir *Tremendous.* The Diction!
> *Clinket.* And to you—Ah, hold, hold—I'm butcher'd, I'm massacred. For Mercy's Sake! murder, murder, ah! [*faints*] (I, 533-48)

At the end of the play a baby is presented and revealed to be Mrs. Towneley's by someone—the father is uncertain but it is not Fossile, who decides to adopt the child. "What signifies," he says, "whether a Man beget his Child or not?"

A great deal of ink has been spilled in identifying the satiric victims in *Three Hours After Marriage*, much of it spilled in vain. The play is understandable without footnotes. The technique of "hiding some sharp personal satire behind a screen of apparent buffoonery" Leo Hughes traces to the practice of the Italian company of comedians in Paris.[26] Personal satire in two instances would have been understood immediately by the London audience; both individuals satirized were longtime antagonists of Pope and the Scriblerians. These were John Dennis, playwright and literary critic, as Sir Tremendous; and Dr. John Woodward, antiquarian collector and society physician, as Fossile. Dennis had been the mock dedicatee of *The Mohocks*, and was mentioned by Gay in *Trivia*: "Here saunt'ring 'Prentices o'er *Otway* weep, / O'er *Congreve* smile, or over D[ennis] sleep" (II, 561-62). He had of course also been victimized by Pope in the *Essay on Criticism*, and had returned the attack.

Woodward is assaulted with the sort of sustained, personal animus that one associates with Pope rather than Gay:
he is vain, pedantic, suspicious, and impotent; even his curtain line on adopting the child, which demonstrates that he
does not know the difference between the genuine and the
fake, is meant to sting.

Despite all his eccentricities, Woodward had many
friends in London, most of them Whigs, and one of them was
Sir Richard Steele himself, governor of Drury Lane. Woodward was his personal physician and confidant. When the
play opened in January 1717, it had a run of seven consecutive playing days and seemed on the way to becoming a success like *The What D'Ye Call It*. Then—nothing. George
Sherburn has traced the "fortunes and misfortunes" of *Three
Hours after Marriage* and shown how the anti-Scriblerians
mobilized opposition to the play, focusing on Pope's supposed
role in writing it.[27] Sherburn is surely mistaken, however, in
believing that Colley Cibber, as Plotwell, was instrumental in
having the show stopped because he objected to the mild satiric thrusts at himself; Cibber was a professional actor and
reveled in publicity, even unfavorable publicity. And as theatre manager, a long run delighted him.

More likely is that Steele simply passed the word down to
the company to scratch the play after the initial run—which
was a good one for a new play, and provided, presumably, two
benefit nights for the author at the peak of the theatre season.
Not a bad deal for Gay. Still, the vehemence and volume of
the opposition is surprising, even when due allowance is
made for the self-serving activities of Addison's Buttonians.
The satire on Phoebe Clinkett the female poet, and by exten-
sion generally on females who aspire to poetry, attracts the
attention of our sensitized times, but it appears to have
stirred not a ripple then. Dennis of course struck back, but
he was given to striking back; it was expected of Sir
Tremendous.

The Scriblerians' continuing quarrel with Woodward had
its roots in serious issues, however much it was overlaid with
farce. Woodward's medical practices were no more ridiculous

than those of any other physician of his time and his patients probably recovered at about the same rate as those of other doctors; in fact, Woodward wrote a book detailing his medical success stories.[28] His antiquarianism, which is now seen as an early attempt at what would become scientific archaeology, was regarded by the Scriblerians as pure pedantry, ridiculed in this play and in the *Memoirs*.[29]

Another line of attack was on the play's alleged bawdry. This was a potentially serious charge, and it may well have been the one that got Steele's attention. Since the turn of the century actors and playwrights had been picking their way with some care. The pseudonymous author of *A Letter to Mr. John Gay, Concerning his Late Farce, Entituled, A Comedy*, who calls himself "Timothy Drub," objects to double entendres such as those already noted that were given to Cibber as Plotwell. Having apparently seen as well as read the play, Drub observes that the actors cleaned it up for performance, leaving out "a considerable load of Obscenity and Prophaness." He especially objects to references to the clergy and allusions to the Bible and the Book of Common Prayer. One "would be apt to imagine, *John*," Drub writes, "that you had made a Sale of your *Religion* to borrow a little *Wit* from your Neighbours."[30] These were charges Steele was bound to attend to, because the royal patent granting him the governorship had specifically complained of the London stage's previous improper "Representations of Human Life," "by indecent and immodest Expressions, by Prophane allusion to Holy Scripture, by abusive and scurrilous Representations of the Clergy, and by the Success and Applause bestowed on Libertine Characters."[31] Timothy Drub had gone through each of these categories, almost as if he were reading the patent. For the Drury Lane management in 1717, I would argue, these allegations were much more important than Pope's politics. (Drury Lane produced the tragedy of that arch-Tory, Delariviere Manley, in May, with a prologue by Steele himself.)

Pope apparently wrote Gay, relaying complaints about *Three Hours after Marriage* that he had heard. Gay replied, accepting responsibility: "I will (if any Shame there be) take it all to myself, as indeed I ought, the Motion [notion?] being first mine, and never heartily approv'd of by you."[32] It was a good, interesting comedy, a farce of ideas; as John Fuller has judged, the characterization has a Jonsonian ring, and Fossile is reminiscent of Morose in *The Silent Woman.*[33] The play also demonstrates Gay's mastery of sight comedy: the walking crocodile and mummy were created for Cibber and Penkethman, who knew how to milk a comic scene dry and did so. Gay received some solace for the play's abbreviated run by counting his handsome royalty from Lintot of forty-three pounds, two shillings, sixpence—quite the largest copyright payment for any of his plays to that time and indicative of Lintot's judgment about the play's popularity.[34] Nevertheless, as an acting vehicle it was dead for Gay's lifetime.

One remark of Timothy Drub in his *Letter to Mr. John Gay* may have stung Gay if he read it: a reference to Gay's expanding silhouette: "I am a good-natur'd Fellow," says Drub, "and almost as Fat as your self."[35] Gay had been living well. He was much involved with the branch of Court society then gathered around the Prince of Wales and Caroline, his vivacious and intelligent wife. Gay, it will be recalled, had been introduced to the couple on his brief sojourn in Hanover and expected good things from them. Tory and Opposition Whig leaders met at their residence because they knew the prince and his father, George I, were bitter enemies, and they hoped to benefit when the prince eventually succeeded to the throne. Gay was also there because he liked the ladies-in-waiting to Princess Caroline, especially Henrietta Howard, Mary Bellenden, and Mary Lepell.

A great figure in this society by virtue of his enormous wealth was James Brydges, Earl of Carnarvon and later Duke of Chandos. Brydges fancied himself a patron of the arts. In September 1717 he wrote Arbuthnot proudly that "Mr. Handle has made me two . . . anthems very noble ones" and invited Arbuthnot (who also gave him medical advice from time to time) to visit him at Canons, his seat in Middlesex.[36] Arbuthnot did so some time during the following winter, and

Gay may have been with him then, because in 1718 or there-abouts he completed his most important collaboration with Handel, the pastoral masque or serenata *Acis and Galatea*. It was Gay's final lesson in the relationship between words and music, the lesson of a master.

The little gem, based on the story in the thirteenth book of Ovid's *Metamorphoses*, tells of the love of Acis for the nymph Galatea, a love that is threatened by the giant Poly-phemus, who also longs for the nymph. This is a work that demands to be heard in performance, for Handel's glorious music but also for Gay's witty and subtle libretto. Roger Fiske judges flatly that Gay "provided Handel with the best dra-matic libretto he ever set."[37] As Bertrand Bronson has ob-served, here are "words and music inseparably united."[38]

Nevertheless, some of Gay's virtues as a lyricist may be noted even by a reader of the text. The plot could scarcely be simpler: The shepherdess Galatea tells Damon of her love for Acis, who conveniently appears, and the lovers are united ("Happy, happy, happy We"). In Part II Polyphemus appears, and receives some advice from Damon, to eschew the rough stuff:

> Would you gain the tender Creature,
> Softly, gently, kindly treat her;
> Suff'ring is the Lover's Part.
> Beauty by Constraint possessing,
> You enjoy but half the Blessing,
> Lifeless Charms, without the Heart.

Polyphemus, inflamed with jealousy at seeing the happy pair together, kills Acis "with a great Stone," but Galatea, who is descended from the gods, secures immortality for Acis, in the form of a river: "The bubling Fountain, lo, it flows; / Through the Plains he joys to rove, / Murm'ring still his gentle Love" (II.113-15).

Gay's lyrics are crystal clear, intelligible at every point but also poetically interesting and dramatically cogent. Han-del accepted Gay's libretto but he may, in the easy atmosphere of Canons, have given Gay some specific lessons on music as a reflection of human modes of feeling. The union of the young lovers is celebrated in the last air of Part One:

> As when the Dove
> Laments her love,
> All on the naked spray;
> When he returns,
> No more she mourns,
> But loves the live-long Day.
> Billing, cooing,
> Panting, wooing,
> Melting Murmurs fill the Grove,
> Melting Murmurs lasting love. (I.57-66)

The transition from lovers' ecstasy to tragedy, or pathos, follows immediately in Part Two with the entrance of Polyphemus; the self-contained world of the lovers is invaded by the world outside, as the chorus sings of love's fleeting joys:

> Wretched Lovers, Fate has past
> This sad Decree, no Joy shall last:
> Wretched Lovers, quit your Dream,
> Behold the Monster, *Polypheme*.
> See what ample Strides he takes,
> The Mountain nods, the Forest shakes,
> The Waves run frighted to the Shores;
> Hark, how the thund'ring Giant roars. (II.1-8)

Handel's resounding music recreates the giant's footsteps as he approaches.

Some of the sight comedy—and sight comedy is generally utilized in Gay's comedies—must depend on the auditor's or spectator's imagination. Polyphemus, for example, is a giant much seized with admiration of his own dimensions, who employs a pine tree for a walking stick ("Thou trusty Pine, Prop of my Godlike Steps"). His carnal passion for his Lilliputian lady love, Acis, is sight comedy waiting for a medium not yet invented, film photography, which could easily combine the divergent pair in one scene.

The serenata apparently did not receive a public performance until 1731, but Carnarvon probably commissioned private presentations at Canons as he did for other works. Whether Gay received any monetary compensation we do not know, but working with Handel on this miniature masterpiece must have been enormously stimulating to Gay's artistic imagination. Better than anyone else, now that Congreve had stopped writing for the stage, he knew how to bring together words and music. *Acis and Galatea* was, as we have already noted, in a sense the completion of Gay's dramatic apprenticeship, on the way to *The Beggar's Opera*.

FIVE

False Starts

Gay was ready to write *The Beggar's Opera* by 1718, in the respect that he possessed the artistic sensibility and experience to do so, but he did not write it. The point is worth reflecting upon. He was at a high point in his literary career: *The Shepherd's Week, Trivia, The What D'Ye Call It* had all been gratifying successes; even *Three Hours after Marriage* played to crowded houses until its untimely suppression. Then, like many another artist riding the crest of his good fortune, Gay tried something he could not do. In face of the fact that everything he had ever written well was in the comic mode, from his first published poem, *Wine*, to *Acis and Galatea*, Gay turned to tragedy, and pastoral tragedy at that, for his next play, *Dione*.

He had been living in most comfortable, even luxurious, circumstances for the preceding several years, traveling to Bath, and to the Continent in 1717 with Sir William Pulteney and his family. In the summer of 1718 Gay and Pope stayed at Lord Harcourt's seat in Stanton Harcourt, Oxfordshire, where they heard of the death by lightning of the farm laborers John Hewet and Sarah Drew, "two much more constant Lovers than ever were found in Romance."[1] Pope and Gay wrote the epitaph for the stone placed over the lovers, which begins:

> When Eastern Lovers feed the funer'l fire,
> On the same Pile the faithful Fair expire;
> Here, pitying Heav'n that Virtue mutual found,
> And blasted both, that it might neither wound.[2]

Pope was in a romantic mood generally and fascinated by the romantic East in particular: Lady Mary Wortley Montagu, with whose charms he was currently smitten, had sojourned in Turkey, where his ardent letters pursued her and from whence she wrote her own incomparable descriptions of that exotic land to Pope. Pope in love, pastoral lovers killed by lightning, Lady Mary in the Mysterious East: it was all enough to drive pedestrian reality back several steps.

In 1719 Gay visited Spa and Paris, perhaps with the Earl of Burlington, the great tastemaker of the Palladian revival and creator of Chiswick House. "I am now rambling from Place to Place," he wrote Henrietta Howard in September of that year. "In about a Month I hope to be at Paris, and the next month to be in England, and the next Minute to see you."[3] Stanton Harcourt and Chiswick, Spa, Paris, and Windsor; these are a long way from Devon and London, the sources of Gay's dramatic imagination to this point.

Or so his next two plays would seem to indicate, which have much classicism but little or no Devon or London in them. He must have been working on *Dione* before or during his trip to Paris because it was ready for production by February 1720, when the Lord Chamberlain, the Duke of Newcastle, personally ordered "that Mr. Gays Pastorall Tragedy be imediately Acted."[4] Gay evidently expected that this would happen, with the Lord Chamberlain's encouragement, because the version of the play that was eventually printed includes a prologue clearly meant to introduce an actual production. It would not, the author wishes to make clear, be in the manner of *The Shepherd's Week* or *The What D'Ye Call It:*

> To night we treat you with such country fare,
> Then for your lover's sake our author spare.
> He draws no *Hemskirk* boors, or home-bred clowns,
> But the soft shepherds of *Arcadia's* downs.[5]

Dione relates the story of unrequited love in Arcadia, in rimed pentameter couplets. When Laura the shepherdess tells us in the opening speech of Act I, "Three times the lark has sung his matin lay,/And rose on dewy wing to meet the day," Gay's reader waits expectantly for the burlesque to come, shaking the poetic dew off the wing of that lark somehow. But *Dione* plods relentlessly on. Menalcas has died of love because Parthenia the resolute virgin spurned him. ("What shepherd does not mourn *Menalcas* slain? / Kill'd by a barbarous woman's proud disdain" [I.ii.25-26].) Now Lycidas pursues Parthenia, even though shepherdess Dione, who secretly loves him, warns him off:

> Rash swain, be wise:
> 'Tis not from thee or him, from love she flies.
> Leave her, forget her.   [*They hold* Lycidas]

But the rash swain will neither leave nor forget her: he is obsessed with Parthenia's charms. Parthenia, on the other hand, feels strongly drawn to Dione, disguised as an androgynous youth, telling him/her:

> Yes, I to thee could give up all my heart.
> From thy chast eye no wanton glances dart;
> Thy modest lips convey no thought impure,
> With thee may strictest virtue walk secure. (IV.iii.ll3-l6)

And so it goes, for five acts, until Lycidas stabs Dione fatally in a jealous rage and then turns the knife on himself in remorse. At the curtain Parthenia invites Laura the shepherdess to share her bower, "And as we sorrowing go, / Let poor *Dione*'s story feed my woe / With heart-relieving tears" (V.iv.29-31). No one sings for Lycidas.

Though mistaken in his choice of mode, Gay is not unintelligent, here or anywhere. His verse for the most part is spare, stripped of the tragic fustian which caught the parodying eye and ear of Buckingham, of Fielding, and of course of Gay himself. Parthenia's meditation on her inner self in Act I illustrates the restrained metaphoric texture of the verse, more like Dryden's practice than that of Pope.

> Most women's weak resolves like reeds, will ply,
> Shake with each breath, and bend with ev'ry sigh;
> Mine, like an oak, whose firm roots deep descend,
> No breath of love can shake, no sigh can bend. (I.iii.29-32)

Why Gay decided to try a tragedy in pentameter couplets, when blank verse tragedies had dominated the London stage for almost half a century, is another matter. It may be that his time in Paris had inspired an interest in rimed tragedy. His poetic "Epistle to William Pulteney," published in 1720 as if written from Paris, contains the exhortation:

> But let me not forget *Corneille, Racine,*
> *Boileau's* strong sense and *Moliere's* hum'rous Scene.[6]

Perhaps Gay thought that rimed tragedy in the manner of the great French exemplars would play, even at this late date in London. When Aaron Hill came to adapt Voltaire's tragedies for the English stage in the next decade he wisely chose blank verse.

There are other clues that Racine was in Gay's imaginative world. As Parthenia's speech indicates, beneath *Dione's* bucolic trappings is a story of frustrated sexuality that possesses considerable power, of a Racinian flavor. Lycidas cannot *not* love Parthenia, no matter what he is told, and Parthenia, as she is careful to insist, cannot love him (because she is a lesbian, though the term was not in use in Gay's time). Gay is portraying a mode of sexuality that had come under his observation at some time in a long career of viewing life from every angle; Jenny Diver in *The Beggar's Opera* is a related character. The name Parthenia derives of course from the Greek, signifying "virgin," "unviolated by man." Dione, a contrasting figure, is the isolated female of eighteenth-century tragedy I have described in another place,[7] who pays for her love with death, here as usual by the knife. The phallic symbolism is sufficiently obvious.

Gay's choice of the pastoral mode for tragedy was fatal, though he probably had Pope's encouragement to try it.

Samuel Johnson ends his "Life of Gay" with this devastating judgment: "There is something in the poetical Arcadia so remote from known reality and speculative possibility, that we can never support its representation through a long work. A Pastoral of an hundred lines may be endured; but who will hear of sheep and goats, and myrtle-bowers and purling rivulets, through five acts?"[8] Who indeed? As it eventuated, no one had the opportunity. The Lord Chamberlain's order was either evaded or ignored by the Drury Lane company—who must have groaned when they saw the script with its pentameter couplets—and *Dione* was never produced.

About this time, interestingly, Gay was also working in the comic pastoral. Sometime in 1720 he published as a broadside *Daphnis and Chloe*, with the subtitle *A Song.*[9] Daphnis, lovesick, has been disdained by Chloe. He overhears her lamenting in the woods:

> How foolish is the Nymph (She crys)
>   Who trifles with her Lovers pain!
> Nature still speaks in Woman's Eyes,
>   Our artfull Lips were made to feign.
> O DAPHNIS, DAPHNIS 'twas my Pride,
> 'Twas not my Heart thy Love deny'd.
>   Come back, dear Youth, again.

After listening to her continuing lament,

> The Youth step'd forth with hasty pace,
>   And found where wishing CHLOE lay;
> Shame sudden lighten'd in her Face,
>   Confus'd, she knew not what to say.
> At last in broken words, she cry'd;
> To morrow you in vain had try'd.
>   But I am lost to Day!

Thwarted sexuality is here given a comic rather than a tragic turn and the eighteenth-century musical public liked it, buying this and at least four other editions in broadside, with music by an unknown hand. Gay continued to be reminded of the attractive power of popular music.

Gay had both *Dione* and *Daphnis and Chloe* included in the handsome folio *Poems on Several Occasions* that Jacob Tonson and Bernard Lintot brought out in 1720. Heading the long list of subscribers were their royal highnesses themselves, the Prince and Princess of Wales. Noble subscribers left, right, and center: the Dukes of Grafton and Devonshire; James Brydges, now Duke of Chandos put his name down for *fifty* volumes. Old friends also subscribed: John Arbuthnot, of course, and Pope and Prior. Charles and Catherine Douglas, the Duke and Duchess of Queensberry, who would be important in Gay's later life, signed up for five copies. Handel ordered a copy for himself.

As the subscription list implied, Gay was much to be seen in fashionable circles now. During the South Sea crisis of 1720 he took a flutter on the stock subscription with a thousand pounds advance on his *Poems.* With all the other stockholders, he watched his paper fortune rise and rise—then fall. After the crash he seems to have unloaded his stock on Pope, perhaps at a loss but certainly not with the catastrophic results recorded by Samuel Johnson: "Gay sunk under the calamity so low that his life became in danger."[10] Not so; Johnson is transferring his melancholy views to the wrong poet. In a poem he published the following year, *A Panegyrical Epistle to Mr. Thomas Snow, Goldsmith,* Gay wryly recalls his pursuit of wealth on Exchange Alley:

> No wonder, if we found some *Poets* there,
> Who live on Fancy, and can feed on Air;
> No wonder, *they* were caught by *South-Sea* Schemes,
> Who ne'er enjoy'd a Guinea, but in Dreams;[11]

Gay is indulging in a bit of poetic license here; he enjoyed several hundred guineas from Tonson's advance, and the tone is not that of a poet sinking under his calamities.

In point of fact, far from destitution's grasp, he was living in Burlington House, the splendid town residence of Richard Boyle, Earl of Burlington, who also maintained Chiswick House, where Gay likewise now dwelled from time to time.

He was angling vigorously for preferment of some kind. Pope had completed the translation of the *Iliad* and was on his way to affluence from its returns. Arbuthnot treated rich hypochondriacs and prospered accordingly. Swift's stipend as Dean of St. Patrick's enabled him to live much as he pleased, and to give generously to charity. Prior enjoyed life under the bountiful hospitality of the earls of Oxford, perhaps as an agreed reward for his political fidelity during the last years of Queen Anne.[12] Only Gay among the great Tory *littérateurs* lacked a steady source of support. In a reflective mood during the summer of 1723 he wrote his friend Henrietta Howard:

I have long wish'd to be able to put in practice that valuable worldly qualification of being insincere, one of my cheif reasons is that I hate to be particular, and I think if a man cannot conform to the customs of the world, he is not fit to be encourag'd or to live in it. I know that if one would be agreeable to men of dignity one must study to imitate them, and I know which way they get Money and places. I cannot wonder that the Talents requisite for a great Statesman are so scarce in the world since so many of those who possess them are every month cut off in the prime of their Age at the Old-Baily.[13]

Great Statesmen as criminals: it may be that something like *The Beggar's Opera* was beginning to form in Gay's mind. He did manage to secure a minor place that year, worth £150 per annum, as commissioner of state lotteries. And he wrote another play, another tragedy. Perhaps this was his way of imitating "men of dignity."

The play was entitled *The Captives*, and the managers at Drury Lane agreed to produce it in January 1724. By then Gay had prepared the way for its reception with more than usual care. Benjamin Victor, a theatrical quidnunc of the highest order, was buzzing about in the London theatre world just now, and he later passed along an anecdote that is probably true in essentials. Victor was a veteran sorter of gossip and his gossip is usually factual.

[Mr. Gay] had interest enough with the late Queen *Caroline*, then Princess of *Wales*, to excite her Royal Highness's Curiosity to hear the Author read his Play to her at *Leicester*-House. The Day was fixed, and Mr. *Gay* was commanded to attend. He waited some Time in a Presence-Chamber with his Play in his Hand; but being a very modest Man, and unequal to the Trial he was going to, when the Door of the Drawing-Room, where the Princess sat with her Ladies, was opened for his Entrance, he was so much confus'd, and concern'd about making his proper Obeysance, that he did not see a low Footstool that happened to be near him, and stumbling over it, he fell against a large Screen, which he overset, and threw the Ladies into no small Disorder. Her Royal Highness's great Goodness soon reconciled this whimsical Accident, but the unlucky Author was not so soon clear of his Confusion.[14]

The master of sight comedy, about to read his tragedy to the ladies, is caught up in a scene from one of his farces.

If it attracted the compassion of Her Royal Highness it was embarrassment well-expended. Gay was calling on all his resources; newspapers reported that free brandy was distributed in the box seats.[15] Drury Lane put its leading players into the cast: Robert Wilks, Barton Booth, Anne Oldfield. No place for comedians Cibber and Penkethman in this one. Gay's Prologue was spoken by Wilks and reveals a certain defensiveness on the author's part, a plea for forbearance: Watch the play and then say whether you like it or not; give it a fair trial:

> Plays are like paintings try'd,
> You first enquire the hand, and then decide:
> Yet judge him not before the curtain draws,
> Lest a fair hearing should reverse the cause.[16]

The Captives is set in that never-never land of the East that appealed to tragic poets, a land in this case called Media. The poetic medium Gay chooses is blank verse, instead of the rimed couplets of *Dione*. A conspiracy is afoot against the Median king, Phraortes, that comes to involve his queen, the proud Astarbe, and the two captives of the title, Sophernes the Persian prince and his long-lost wife, Cylene. The queen is mad with love for Sophernes, as is de rigueur in such situations, and confesses her passion to the captive prince:

> For only you I could renounce a kingdom,
> For you, ev'n in the wild and barren desart
> Forget I was a Queen; ev'n then more happy
> Than seated on a throne. Say, wilt thou chuse
> Or liberty, and life, and poor *Astarbe*,
> Or dungeons, chains, and ignominious death! (II,viii.88-94)

Liberty and Astarbe or dungeons, chains, and death? Since Sophernes at this point does not realize his wife Cylene is still alive the choice would seem to be obvious, to those who do not know baroque tragedies. But Sophernes has given his word to Phraortes that he will not "pass beyond my bounds prescrib'd," i.e., escape, and he turns the proposition down. This naturally infuriates the queen who vows revenge. After many convolutions of the plot, Cylene appears, saves her husband's life by a deception, and proudly confronts the queen with what she has done:

> If 'tis a crime when innocence is wrong'd
> To snatch it from the rage of credulous Power;
> If 'tis a crime to succour the distrest,
> If 'tis a crime to relieve injur'd virtue;
> If 'tis a crime to be a faithful wife;
> These crimes are mine. For I have sav'd my husband.
> (IV.x.50-55)

This is the sort of tragic hot-air balloon, with its embellishments of anaphora, that Gay had once rejoiced to deflate. When young Henry Fielding surveyed baroque tragedy for burlesquing in his *Tom Thumb*, he included *The Captives*.[17]

In the denouement, the queen's complicity in the conspiracy is revealed; she stabs herself, and the happy Persian couple are reunited and forgiven by the king, they not having participated in the attempt on his life. Sophernes is awarded the last word: he counsels patience and fortitude:

> Since 'tis not giv'n to mortals to discern
> Their real good and ill; let men learn patience:

Let us the toils of adverse fate sustain,
For through that rugged road our hopes we gain.
(V.ix.25-28)

Tragedy of *The Captives'* sort was achieving a limited success in the eighteenth century: typically, a female character, or in this instance two female characters, are depicted in a stressful situation involving love and marriage. The setting is distanced in either space or time or both: it is somewhere far from England, or takes place at a time much earlier than the present. Death, usually by some form of stabbing, is the invariable outcome for the female lead. In *The Captives* Gay relieves some of the tragic sting by having the young couple spared to live, presumably, happily ever after. Some tragedies of this sort were staples of the repertory, such as John Banks's *The Unhappy Favorite*, which dramatizes Queen Elizabeth's supposed love for Essex. *The Captives* follows the standard pattern by having female characters direct and control the action.[18]

The Captives must have been produced just as Gay wanted it done. As an established author, he was in a position to make his views known, and he was writing for a company he had worked with off and on for more than ten years. Gay's most recent editor has concluded that he and the Drury Lane company were experiencing disagreements during the early 1720s and that he rewrote Thomas Wright's old play, *The Female Vertuoso's* as *No Fools Like Wits*, for production at Lincoln's Inn Fields in a gesture of hostility. It is impossible to prove negatives, of course, but one may be reasonably confident that Gay had nothing to do with the revival of *No Fools Like Wits*,[19] and that his relationships with Drury Lane in the early 1720s were tolerably agreeable.

The Royal Company of Comedians at Drury Lane was a repertory company with a good sense of itself, experienced and making money. Benjamin Victor, then at the beginning of a long career in the theatre, recalled years later how the three managers conducted the company at this period—Steele, in ill health, had by 1724 retired to Wales. Victor especially admired "their regular, and masterly Manner of governing their Rehearsals, over which one of the three Managers presided weekly."

If a new Play was coming on, the first three Readings fell to the Share of the Author. . . . The Readings over, there followed a limited Numbers of Rehearsals, with their Parts in their Hands, after which a distant Morning was appointed for every Person in the Play to appear perfect, because the Rehearsal only then begins to be of Use to the Actor.[20]

John Rich at Lincoln's Inn Fields felt that Gay's tragedy with established actors and royal favor might attract the customers; he set up a formidable slate of plays in competition with *The Captives*, offering seven different selections against the first (and last) seven performances of the run. His strategy in opposing *The Captives* provides an apt illustration of the manner in which the rival companies would attempt to deal with the competition. Rich began with Vanbrugh's perennial favorite, *The Pilgrim*, on opening night of *The Captives*, followed by *Measure for Measure*, and on Gay's first benefit (third) night, by Farquhar's always popular *The Recruiting Officer*. There was a Rich irony in Lincoln's Inn Fields covering Gay's play with *The Recruiting Officer*, which had been one of the great money-makers for the Drury Lane company ever since its premiere there in 1705. Anne Oldfield, now playing Cylene the faithful wife in *The Captives*, had created the role of Silvia in *The Recruiting Officer* nineteen years earlier, and Wilks had been the original Captain Plume. Gay and the Drury Lane troupe watched glumly as Rich ran up one of the largest profits of the season, £160, from Farquhar's play, even though the Prince and Princess of Wales were seeing *The Captives* that night.[21]

Rich kept up the pressure, countering on January 18 with Addison's *The Drummer*, which had also received its premiere at Drury Lane, Congreve's *The Double Dealer*, and *The Merry Wives of Windsor*. Two Shakespeares and one excellent play each by Congreve, Farquhar, and Vanbrugh in eight days' time: this was as competitive as Rich could make it (and must have strained his company to the limits of their abilities and endurance). Opera was also playing at the King's, Haymarket. The competition of Shakespeare, comedy, and opera was probably too much for Gay's frail vehicle, which closed on 23 January. Seven performances was a good but not an outstanding run for a tragedy and Gay made it to his second benefit night, though Pope's collaborator Fenton, who had good sources, wrote that "Gay's play had no success. I am told he gave thirty guineas to have it acted the fifth night"[22] (against Congreve's *Double Dealer*). No receipts are available for Drury Lane performances during this period so one cannot be precise about the gross, but, significantly, the take for Lincoln's Inn Fields held steady, at a high level, during the run of *The Captives*.

Fenton also reported that the plot of *The Captives* was Gay's "own invention,"[23] but critics have at various times affected to discern the influence of Southerne's *Oroonoko*, of Congreve's *The Mourning Bride*, of Dryden's *Aureng-Zebe*, of *Macbeth* and *Julius Caesar*.[24] A commentator has found references in the play to the recent trial of the Jacobite Bishop Atterbury, though he adds, correctly, that it is strange these references were not noticed at the time.[25] Peace to all such, but the fact is that *The Captives* is a perfect tissue of baroque tragic commonplace, in action, theme, and characterization. That is its problem, that is Gay's problem in writing baroque tragedy, as the Scriblerian in him must have known.

The poet Edward Young's statement in a letter to Lady Mary Wortley Montagu that *The Captives* brought Gay a thousand pounds must be discounted, unless we are to suppose some sort of royal gift.[26] If Princess Caroline was moved to financial bounty by Gay's pratfall into her screen, no record of the generosity has been found. He received the receipts from the two benefit nights, less the house charges in each case of about fifty pounds, for a total almost certainly less than two hundred pounds.[27] Tonson, now Gay's bookseller, may have given him more for the copyright than Lintot had done for his last play, but *The Captives* went to only one edition. It was no doubt just as well that he did not have more of a financial return for his efforts: he might have been encouraged otherwise to continue writing tragedies. *The Captives* is a well-constructed drama and has less tragic fustian than most other contemporary examples of the genre, but tragedies were not doing well at the box office, though literary critics kept on deploring audience taste and calling for more of them. Gay determined to return to comedy. It is almost as if Anne Oldfield, speaking the epilogue to *The Captives*, were voicing Gay's own genuine inner feelings:

> Shall authors teaze the town with tragick passion,
> When we've more modern moral things in fashion?
> Let poets quite exhaust the Muse's treasure;
> Sure Masquerades must give more feeling pleasure,
> Where we meet finer sense and better measure;
> The marry'd Dame, whose business must be done,
> Puts on the holy vestments of a Nun;
> And brings her unprolifick spouse a son.[28]

Disguises, naughty liaisons, illegitimate babies, role reversals: comedy. That was Gay's road to success.

SIX

The Beggar and His *Opera*

As if they were voicing confidence in Gay's comic muse, the Drury Lane company played *The What D'Ye Call It* as an afterpiece on 23 January 1724, the night after *The Captives* closed. It was a compliment, but the performance carried no financial reward, probably not even for the company, because, in the mysterious way of audience taste, pantomimes rather than farces were the entertainment paying customers wanted that season. Significantly, Gay was involved in the production of a pantomime recognizably kin to *The Beggar's Opera*, during the following theatrical season.

Meanwhile, thoughout 1724 and the year following, Gay hunted financial stability from preferment, *substantial* preferment. His post as Commissioner of the Lottery yielded £150 a year for minimal duties; that stipend was enough to live on with modest comfort in the country—most country parsons made considerably less—but not enough for life in the aristocratic circles in which he now moved. He was staying with the Earl of Burlington at Burlington House and Chiswick; with the Duke and Duchess of Queensberry at their London address, Queensberry House in Burlington Gardens, and at their country house in Amesbury, Wiltshire. In September 1724 he took the waters at Bath, planning to return to London in the entourage of Lord Scarborough. Tips to the servants alone would probably eat up £150 a year in that environment.

His credit was presumably still high with the Prince and Princess of Wales, with the Princess Caroline on his own merits and with the Prince on the merits of Henrietta Howard, the Prince's mistress. Sir Robert Walpole, by 1724 firmly in control of the government, was cultivating Princess Caroline.[1] Preferment for Gay could conceivably come from one of several directions, or so he believed.

Pope was very skeptical. So was Swift, if the reference to "beggars" applies to Gay, as it may well do, in his letter to Pope of 19 July 1725: "I am frighted to think what I should do in London, while my Friends are all either banished or at-tain[t]ed or beggars, or retired."[2] In that summer Pope was happily retired to Twickenham, supervising work on his grotto there, having seen the translation of the *Odyssey* through the press. His attitude toward Walpole was blowing warm and cool. In May he wrote Gay's old Devon schoolmate William Fortescue, observing of Walpole, "I am much more his Servant, than those who would flatter him in their Verses."[3] Gay was with Pope at Twickenham in June, in Ames-bury with the Queensberrys later in the summer, and back in London in September, following up a lead from Fortescue about possible preferment. Fortescue possessed, or was thought to possess, some leverage with Walpole. When ar-rangements did not appear to be working out in Gay's favor, he and Pope wrote Fortescue a joint letter about Gay's situa-tion. "I know I have sincerely your good wishes upon all oc-casions," Gay wrote. "One would think that my friends use me to disappointments, to try how many I could bear; if they do so, they are mistaken; for as I don't expect much, I can never be much disappointed."[4] Brave words. Pope goes on to elaborate on this in his portion of the letter, including advice by indirection to Gay: " 'Blessed is the man who expects noth-ing, for he shall never be disappointed,' was the ninth beati-tude which a man of wit (who, like a man of wit, was a long time in gaol) added to the eighth; I have long ago preached this to our friend [Gay]; I have *preached* it, but the world and his other friends *held it forth*, and exemplified it. They say, Mr. Walpole has friendship, and keeps his word; I wish he were our friend's friend, or had ever promised him anything." The reference to the jailed wit is significant. Perhaps it constitutes a joke among intimates, because Gay had written and seen published a ballad about jail the previous winter. The ballad had earlier been used in a theatrical production, a pantomime, at Drury Lane. The ballad and the pantomime in which it was performed in 1724 point the way toward *The Beggar's Opera* in several different theatrical respects.

The ballad has a title and a richly descriptive subtitle: "Newgate's Garland: Being a New Ballad, Shewing How Mr. *Jonathan Wild*'s Throat was cut, from Ear to Ear, with a Penknife by Mr. *Blake*, alias *Blueskin*, the bold Highwayman, as he stood at his Trial in the Old-Bailey."[5] Mr. Blake, Joseph Blake, had in fact attempted unsuccessfully to kill Wild in this manner. Wild had arranged Blake's arrest and that of his companion Jack Sheppard, for the reward offered. Wild had "peached" them, to use the cant vocabulary: turned them in. Wild himself was superintending a band of "thief-takers" at the time, acting just within the bounds of the law. Gay may possibly have met him in a tavern at Windsor.[6] The situation seems an obvious prefiguring of that in *The Beggar's Opera*. It is indeed just such a prefiguring. Gay was back from Media and Arcadia, into the London he knew well, the London of *The Mohocks* and *Trivia*.

The use of Gay's ballad on the stage at Drury Lane is important. "Newgate's Garland" and the vehicle in which it was contained, a pantomime, deserve more attention than they have received with respect to their place in Gay's dramatic career. As Roger Fiske has written, "in the eighteenth century pantomimes and operas were composed by the same composers and sung by the same singers."[7] The conjunction here of pantomime and Gay's ballad is, I would argue, a significant step on the way to *The Beggar's Opera*.

"Newgate's Garland" was sung in a pantomime written, and presumably danced, by John Thurmond: *Harlequin Sheppard*. This was a Drury Lane entry in the increasingly strenuous competition in pantomimes during the season of 1724–25. Topical to the moment, the pantomime was produced on 24 November 1724, less than two weeks after Jack Sheppard's hanging on the sixteenth of that month. The topicality is itself significant. Did Gay write his ballad for Thurmond's pantomime? Thurmond was dancing master at Drury Lane and author of a series of pantomimes produced there between 1723 and 1727.[8] Drury Lane had played his *The Captives* earlier in 1724; Gay would have known Thurmond. Gay had been involved with the Drury Lane company in one way or another almost continuously at least since 1713 and probably since 1712. It seems likely that he composed the ballad for Thurmond's use or offered it to him just after he had composed it, because the earliest known version is the one included in the printed text of *Harlequin Sheppard* itself, rather than the several printings in broadside.[9] The text was published simultaneously with the first production of the pantomime to stimulate attendance, as had become customary.

Gay's ballad treats the deeds of Sheppard's colleague in crime, Joseph Blake, alias Blueskin, whereas the pantomime itself focuses on Sheppard, here as Harlequin, the traditional central figure of the form. Thurmond probably danced Harlequin himself.[10] This was to be a realistic pantomime, however, or at least a less fantastic production than the usual run of pantomimes, as the title page of the printed text indicates: *Harlequin Sheppard. A Night Scene in Grotesque Characters: As it is Perform'd at the Theatre-Royal in Drury Lane. By John Thurmond, Dancing-Master, with New Scenes Painted from the Real Places of Action. To Which is Prefix'd an Introduction, Giving an Account of Sheppard's Life. With a Curious Frontispiece representing Harlequin Sheppard.*[11] The title page itself constitutes almost a guide to the production; sold as a theatre program or libretto, at sixpence the text was a bargain. The "grotesque characters" were choreographed by John Thurmond against new, realistic scenery based on "Real Places of Action."[12] The "curious frontispiece," a copper engraving, depicts Harlequin Sheppard in tights, immured at Newgate with his legs in fetters, which are padlocked to the floor. This frontispiece illustrates the opening scene of the pantomime, which goes on to dramatize in ten musical scenes Sheppard's escape from Newgate and subsequent events in his brief career, ending with his final arrest. The music, now largely lost, may have been done by Henry Carey, who was working at Drury Lane and whose tune for the ballad "Sally in our Alley" Gay borrowed for *The Beggar's Opera*.[13]

The Introduction presents a synopsis of Sheppard's life; it is in fact an excellent example of a criminal biography, that popular genre that Richetti, McKeon, and others have identified as an important contributor to the development of the novel.[14] The anonymous author describes Sheppard's apprenticeship to an indulgent carpenter, who at first forgives Sheppard's youthful rogueries (Sheppard was only twenty-two when he was executed). "But *Sheppard* left his Master . . . and got acquainted with *Blake* alias *Blueskin, Field, Doleing,* and *Sykes* alias *Hell and Fury*" (p. 6). Blueskin, Hell and Fury—the author's dwelling on criminals' nicknames looks forward to Gay's own exuberant catalogue of characters in his *Opera.* Sheppard, the Introduction relates, also became acquainted with Elizabeth Lyon, alias Edgeworth Bess, who shared the booty of his robberies with him but eventually betrayed him to Wild and thus to the authorities. "On *Monday* the 16th day of *November,* [Sheppard] was carry'd to *Tyburn* where he was Executed. He was cut down by a Soldier, and the Mob carry'd his Body to the *Barley-Mow* in *Long-Acre,* where he was expos'd to the View of all that came; and bury'd the same Evening in St. *Martin's Church-Yard*" (p. l2). Gay's lodgings in Whitehall were only a few hundred yards from the churchyard, the site now occupied by the National Gallery of Art.

The pantomime generally follows the order of events described in the Introduction, beginning, however, with Sheppard's escape from the Newgate cell of the frontispiece rather than with his earlier crimes, and ending with a scene in a tavern. This being a pantomime, the emphasis is on Sheppard's agility: the dancer portraying him is in almost constant motion. The third scene (the scenes are not numbered in the text) interrupts Sheppard's flight up chimneys and over rooftops to introduce an incident that is not included in the introductory narrative: "Enter two People as from the *Old Baily* in Surprize, one with a Pen-knife in his Hand, who makes Signs that one of the Prisoners had cut a Man's Throat.

Immediately the Prisoners Re-enter, and *Blueskin* exulting, imagining that he had cut *Jonathan Wild*'s Throat effectually. Some of the Keepers bring across *Jonathan Wild*, with his Throat cut. Some of the Prisoners sing the following Song." The song, Gay's ballad, is annotated: Sung by Mr. Harper. It is not clear which character John Harper is portraying. The tune is "The Cut Purse" or "Packington's Pound," a popular tune from Tudor times, which Ben Jonson used in *Bartholomew Fair* and which Gay himself was to employ again in *The Beggar's Opera* as Air 43 in Act III.[15] Roger Fiske has pointed to the importance of this particular tune: this is Nightingale's song from *Bartholomew Fair*, every verse of which has the refrain:

> Youth, Youth, thou had'st better been starv'd at Nurse,
> Than for to be hang'd for cutting a Purse.

Gay, Fiske argues, "could count on people associating [the tune] with Jonson's words and appreciating its relevance."[16] This is the sort of musical resonance, Dugaw's "critical instant," that Gay was to draw on, as will be seen, in *The Beggar's Opera*.[17]

John Harper, who had performed at Drury Lane since the 1721–22 season, as the singing prisoner does not realize when he sings Gay's ballad that Wild is still alive:

> YE Gallants of *Newgate*, whose Fingers are nice,
> In diving in Pockets, or cogging of Dice,
> Ye Sharpers so rich, who can buy off the Noose,
> Ye honester poor Rogues, who die in your Shoes,
>   Attend and draw near,
>   Good News ye shall hear,
> How *Jonathan*'s Throat was cut from Ear to Ear;
> How *Blueskin*'s sharp Penknife hath set you at Ease,
> And every Man round me may rob, if he please.

Blueskin, according to the second stanza, has "made a sad Widow of *Jonathan*'s Wife. / But Forty Pounds paid her, her Grief shall appease."

Gay then introduces an audacious transition from low life
to high life in the third stanza, a foretaste of that transvaluation of values that would constitute the basic structure of
The Beggar's Opera. He also sets up the equation with which
he was to open the *Opera:* all occupations are much the same,
conspiracies to defraud:

> Knaves of Old, to hide Guilt, by their cunning Inventions,
> Call'd Briberies Grants, and—plain Robberies Pensions;
> Physicians and Lawyers (who take their Degrees
> To be Learned Rogues) call'd their Pilfering—Fees;
>   Since this happy Day,
>   Now ev'ry Man may
>   Rob (as safe as in Office) upon the High-way.
> For *Blueskin's* sharp Penknife, &c.

The use of dashes in lines two and four appears to serve
the purpose of a stage direction, calling on the singer to pause
and thereby emphasize the transvaluation. Presumably the
other prisoners come in as a chorus on the refrain, "For *Blueskin's* sharp Penknife, &c." The next stanza continues the
transvaluation—more corruption in high places:

> Some cheat in the Customs, some rob the Excise,
> But he who robs both is esteemed most wise;
> Church-Wardens, too prudent to hazard the Halter,
> As yet only venture to steal from the Altar:
>   But now to get Gold,
>   They may be more bold,
>   And rob on the High way since *Jonathan's* cold.
> For *Blueskin's* sharp Penknife &c.

Gay's skill as a lyricist is highlighted here: clarity, brev-
ity, wit. Halter, altar, the transvaluation extends even to end
rimes. In fact, the case could be made that the highwaymen
were *more* honest, being less hypocritical than the learned,
and the singer makes that case:

> Some, by publick Revenues, which pass'd through their Hands,
> Have purchas'd clean Houses, and bought dirty Lands,

> Some to steal from a Charity think it no Sin,
> Which, at home (says the Proverb) does always begin;
>   But, if ever you be
>   Assign'd a Trustee,
>   Treat not Orphans like Masters of the Chancery,
> But take the High-way, and more honestly seise,
> For every Man round me may rob, if he please.

Instead of defrauding widows and orphans, like a trustee or a lawyer, get on the highway and be an honest robber. The argument is crystalline, and is both an echo of the corrupt justices in *The What D'Ye Call It* and a proleptic echo, so to speak, of the Beggar's moral in the *Opera*: "that the lower Sort of People have their Vices in a degree as well as the Rich: And that they are punish'd for them."

After Harper's song the focus returns to Sheppard who is "discover'd coming from Top of Newgate . . . by the help of a Blanket." The mob pursues him, and, several scenes later, he takes refuge in an alehouse, drunk, where Frisky Moll greets him. Moll and Sheppard dance, then the constable and others seize him, having been tipped off by the alehouse boy. "The Entertainment concludes with a Canting Song sung by Frisky Moll. The words by Mr. Harper." Frisky Moll's canting song is a virtual anthology of criminal argot, carefully footnoted in the printed text, illustrating again how the text must have served as a sort of libretto for the audience. Verse three of her song, for example, runs:

> I Frisky Moll, with my Rum Coll, 8
> Wou'd Grub in A Bowzing Ken 9
> But ere for the Scran he had tipt the Cole, 10
> The Harman he came in. 11

The footnotes explain: 8 clever thief; 9 wou'd eat in an Alehouse; 10 Before the Reckoning was paid; 11 the Constable.

Pantomimes were universally execrated by the critics, as being debased foreign imports catering to the depraved taste of the public for music and spectacle. The combination of spectacle and music attracted customers, however, and Gay was fully aware of this: the realization had been forced upon him. In November 1723, shortly before his *The Captives* opened, Drury Lane had produced Thurmond's *Harlequin Doctor Faustus*. Lincoln's Inn Fields answered it with a pantomime of their own, *The Necromancer; or Harlequin Doctor Faustus*. Both were successes, immortalized in *The Dunciad* (III, 231ff.) and "frequented," according to Pope's despairing note to the passage there, "by the first Quality of *England*, to the twentieth and thirtieth times."[18] Gay ruefully admitted the drawing power of the rival Faustuses, putting the question into Anne Oldfield's mouth in his Epilogue to *The Captives:*

> Will Poets ne'er consider what they cost us?
> What tragedy can take, like Doctor *Faustus*?

Thurmond's *Harlequin Sheppard* was different from the usual run of pantomimes, because it had a local setting and was based on a contemporary incident. Rich replied to it with a successful revival of Beaumont and Fletcher's *The Prophetess*, and *Sheppard* folded after a week's run, the performance greeted, according to a contemporary observer, "with a universal hiss."[19] It may be that audiences did not want a topical pantomime, preferred the Faustian fustian. Gay, who must have seen *Harlequin Sheppard*, kept his mouth shut about his role in the pantomime, except perhaps to his intimates, and his ballad was published anonymously.[20]

Nevertheless, *Harlequin Sheppard* clearly provided him ideas that would be worked out in *The Beggar's Opera*. Here were underworld characters, "grotesque characters," in a realistic underworld setting that included Newgate prison, acting—or dancing—in a silent drama of money and betrayal, with songs that comment on the action, performed to ballad tunes. One aspect that could be addressed only obliquely in a pantomime was language, but it is interesting that Gay chose to cast his ballad in standard English rather than attempt to reproduce an underworld dialect, as Harper did in his song, a choice Gay was to make again in *The Beggar's Opera*.

Jonathan Wild did not die from Blueskin's ministrations with the penknife: he lived to "hazard the halter" at Tyburn on 24 May 1725, where Gay could have seen him and where young Henry Fielding did in fact see him die: "I had the Curiosity," Fielding recalled years later, "to see the late *Jonathan Wild* go to the Gallows; but instead of taking any Pleasure in beholding so *notorious a Criminal* brought to Justice, I was shock'd at the Barbarity of the Populace, who pursued him in his last Moments with horrid Imprecations, and even with brutal Violence."[21] This was the London mob, urban violence that Gay knew well from his days as a mercer's apprentice even if he did not discuss it these days over tea at Chiswick.

There his current project was much more acceptable fare for polite conversation. In October 1725 he explained it succinctly in a letter to his friend, Brigadier James Dormer: "I have employ'd myself this summer in study, & have made a progress in it. What I am about is a Book of Fables, which I hope to have leave to inscribe to Prince William. I design to write fifty, all entirely new, in the same sort of verse as Prior's tales. I have already done about forty, but as yet there are very few of my friends know of my intention."[22] Gay was making a determined bid for preferment, to the Prince and Princess of Wales by way of their son, Prince William. As the Duke of Cumberland in 1745 he would be the nemesis of Bonnie Prince Charlie and the Jacobites at the battle of Culloden, "Butcher Cumberland." Now he was four years old, of uncertain literary interests. Pope continued dubious, writing Swift, "Our friend Gay is used, as the friends of Tories are by Whigs, (and generally by Tories, too)."[23] Swift was putting finishing touches to *Gulliver's Travels*, his "Materials," as he told Pope in the famous letter, "Towards a Treatis proving the falsity of that Definition *animal rationale;* and to show it should be only *rationis capax.*"[24] It is of interest that the two Scriblerians Gay and Swift were working independently on beast fables at the same time.

Gay enjoyed assuming the role of a talking animal, an *animal rationale,* as he had demonstrated years before in the splendid letter from "Horse" to the Blount sisters.[25] Although the *Fables* are not dramatic as such, they utilize the characterizing concision, the verbal pointedness an effective comic dramatist must possess. They present dramatic situations; good training for comedy. Animals talk freely to other animals in Gay's work, and humans and animals exchange barbed observations, like Gulliver among the Houyhnhnms.

Fable 23, "The Old Woman and her Cats," provides an amusing example of this interchange, which cat-owners at least will appreciate. The opening couplet might even be seen as evidence that Gay was mulling over the *Opera* in his mind: "WHO friendship with a knave hath made / Is judg'd a partner in the trade."[26] The Old Woman, "An untam'd scold of fourscore years," complains to her numerous brood of cats, who are hungry and mewing for food, that they have brought troubles on her by attracting crowds of naughty boys. This accusation does not sit well with the cats. Their spokescat replies. "To hear you prate would vex a saint, / Who hath most reason of complaint?"

> 'Tis infamy to serve a hag;
> Cats are thought imps, her broom a nag;
> And boys against our lives combine,
> Because, 'tis said, your cats have nine.

The fine copper plate by Vandergucht completes the dramatic situation, as it were: it shows woman and cat facing off, neither pleased with the other.

In Fable 50, last in the planned volume, "The Hare and many Friends," Gay perceptively dramatizes his own situation as a beggar for preferment. It is a melancholy vision.

> Friendship, like love, is but a name,
> Unless to one you stint the flame.
> The child, whom many fathers share,
> Hath seldom known a father's care;
> 'Tis thus in friendships; who depend
> On many, rarely find a friend.
> A Hare, who, in a civil way,
> Comply'd with ev'rything, like *Gay,*

> Was known by all the bestial train,
> Who haunt the wood, or graze the plain:
> Her care was, never to offend,
> And ev'ry creature was her friend.[27]

When hound and hunter pursue her to exhaustion, however, she finds the beasts all have excuses for not helping. The horse refers her to the bull; the bull has pressing responsibilities: "Love calls me hence; a fav'rite cow/Expects me near yon barley mow." The goat fobs her off on the sheep, who "Said he was slow, confest his fears;/For hounds eat sheep as well as hares." Finally she turns to the calf; though youthful the calf can manufacture excuses as adroitly as his elders:

> Shall I, says he, of tender age,
> In this important care engage?
> Older and abler past you by;
> How strong are those! how weak am I!
> Should I presume to bear you hence,
> Those friends of mine may take offence.
> Excuse me then. You know my heart.
> But dearest friends, alas, must part!
> How shall we all lament! Adieu.
> For see the hounds are just in view.

With this vision of charity beginning, and remaining, at home, Gay ended his gift for little Prince William. Jacob Tonson and James Watts published the *Fables* in 1727, in a sumptuous edition with plates designed by William Kent, Lord Burlington's artist-in-residence, and executed by the best engravers in London. Here was a gift fit for a king, or for the Duke of Cumberland, as he now was.

Gay was living at his lodgings in Whitehall, attempting to adjust his expectations to reality. "I expect nothing," he wrote Swift in February 1727, "& am like to get nothing." "The contempt of the world," he continued in his philosophic mood, "grows upon me, and I now begin to be richer and richer, for I find I could every morning I wake be content with less than I aim'd at the day before."[28]

Pope was engaged just at this time in overseeing the printing of the so-called Pope-Swift *Miscellanies,* in which, he wrote to Swift, "methinks we look like friends, side by side, serious and merry by turns, conversing interchangeably, and walking down hand in hand to posterity."[29] What Pope fails to mention in this letter, which obviously has Prince Posterity as an information addressee, is that works by Gay and Arbuthnot are collected in the *Miscellanies* without attribution, to the continuing puzzlement of bibliographers. Included in the third volume was "Newgate's Garland."

Swift came over from Ireland and was with Pope at Twickenham in May of 1727, enjoying in his restrained manner the fame of *Gulliver's Travels.* In June King George I died suddenly while on the Continent, to be succeeded in due course by the Prince of Wales. After hearing the news, Pope commented to a correspondent on "the Disparity of men from themselves in a weeks time: the desultory leaping and catching of new motions, new modes, new measures: and the strange spirit and life, with which men broken and disappointed resume their hopes, their sollicitations, their ambitions!"[30] One of those disappointed men, though Pope does not mention his name, was John Gay. Pope wrote Henrietta Howard, "What does Gay do? or what will be done for him?"[31] Would his hopes for preferment finally be fulfilled by the accession of the Prince and Princess of Wales? Would the *Fables* be his admission ticket to a place at Court?

The short reply is no. When the notice of appointments appeared in October, Gay was listed as Gentleman Usher to the Princess Louisa, who was just two years old. The stipend was £150, exactly what he received for his post with the Lottery. Gay felt that the appointment was insulting and he declined it. He explained to Swift: "I was appointed Gentleman-usher to the Princess Louisa, the youngest Princess; which, upon account that I am so far advanc'd in life, I have declin'd accepting; and have endeavour'd, in the best manner I could, to make my excuses by a letter to her Majesty. So now all my expectations are vanish'd; and I have no prospect, but in depending wholly upon my self and my own conduct." No supplications for place now; Gay had set a more important project in motion. "You remember," he continued, "you were advising me to go into Newgate to finish my scenes the more correctly—I now think I shall, for I have no attendance to hinder me; but my Opera is already finished."[32] The beggar had an opera.

SEVEN

The Beggar's Opera in Theatre History

Hearing of Stella's illness, Swift had departed for Dublin in September 1727. Before he left he had read scenes from *The Beggar's Opera*, which was finished, if we can trust the text and dating of Gay's letter to him,[1] by late October 1727. How long had it been in active preparation, one may ask, actually in the stage of composition, and what influenced Gay in writing it?

Many years before, in the Scriblerian days of 1716, Swift had written to Pope about what Gay might do: "what think you of a Newgate pastoral, among the whores and thieves there?"[2] Swift presumably meant a pastoral poem, a comic urban pastoral of the sort he himself wrote in "Description of the Morning." *Trivia* itself is close to a Newgate pastoral poem at times; the scene in that work quoted earlier of the apprentices' football game is a kind of *Shepherd's Week* episode in urban dress. Gay was certainly capable of writing a Newgate pastoral if he wished to do so.

His instinct was for the stage, however, as Swift's was not. Gay had been writing ballads intended for or employed in stage performance off and on over the years, as we have seen; most recently and importantly "Newgate's Garland" for Thurmond's pantomime, *Harlequin Sheppard* in 1724. He had been in and around music for a long time, from his years as an apprentice, from the days of Aaron Hill and the *British Apollo*,[3] and especially from the beginning of his association with Handel. An eighteenth-century legend, which I have not been able to verify, says that Gay could play the flute, that is,

what we could call the recorder.[4] Although there is no reason
to believe that he had musical training, he was on the other
hand a most sophisticated listener with considerable experience at adapting words to musical settings. He had a good poetic ear and a good musical ear; the combination does not
occur so frequently as one might suppose. As far as the musical side of his experience is concerned, he was fully ready
by 1727 to compose a ballad opera, a genre that he was in the
process of inventing.

As for literary "influences," that happy hunting ground of
scholars who believe that playwrights write plays by surrounding themselves with books, from which they make appropriate selections, as for these, in spite of assiduous
searching, not much has turned up. Richard Brome's *A Jovial
Crew, or The Merry Beggars*, a Caroline comedy that was revived frequently after the Restoration and that the Drury
Lane company had been playing for more than twenty years,
has often been mentioned as it features songs and deals with
beggars. But it has nothing whatever to do with *The Beggar's
Opera* (which after all includes only one beggar: the author
poet). Set in the country and full of rural jokes, jollity, and
folklore, *A Jovial Crew* is much closer to *The Wife of Bath* in
spirit than to the *Opera*. It was adapted in 1731 as a ballad
opera, after the success of Gay's work, and had a long stage
life of its own, but the influence is all the other way around.[5]
Christopher Bullock's *A Woman's Revenge, or A Match in Newgate*, produced in 1715—Bullock was one of the actors who de-
fected from Drury Lane to Rich's company that year—depicts
bawds and criminals in Newgate, but the parallels of plot and
character are not at all convincing, and neither *A Jovial Crew*
nor *A Woman's Revenge* resembles the *Opera* in language, of
dialogue or song. It is entirely possible, however, even probable, that Gay as an ambitious dramatist *saw* both of these
plays, as an aspiring cinematographer today would screen every film he could lay hands on. With the London repertory
theatres, one could see most of the standards every season or
two, recognizing that the form in which one saw a particular

play was that which the managers had given it: Nahum Tate's adaptation of *Lear* with a happy ending, for example.

To correct impressions of drama altered for the play-house, one could buy the play in its original form. Printed versions of almost all the plays produced on the London stage were available at the booksellers, soon after or during opening night. In imitation of the 1709 Rowe edition of Shakespeare, collected editions of plays were also becoming increasingly common—even pirated editions from The Hague, with London on the title page. All this was catering for the rising literacy rate in London and the provinces, and the evolving provincial and colonial book trade that supplied a growing literate public.[6] The books were available to Gay if he had wished to use them.

Beyond that, though, on the subject of literary influence, beyond his own important participation in *Harlequin Sheppard*, one comes back to the astute comment of Gay's most recent biographer: "All we need to say is that a succession of such plays no doubt forced him to recognize the possibilties of the subject and to speculate on his own ability to handle it."[7]

It was probably in the summer of 1727, with Swift and Pope at hand to remind him of reality, when Gay finally understood substantial preferment was not likely to come in his direction. After the king's sudden death in June some persons were out of employment and others were in. One person most securely in was Sir Robert Walpole, who was cultivating the new queen and making himself indispensable to the new king.[8] As Irving has pointed out, Gay's friend Henrietta Howard, the king's mistress, the classic Other Woman, did not stand to be much help to him with the king's wife. Pope himself called on Walpole in August, and Pope was in touch with his and Gay's good friend, William Fortescue, who saw the first minister frequently. Pope and Fortescue were both sensitive men, good readers of others' intentions. They must have known that Walpole was not going to bestir himself on Gay's account and that without Sir Robert's acquiescence, at the least, little in the way of place or profit was going to be his.

Pope's and Swift's attitude toward Gay's place-seeking perhaps differed somewhat at this particular juncture. Swift had committed himself in *Gulliver's Travels* as a satirist of Walpole's political methods—and everyone recognized what he was up to.[9] Pope was still trimming his sails a bit in 1727; in fact, as recently as 1725 he had accepted a two-hundred pound grant from the Treasury, that is, from Walpole's government though technically from the King,[10] which he kept discreetly quiet about. Both Swift and Pope, however, still hoped that Gay might receive something from the Court and were angered when he was, as he and they thought, fobbed off with the appointment as Gentleman Usher to the baby princess. Why, asks Bertrand Goldgar, a scholar who has studied this issue carefully, were Gay and his friends so shocked that he did not find favor? After all, Gay had no family connections, not much money, little political acumen. "The answer seems to be . . . that as 'men of wit' they regarded patronage as their due and honestly expected those in power to support them regardless of 'party,' and as humanists they expected poets, the teachers of virtue, to play some role in the circles of power."[11] Such dreams of influence might possibly have proved true when Robert Harley was a Scriblerian and also Lord Treasurer—though Swift the realist was capable of a good deal of self-deception when it came to practical politics—but it was certainly not true in 1727.[12] Fortunately, as his friends recognized, Gay possessed artistic talent that in proper combination with circumstance could amount to genius, and he was about to make use of that talent.

Some time in that early summer of 1727, then, Gay probably began working seriously on *The Beggar's Opera*. The *Fables* had occupied him through the spring, and, as we have seen Fable 50, The Hare and many Friends, itself reflects his conviction that friends in high place would not help him in the day of trouble. It was time to help himself. He may have written the work rapidly, and even though Pope and Swift were around it was not to be a collaborative effort. Pope, speaking to Spence a few years later, was careful to underline that fact: "He began on it, and when first he mentioned it to Swift the Doctor did not much like the project. As he carried it on he showed what he wrote to both of us, and we now and then gave a correction or a word or two of advice, but 'twas wholly of his own writing. When it was done, neither of us thought it would succeed. We showed it to Congreve, who after reading it over, said, 'It would either take greatly, or be damned confoundedly.' "[13]

By October he had apparently finished the *Opera*. It was an odd kind of work he had produced, not much like anything else in the drama, but the genius that informs it is distinctly a Scriblerian kind of genius, combining social satire, political satire, and literary burlesque, as Pope was combining the same ingredients just at this time in the first version of *The Dunciad*, and as Swift had recently done in *Gulliver's Travels*. The three works are utterly different, but they are recognizably kin, too.

Once he had written it, he was faced with getting the piece onto the stage. It was tough going to have a new play produced in one of the two patent theatres in those days, even for an experienced dramatist like Gay.[14] Drury Lane, which had produced his earlier plays and whose actors and actresses he consequently knew well, was the obvious place to start. Because of its subsequent astonishing success, the first production of *The Beggar's Opera* is so beclouded with theatre gossip, partisan comment, and *parti pris* recollection as to make certainty about what actually happened almost impossible to come by. Colley Cibber always appears center stage as the Dunce who turned down the hit of the century for Drury Lane, in a fit of pique or vanity. But Cibber was only one of three managers there; Wilks and Barton Booth must have turned it down, too, or at least have agreed with Cibber's decision. Why did they do so?

Naturally Cibber does not dwell on, or even mention the decision in his *Apology*, which must constitute a principal source, maddeningly organized and discursive though it be, for what was going on in the London theatres during his

lifetime. There is no evidence at all, however, there or elsewhere to support the contention that the Drury Lane
managers in general or Cibber in particular were displeased
with Gay at this time. They had, after all, kept his pastoral
turkey *The Captives* running for seven performances in 1724,
against the strenuous competition of Lincoln's Inn Fields. *The
What D'Ye Call It* was in their repertory, ready to make money
for them when audience taste for farces returned. On balance
the three managers probably regarded Gay with about the
same enthusiasm as that with which they regarded living
dramatic authors in general, that is to say, guarded, luke-
warm. Dead writers were preferable because one did not have
to pay them for author's benefit nights or listen to their an-
noying complaints about the production. John Gay, in their
eyes, was a typical living author; no better than the rest, perhaps, but no worse.

Nor is there much to say for the supposition, frequently
voiced, that Tory political satire in the *Opera* frightened the
Whiggish triumvirate of managers. The *Opera* was swept up
after its production into the political storm, along with everything else written by Gay and the other Scriblerians, but this
was later, in the period between 1728 and 1730 to which Bertrand Goldgar has given the title, "The Triumphs of Wit," the
triumphant wit being that of the Scriblerians, of course.[15] In
truth, *The Beggar's Opera* does not embody much specific political satire, Tory or Whig. Received opinion is always difficult to counter or alter, but in this case received opinion
wants changing. The biographer W. H. Irving, so right on so
many judgments about Gay is simply mistaken when he as-
serts that "Gay proposed to make his play somewhat of a theatrical *Craftsman*," that is, a vehicle of propaganda for the
Tory and dissident Whig opposition.[16]

It was later converted into such a vehicle, as we shall see,
by among others Swift in *The Intelligencer* and by *The Craftsman* itself, but this was after the fact, several weeks after the
opening. There are, to be sure, political references salted here
and there through the play that would have drawn laughs.
Peachum's reference, for example, in I.iii, to "*Robin* of *Bag-*

shot, alias *Gorgon*, alias *Bluff Bob*, alias *Carbuncle*, alias *Bob Booty*." This bit of verbal exuberance—note its resemblance to the list of aliases seen earlier in the Introduction to *Harlequin Sheppard*—is invariably footnoted heavily, and explained in ponderous academic lectures as a reference to Robert Walpole, which of course it is. But the dialogue that follows effectively draws the teeth of the satire:

> Mrs. *Peachum.* What of *Bob Booty*, Husband? I hope nothing bad hath betided him. You know, my Dear, he's a favourite Customer of mine. 'Twas he made me a Present of this Ring.
> *Peachum.* I have set his Name down in the Black-List, that's all, my Dear; he spends his Life among Women, and as soon as his Money is gone, one or other of the Ladies will hang him for the Reward, and there's forty Pound lost to us for-ever. (I.iv.1-7)

So much for Bluff Bob, who has one line of dialogue in the entire opera. If Gay intended Bob Booty for political satire with Walpole as the satiric victim he was remarkably inept in his dramaturgy. And likewise with Macheath, who is also often said, following *The Craftsman*'s guidance, to represent Walpole. The male lead, the hero, who enjoys to the end the steadfast love of both Lucy Lockit and Polly Peachum? Macheath as Walpole as satiric victim? The identification will not bear dramatic analysis. In *Polly*, it can be argued; but not in *The Beggar's Opera*.

The script presented to the three managers, assuming it resembled the version that finally appeared in print, had almost nothing in it to frighten Cibber and his colleagues, nothing that would have sent a Court Whig out of the theatre at the first interval. And in point of fact the Court Whigs paid to see *The Beggar's Opera* when it was produced, along with everyone else. It was not topical satire that kept the Drury Lane managers from accepting Gay's proposal. What then was it?

An informed guess is that the script Gay showed Cibber, Wilks, and Booth impressed those theatre professionals as being too out-of-the-way, too experimental, too nonstandard for commercial success. It was a what-d'ye call it. They had a point: *The Beggar's Opera* is out-of-the-way, experimental, and nonstandard. That is part of its glory: its dazzling originality; it is as original in its own way as *Gulliver's Travels* or the *Dunciad*. But the very originality must have worked against its chances with the managers, who could have said: "Interesting, yes. Original, no doubt about that. But risky. Will it take?" Leo Hughes has made the cogent suggestion that they may have been right, "that the history of Gay's ballad opera—and therefore of ballad and comic opera in general—might have been different if Cibber and his partners at Drury Lane had accepted the play."[17] The Drury Lane audience did not expect or relish novelty: one went to Lincoln's Inn Fields for novelty. The audience at Drury Lane had greeted the realistic pantomime *Harlequin Sheppard*, which included Gay's satirical ballad, with "a universal hiss." It is entirely possible that they might have hissed *The Beggar's Opera*, too, as being out of place at Drury Lane.

Another aspect that may have discouraged Cibber and his colleagues is also a part of the *Opera's* glory: its musicality. The title proclaims it to be an opera. Opera is what was being produced at the King's theatre in the Haymarket, at enormous expense, opera in Italian, but opera all the same. Drury Lane employed music and musicians—though less than had been so twenty years earlier—and had even been venturing hesitantly into pantomime, as we have seen, in response to Rich's success with the form at Lincoln's Inn Fields. The company could accommodate the occasional song but to take on a piece with at least one song in every scene may have seemed daunting to a group of actors and actresses who had been together for a quarter-century or more and who were beginning to look their age. The music was not difficult, Gay could have told them, mostly popular tunes, but even so there was a great deal of it, and Drury Lane, the managers may have decided, was simply not a musical theatre, not a place for an opera, a beggar's or anyone else's.

Finally, and perhaps most important, the Drury Lane company was flourishing in the autumn of 1727, while Lincoln's Inn Fields wilted. The Coronation took place on 11 October, with all its pageantry. *Everyone* who was Anyone was in Town. Competition at the two theatres was fierce. Like duellers, on 4 November *both* houses played Rowe's old warhorse favorite, *Tamerlane*, toe to toe, as it were. Challenging simultaneously Italian opera at the King's Theatre and pantomime at Rich's house, Drury Lane mounted a production of *Henry VIII* in honor of the recent succession of George II, which incorporated important elements of spectacle as Benjamin Victor reported: "on the Account of their present Majesties Coronation, a pompous representation of [Henry's] Ceremony was introduc'd into that play."[18] With copious advertising, *Henry VIII* became the hit of the new season. The King, Queen, the Princess Royal, and Princess Carolina attended a performance on 7 November and, according to *The British Journal* of 11 November, "seemed very well pleased with the Performance."

Fighting Shakespeare with Shakespeare, Rich ran *The Jew* [i.e., *The Merchant*] *of Venice* against *Henry VIII* on 13 November and grossed only eighty-six pounds plus shillings, just thirty-six pounds over the house charges of about fifty.[19] The *Daily Post* reported that day that *Henry VIII* "with the magnificent Coronation of Queen Anna Bullen, . . . still continues to draw numerous Audiences, which is owing to the Excellency of the Performance, and the extraordinary Grandeur of the Decorations."[20] *Macbeth*, with Quin in the title role, grossed a meager thirty-one pounds at Lincoln's Inn Fields on 17 November, not even enough to pay the house charges. In desperation Rich mounted a pantomime *Harlequin Anna Bullen* in December, which fizzled.[21] The money poured into Drury Lane. It was in this prosperous context, then, that the managers read Gay's script of *The Beggar's Opera*, and told him no. It was a decision they would soon come to regret.

At some point in the negotiations for production, Gay's friends Catherine and Charles Douglas, Duke and Duchess of Queensberry, seem to have come to his assistance. A likely time would have been after the Drury Lane managers had turned him down. Gay would find that the Queensberrys did not at all resemble those fair-weather friends of the Hare in Fable No. 50, who abandoned him to the hunter in his day of trouble. They were both young, he not yet thirty and she even younger, and they had been married only since 1720. Catherine Douglas was a Hyde, second daughter of the fourth Earl of Clarendon and granddaughter of the historian. Charles had succeeded his father, the second duke, in 1711, and had inherited estates in England and vast acreage in the border country of Scotland, along with the pink sandstone castle at Drumlanrig built by his grandfather, the first duke. This young noble couple would prove to be Gay's loyal, lifelong friends, ready to stand by him even if friendship cost them considerably in terms both social and financial.[22]

Precisely what *The Beggar's Opera* cost the duke and duchess, if anything, before its opening is difficult to assay. The duchess may have guaranteed some or all of the costs of production to John Rich; the evidence for this is uncertain.[23] Robert D. Hume, writing of young Henry Fielding's entry into the theatrical world, is skeptical about the potential influence of the nobility on theatre managers. Authors, he writes "cadged introductions and recommendations from . . . persons of social distinction—though whether such recommendations really helped is doubtful."[24] Still, Rich was in dire financial straits and a guarantee might conceivably have attracted his eye, which was on the main chance as always. Benjamin Victor, a principal source for information about the production, does not refer to any subsidy. He notes, however, that the Drury Lane managers "peremptorily rejected this Opera." "Nay, it was currently reported that the happy Manager [Rich], who perform'd it, gave it up after the first Rehearsal, and was with some Difficulty prevailed on to make the Trial."[25] Rich may or may not have been reluctant to take the *Opera* on, but he certainly would have *appeared* reluctant if the duchess had agreed to foot the bill. Any difficulties in rehearsal would have allowed him to raise the ante, like a Peachum from Gay's opera. Rich also had the continuing problem of competition from Drury Lane to nag his days and nights. The other house had followed up its triumph with

Henry VIII by reviving Vanbrugh's *The Provok'd Husband*, as edited and altered by Cibber. Critics protested, but audiences loved it: beginning 10 January 1728 it ran for twenty-eight nights successively, an unprecedented hit. This was enough in itself to make any rival manager nervous. Could the unknown comic opera by Gay face up to this sort of competition? Rehearsals continued.

Lavinia Fenton, destined for theatrical immortality, was selected to play Polly Peachum, though she had barely two years' experience on the stage. Rich had cast Fenton as Cherry in *The Beaux Stratagem* during the previous season; she had also played Ophelia and appeared as an entr'acte singer and dancer. Someone right for the ingenue part of Cherry who could sing would be right for Polly as well. Thomas Walker, strictly a journeyman actor to this date, was chosen for the part of Macheath instead of James Quin, the leading actor of the company, who apparently rejected the role.[26] The other parts Rich filled out with the regulars of his company, not a distinguished group of actors, but adequate. As its stage history affirms, adequate actors will do well in *The Beggar's Opera*, good actors will do superbly.

But this was in the future. Right down to opening night there was every reason for Rich and his company to have second thoughts about presenting a new production. Drury Lane's *The Provok'd Husband* was demolishing competition. The premiere of John Sturmy's *Sesostris* grossed only sixty pounds on opening night (17 January) at Lincoln's Inn, dragged on for a second author's benefit of forty-seven pounds on the 23rd and closed forever on the 27th of January 1728.[27] *The Beggar's Opera* was next up. It was not a promising atmosphere for Gay's new play.

The author and his friends were naturally apprehensive. Congreve's judgment (that "It would either take greatly, or be damned confoundedly") was scarcely an opinion to calm Gay's nerves, and the tension communicated itself to Congreve, too. Pope wrote Swift: "John Gay's Opera is just on the point of Delivery. It may be call'd (considering its Subject) a Jayl-Delivery. Mr. Congreve (with whom I have commemorated

you) is anxious as to its Success, and so am I; whether it suc-
ceeds or not, it will make a great noise, but whether of Claps
or Hisses I know not. At worst it is in its own nature a thing
which he can *lose* no reputation by, as he lays none upon it."[28]
This is a friend talking to a friend about another friend, but
one guesses that Gay longed more fervently for his opera's
success than was evident to Pope. The theatre had been the
locus of his principal literary ambitions for more than fifteen
years; he had, he felt, been publicly humiliated by the Court.
What better way, what *other* way to settle accounts than by
writing a successful play?

About six o'clock on the night of Monday, 29 January
1728, as was the custom, the author appeared at the theatre,
hoping for the best. Pope, and an entourage of friends also
turned up at Lincoln's Inn Fields, along with, the *Daily Journal* later reported, "a prodigious Concourse of Nobility and
Gentry."[29] Gay had of course peddled tickets genteelly to all
his friends; this was also customary. Seated in their box seats,
Gay and his associates awaited the verdict of the Town with
trepidation, as the orchestra launched into the overture, composed and conducted by the competent musical director of
Lincoln's Inn Fields, Dr. John Christopher Pepusch. As Pope
later recalled it to Spence:

We were all . . . in great uncertainty of the event, till we were very
much encouraged by overhearing the Duke of Argyle, who sat in the
next box to us, say, "It will do—it must do! I see it in the eye of
them." This was a good while before the first act was over, and so
gave us ease soon, for that Duke, beside his own good taste, has as
particular a knack as any one now living in discovering the taste of
the public. He was quite right in this, as usual. The good nature of
the audience appeared stronger and stronger every act, and ended in
a clamour of applause.[30]

Benjamin Victor's recollection confirms the tension, and also
confirms that indecision on the part of the audience so tor-
turing to a cast, especially on opening night: "On the first
Night of Performance, its Fate was doubtful for some Time.

The first Act was received with silent Attention, not a Hand moved; at the End of which they rose, and every Man seemed to compare Notes with his Neighbor, and the general Opinion was in its Favour." This must have been about the time the Duke of Argyle delivered the memorable aside that Pope and Gay picked up in the next box, but "silent Attention" is not enough. Victor continues: "In the second Act they broke their Silence, by Marks of their Approbation, to the great Joy of the frighted Performers, as well as the Author; and the last Act was received with universal Applause."[31] Act II opens with the great tavern scene, the musical and dramatic strategy of which will be discussed in the following chapter. Act I closes with the quiet love duet of Macheath and Polly, "Parting," as Gay's stage direction indicates, "and looking back at each other with fondness; he at one Door, she at the other" (I.xiii.70-73). It is a notably understated act closing, one that does not draw much applause in modern productions. Victor's recollection accords with the dramatic logic of the *Opera*.

In the first week Gay's fortune was assured. On Thursday 1 February the *Daily Journal* reported succinctly on "Mr. Gay's new English Opera, written in a Manner wholly new, and very entertaining, there being introduced, instead of Italian Airs, above 60 of the most celebrated old English and Scotch tunes. . . . [N]o Theatrical Performance for these many Years has met with so much Applause." The opposition newspaper, *The Craftsman*, which would soon undertake its explication of the *Opera*'s latent political comment, contented itself in the initial week with recording on 3 February for the first time that witticism that has become standard: The *Opera* "has met with a general Applause, insomuch that the Waggs say it has made *Rich* very *Gay*, and probably will make *Gay* very *Rich*."[32] It is worth reiterating that the re-education campaign of the opposition, the program of finding and pointing out specific political propaganda, did not begin until *The Beggar's Opera* was securely established as a hit.

By 15 February Gay was feeling sufficiently confident to write Swift a letter that signalizes his triumph and also reflects the deep satisfaction he was receiving from that triumph. It is worth quoting in full:

Dear Sir / I have deferr'd writing to you from time to time till I could give you an account of the Beggar's Opera. It is Acted at the Playhouse in Lincoln's Inn fields, with such success that the Playhouse hath been crouded every night; to night is the fifteenth time of Acting, and 'tis thought it will run a fortnight longer. I have order'd Motte to send the Play to you the first opportunity. I made no interest either for approbation or money nor hath any body been prest to take tickets for my Benefit, notwithstanding which, I think I shall make an addition to my fortune of between six and seven hundred pounds. I know this account will give you pleasure, as I have push'd through this precarious Affair without servility or flattery. As to any favours from Great men I am in the same state you left me; but I am a great deal happier as I have no expectations. The Dutchess of Queensberry hath signaliz'd her friendship to me upon this occasion in such a conspicuous manner, that I hope (for her sake) you will take care to put your fork to all its proper uses, and suffer nobody for the f[uture] to put their knives in their mouths.

Gay's comment on the generosity of the duchess is apparently the ultimate source of later speculation about her subsidizing rehearsals, but it could refer to many other manifestations of the noble lady's warm heart. The advice to Swift on minding his table manners is of course a delightful aside between old friends. Gay continues:

Lord Cobham says that I should [have] printed it in Italian over against the English, that the Ladys might have understood what they read. The outlandish (as they now call it) Opera hath been so thin of late that some have call'd that the Beggars Opera, & if the run continues, I fear I shall have remonstrances drawn up against me by the Royal Academy of Musick. As none of us have heard from you of late every one of us are in concern about your health. I beg we may hear from you soon. By my constant attendance on this affair I have almost worried myself into an ill state of health, but I intend in five or six days to go to our Country seat at Twickenham for a little air. Mr. Pope is very seldom in town. Mrs Howard frequently asks after you, & desires her compliments to you; Mr. George Arbuthnot, the Doctor's Brother is married to Mrs. Peggy Robinson. I would write more, but as to night is for my Benefit, I am in a hurry to go out about business. / I am Dear Sir / Your most affectionate / & obedient Servant / J. Gay[33]

"I have push'd through this precarious Affair without servility or flattery." It is as if Gay is seeking to underline his independent action to Swift, whom he knew to have been skeptical about his search for preferment.

Gay sold the copyright to John Watts, for an unknown but no doubt substantial sum. Watts was by then the leading publisher of dramatic authors. He began publishing editions on 14 February, "To which is Added, The MUSICK *Engrav'd on* COPPER-PLATES," as the title page of the first edition indicated. Watts must have had to push his engravers and printers hard to produce the edition just sixteen days after the opening but it was well worth the effort: edition followed edition, in varying states which have puzzled bibliographers ever since.[34]

Gay's remark to Swift about this being his benefit night and having to see about his business may stem from the slim returns of the first author's benefit, which dipped mysteriously from opening night (£169 to £161), then leaped to £175 on the fifth night. On his benefit night on 8 February the take was again down to £165, even though the *Daily Journal* that day commented the show "meets with that universal Applause, that no one third Part of the Company that crowd thither to see it, can get Admittance." These were spectacular receipts—the opening of *Sesostris* in January, it will be remembered, grossed only sixty pounds, barely enough to cover the house charges. Although Rich's books are difficult to interpret, it may be that he was at first skimming some off the top for his own use, as it were, before reporting the gross on benefit nights to Gay. This, then, would account for Gay's anxious attention to business on benefit night: so that he could verify the totals himself.[35]

Rich was shoehorning that happy third part of the crowd into every square inch of space he could clear. On the 23rd of

March, for example, the *Opera* grossed £194, with 238 spectators in the boxes, *98*(!) on the stage, 302 in the pit, 65 in the slips (extensions of the boxes), 440 compressed into the first gallery, 196 in the second gallery, and 2 paying customers in a category not yet explained by scholarship, but the comfort of which imagination can conjure up: "pidgeon holes."[36] A total of 1,341 in the audience. For comparison, a year earlier on 13 March 1727 Rich had taken in £133 for a performance of *Hamlet* with Quin in the title role playing to 891 in the audience—7 on the stage and no one in pidgeon holes. A routine performance of *The Beggar's Opera* came out 50 percent ahead, in terms of both audience and receipts.

Precisely how much came to Gay of these receipts is impossible to say: his own estimate in mid-February to Swift of between six and seven hundred pounds may or may not be accurate. If he had his wits about him and insisted on additional benefit nights or some similar arrangement, it is on the low side. The figure to precise pounds, shillings, and pence that is quoted so confidently by both his latest biographer and editor has no relationship to reality, however, and will not be given further life here.[37]

Consecutive performances of the *Opera* continued through February and early March. On 22 February the Royal Family attended a command performance: their entourage took up twenty-eight box seats, plus a place for a Yeoman of the Guard in the pit.[38] The company performed it on the 7th of March and gave it a brief rest, offering James Carlisle's *The Fortune Hunters*, "Carefully Revis'd, with Fenton as Nanny." The star system was working: receipts for the revival were a most satisfactory £131. But the temptations of the *Opera's* gross were too much, and it was back on the stage the following Monday. Drury Lane, meanwhile, was attempting to counter Gay's success, which had overshadowed even the bonanza of *The Provok'd Husband*. In a rare deviation from previous form, the Drury Lane managers produced a new play: young Henry Fielding's *Love in Several Masques*. This intrigue comedy was given its first performance on 16 February 1728, in the very teeth of the *Opera's* success and ran only four nights, "neither a success nor a fiasco."[39] After this Cibber and his colleagues returned to the tried and true, running repertory standards: *Hamlet, The Funeral, The Way of the World, The Man of Mode*. The success of Gay's *Opera* would soon shake both Drury Lane and Lincoln's Inn Fields out of their extreme conservatism by encouraging competition for new work, but that was still in the future.

Now Rich could watch the money roll in, and the Opposition could be about showing how *The Beggar's Opera*, correctly interpreted, represented a frontal attack on Sir Robert Walpole and his ministry. Swift wrote Gay on 26 February, in reply to Gay's account of the *Opera*'s success: " Does W[alpole] think you intended an affront to him in your opera. Pray God he may, for he has held the longest hand at hazard that ever fell to any Sharpers Share and keeps his run when the dice are changed."[40] The strength of Swift's feeling about Walpole is not in dispute, but this letter, which is frequently cited as proof that Gay *did* intend an affront to Walpole in the *Opera*, seems on the contrary to be evidence that he did not. Swift had read at least part of the *Opera* in manuscript; he asks Gay if Walpole thinks that Gay intended an affront. Surely if Swift had known that Gay intended an affront he would have written "knew you intended" or "believed you intended." The comment appears to be, rather, a query set off by *The Craftsman*'s famous blast of 17 February—which Swift could have seen by 26 February. Swift seems to be telling Gay that Walpole may have taken offense where no offense was intended, and that Gay should be happy about it.

The sequence of events that the opposition set in motion to convince the public that the *Opera* was anti-Walpole propaganda is interesting in its own right as an effective use of the print medium in politics. How far Gay himself was involved is a matter for conjecture, but his financial interests were at least carefully protected, and there is every reason to believe that he knew what was going on. *The Craftsman*, after its initial, good-humored comment about Rich and Gay on 3 February, waited until the opera was well established, the printed edition had been placed on sale, and Gay had received his benefit for the fifteenth performance to publish on 17 February the richly ironic letter by "Phil. Harmonicus" to *The Craftsman*'s putative editor, "Caleb D'Anvers." Harmonicus identifies *The Beggar's Opera* as "the most venemous [sic] *allegorical Libel* against the G[*overnmene*]*t* that hath appeared for many Years past." He explains that Macheath represents Walpole, and that Peachum and Lockit *also* represent Walpole and his brother Horatio. "Harmonicus" demonstrates how to read the *Opera* for innuendo, of which he finds plenty.

A few weeks later, in the middle of March, Harmonicus's letter was republished as part of a little guide or do-it-yourself kit for Walpole-bashing, appended to the "second edition" of Christopher Bullock's *Woman's Revenge*.[41] Bullock, one of a family of actors, had died in 1722 but his widow Jane was the highest paid female actor on the Lincoln's Inn payroll in the late 1720s and republication of the play may have brought her some copy money. What the customers presumably wanted, however, was the reprinted letter, here appearing as *A Compleat Key to the Beggar's Opera*, by "Peter Padwell of Paddington, Esq;" a "Town Pastoral to Mrs. Polly Peachum"—a verse satire with Walpole the satiric victim—and, significantly, Gay's "Newgate's Garland." The opening lines of the "Garland's" last stanza with a reference to William Wood and the Irish coinage scandal, which Swift had celebrated in *The Drapier's Letters*, would have evoked echoes in Dublin:

> What a Pother has here been with *Wood* and his Brass,
> Who would modestly make a few Half-pennies pass?

Perhaps they did evoke such an echo. Jonathan Swift in the other island was about to reinforce the attacks on Walpole, with his own satiric touch. Swift employs a somewhat different strategy from that of the "Key," although also an ironic one, for his Irish audience in an essay published in the Dublin *Intelligencer* in May 1728. The essay is to be seen in the context of Swift's pamphlet battles with the Walpole ministry and their Irish representatives, of which the *Modest Pro-*

posal (1729) would be the crowning jewel. Swift simply co-opts Gay for his side. He, Swift, writes satire, he contends, only for personal satisfaction. "If I ridicule the Follies and Corruptions of a *Court*, a *Ministry*, or a *Senate*, are they not amply paid by *Pensions*, *Titles*, and *Power:* while I expect, and desire no other Reward, than that of laughing with a few Friends in a Corner?" He continues, "My Reason for mentioning *Courts*, and *Ministers* (*whom I never think on, but with the most profound Veneration*) is, because an Opinion obtains, that in the *Beggar's Opera* there appears to be some Reflections upon *Courtiers* and *Statesmen*, whereof I am by no Means a Judge."[42]

Unlike Phil. Harmonicus, Swift does not spell out the Reflections for his audience. Rather, he contends that Gay's merit and his fourteen years' attendance at Court have been overlooked and he has "failed of Preferment," which of course was true. "It must be allowed, That the *Beggar's Opera* is not the first of Mr. Gay's Works, wherein he hath been faulty, with Regard to *Courtiers* and *Statesmen*. For to omit his other Pieces, even in his Fables, published within two Years past, and dedicated to the Duke of Cumberland, for which he was promised a Reward, he hath been thought somewhat too bold upon the *Courtiers*." Swift here sends the readers of the *Fables* back to their volumes, to seek out innuendoes that to that moment no one had recognized. After a discussion of recent attacks on the morality of the *Opera*, Swift in his inimitable backhanded manner focuses attention on the transvaluation of values dramatized in the work: "This *Comedy* contains likewise a *Satyr*, which without enquiring whether it affects the present Age, may possibly be useful in Times to come. I mean, where the Author takes the Occasion of comparing those *common Robbers of the Publick*, and their several Stratagems of betraying, undermining and hanging each other, to the several Arts of *Politicians* in Times of Corruption" (p. 36). Times of Corruption. Not *these* times, not the present Age, of course. It is the rhetorical device of praeteritio, saying by affecting not to say; one of Swift's favored techniques. "Disingenuous,"

Bertrand Goldgar has termed Swift's arguments in *The Intelligencer.*[43] Disingenuous they are, but ingenious.

Benefiting from the political guidance of *The Craftsman* and Swift, audiences now knew when to laugh and when to glance significantly at politicians in the theatre boxes. It all added to the fun, and Gay had provided the perfect cue with Lockit's song in Act II:

> When you censure the Age,
> Be cautious and sage,
> Lest the Courtiers offended should be:
> If you mention Vice or Bribe,
> 'Tis so pat to all the Tribe;
> Each crys—That was levell'd at me. (II.x.21-26)

By this time vendors were selling mezzotint engravings of Lavinia Fenton and Thomas Walker as Polly and Macheath; Gay sent Swift, at Swift's request, a pair of these predecessors of publicity shots. Gay was in an ebullient mood, writing the Dean in March:

On the Benefit day of one of the Actresse's last week one of the players falling sick they were oblig'd to give out another play or dismiss the Audience, A Play was given out, but the people call'd out for the Beggar's Opera, & they were forc'd to play it, or the Audience would not have stayd. I have got by all this sucess between seven & eight hundred pounds, and Rich, (deducting the whole charges of the House) hath clear'd already near four thousand pounds. In about a month I am going to the Bath with the Dutchess of Marlborough and Mr. Congreve, for I have no expectations of receiving any favours from the Court.[44]

The two lovers and Gay found a production of the *Opera* playing in Bath when they arrived there. Swift as an author was annoyed at the disproportionate size of Rich's bonanza, writing Gay that "I think that rich rogue Rich Should in conscience make you a present of 2 or 3 hundred Guineas." It was time for Gay to provide for himself: "Ever preserve Some Spice of the Alderman [i.e., financial acumen] and prepare against age and dulness and Sickness and coldness or death of friends. A whore has a ressource left that She can turn Bawd: but an old decayd Poet is a creature abandond."[45] With the politicization of the *Opera* Gay must himself abandon all hope of preferment, as he knew. The Government wisely chose not to attempt to refute the innuendoes—that would have been fulfilling Lockit's prediction in his song— but decided to move against the work on moral and aesthetic grounds. Dr. Thomas Herring, chaplain at Lincoln's Inn, preached a sermon in March against the morality of *The Beggar's Opera*, contending that the favorable presentation of criminals in the work would encourage crime.

Pope and Gay recognized that Herring's sermon was a political plant—Swift said as much in his *Intelligencer* essay— but his contentions were taken seriously, then and later. Daniel Defoe, perhaps still smarting from his encounter with the Mohocks, complained in a pamphlet that "Every idle Fellow, weary of honest Labour, need but fancy himself a *Macheath* or a *Sheppard*, and there's a Rogue made at once."[46] Samuel Johnson felt compelled to refute such criticism in his "Life of Gay" in *Lives of the Poets:* "The play, like many others, was plainly written only to divert, without any moral purpose, and is therefore not likely to do good; nor can it be conceived, without more speculation than life requires or admits, to be productive of much evil. Highwaymen and housebreakers seldom frequent the playhouse."[47]

The next chapter will examine the moral content, if any, of *The Beggar's Opera*, but it is a fact that, Johnson to the contrary notwithstanding, many people continued for a long time to brood about its tendency to deprave. A biographer of Gay writing in the 1820s presented a long discussion of Herring's sermon, concluded that he was correct, and regretfully summed up Gay's career after the *Opera*'s success this way: Gay "had a pleasing turn for poetry," but "unhappily falling into the hands of Swift and Pope and their set, he was promoted into a walk, which rendered his talents a snare to himself, and in general a nuisance to his fellow creatures. . . . Let his example prove a warning to others, and it will not have been in vain."[48]

Another line of attack on *The Beggar's Opera* by the government's followers was aesthetic: that the opera was a debased form of entertainment. This could be and sometimes was associated with the charge of immorality. The *London Journal* of 23 March 1728, for example, viewed the declining interest in opera as a symptom of failing aesthetic taste: "I would not be thought here to speak with any Prejudice or Ill-will to the *Beggar's Opera*, in which I am willing to allow there is a great deal of true low Humour." Just what the audiences, unfortunately, wanted. These charges were perhaps motivated primarily by politics, but they had a residual sting and no doubt some persuasive effect.

Those of the aristocracy who took a dim view of the stage found their opinions amply confirmed that spring. The Duke of Bolton attended a performance of the *Opera* on Monday, 8 April, when Gay also had a box seat there.[49] The Duke came to the next two performances and brought his duchess to the *Opera* on Saturday 13 May. On 22 June *The Craftsman* reported, "To the great Surpize of the Audience, the Part of *Polly Peachum* was performed by Miss WARREN, who was very much applauded; the first Performer being retired, as it is reported, from the Stage." Retired indeed: "The D[uke] of Bolton," Gay informed Swift, "I hear hath run away with Polly Peachum, having settled 400£ a year upon her during pleasure, & upon disagreement 200£ a year."[50] Lavinia Fenton was "now in so high vogue," Gay had written Swift, "that I am in doubt, whether her fame does not surpass that of the Opera itself."[51] Lavinia had struck paydirt; eventually the duke would make her his duchess, but these were unseemly doings, even for the nobility. A good many individuals, in all classes, felt that the theatre was no better than it should be. Perhaps some kind of systematic censorship was in order.

EIGHT

The *Opera* as Work of Art

The *Daily Journal* got the matter right when it wrote of "Mr. Gay's new English Opera" in the issue of 1 February 1728. Like all great works of art, *The Beggar's Opera* possesses differing meanings for different members of the audience—every audience; its significance will not be exhausted in any single discussion. However, the three terms used by the *Journal*, new, English, and opera, provide convenient guideposts to what it was that Gay delivered to the reluctant—and soon to be gay—John Rich.

There is nothing entirely new in the theatre, of course. Readers of this book will remember that the use of music, popular and/or traditional music, was a strategy Gay had adopted at the very beginning of his dramatic career, with the songs in *The Mohocks,* and had continued in most of his later plays except for his tragedies. He had worked with—and learned from—Handel on *Acis and Galatea.* Handel's setting for " 'Twas when the Seas were roaring" from *The What D'Ye Call It* was being reprinted for popular sale—Gay would employ the tune again in the *Opera.* Most recently he had written a ballad for performance in the pantomime *Harlequin Sheppard,* sung to an old favorite tune, "The Cut-Purse," or "Packington's Pound," which he would also use again in the *Opera.* One imagines Gay humming tunes to himself as he wrote. Music was never far from the center of his artistic creativity.

Music had a place in the English theatre at least since Elizabethan days, as Shakespeare's songs remind us. By the latter part of the seventeenth century music was becoming increasingly important, and composers and playwrights were collaborating to produce music in plays that possessed, as Dianne Dugaw has explained, a life separate from but complementary to the action of the plays themselves. Musical references accompanied literary intertextuality. "Thus, the 'songish parts' in late-Restoration plays constitute a separate level of performance that does not emanate from, but rather parallels the dramatic level of the play."[1] Although the use of music in the legitimate theatre began to decline after the turn of the eighteenth century, as opera grew increasingly important,[2] it was precisely to this use of "songish parts" with resonances of their own that Gay returned in *The Beggar's Opera*.

It has been observed[3] that Parisian popular tunes had been used for years in *comédie en vaudeville* at the Théâtre de la Foire, which Gay could have seen on one of his visits to the city, and that a troupe from France presented a performance in London in May 1726. There is nothing entirely new in the theatre; the notion of employing popular tunes in a topical setting was in the air: Gay himself had already participated in one such undertaking in *Harlequin Sheppard*. But the overriding truth is that the audiences who came to the first performances of *The Beggar's Opera* felt that it was, as the *Daily Journal* put it, "written in a Manner wholly new." A stage comedy with music organic to its plot development—not incidental or entr'acte music—seemed to the audiences at Lincoln's Inn Fields to be something new. They were correct: it was new. Musical comedy was being invented.

The Beggar's Opera was new, then, and it was also English: English because the tunes were native ones for the most part—"British" would be a more accurate term since some of the popular tunes were Scottish—and English because the dramatic vehicle is written in that language. Interesting stage performances bringing together music and spoken or sung English had appeared on the late seventeenth-century stage, most notably in the dramatic operas of Dryden and

Purcell, but also, as Curtis Price has shown, in plays with musical scenes integral to the plot such as Thomas Durfey's *Massaniello* (1699).[4] These proved to have no future in the London theatre; during the first decade of the eighteenth century, opera in Italian came to dominate the musical stage,[5] with, as we have seen, Aaron Hill and probably his secretary John Gay assisting in the process by producing Handel's *Rinaldo*.

Lowell Lindgren has demonstrated, however, that opera in English was making a return engagement: Giovanni Bononcini's *Camilla*, with an English libretto, found considerable success among London audiences during 1727 and can legitimately be seen as a predecessor of Gay's *Opera* in its surprising "Englishness."[6]

Singers from abroad were imported at ruinous fees for these performances, especially and notoriously the flute-voiced *castrati* from Italy; the theatre companies themselves were stripped of what native British musical talent they possessed. Colley Cibber recalls his plight in playing Sir Courtly Nice in Crowne's play of that name, which required a singing part that "I, alas! could only struggle thro', with the faint Excuses, and real Confidence of a fine Singer under the Imperfection of a feign'd, and screaming Trebble."[7] The Royal Academy of Music at the King's Theatre, Haymarket, continued to dominate the London musical stage, enjoying support from the royal family who were attuned to opera because of their German background and with Handel providing his genius to the enterprise. Opera, however, was enormously expensive then, as it still is, and even Handel could not keep it going indefinitely.[8] *The Beggar's Opera*, seen as a continuation of the British musical tradition, appeared for a while to offer hope for that tradition. A few years after its debut, Hill addressed to Handel a famous letter, proposing that he write operas in English.[9] But this was not to be. Although revived and imitated times without number, *The Beggar's Opera* made little permanent contribution to English music as such. A historian of opera has put the matter in this way: "In a century which, to speak mildly, was not the Golden Age of British music, the ballad opera appeared as a vigorous but solitary gesture of revolt against foreign musical domination; but it lacked the principle of growth within itself, nor did external conditions favor the rise of an independent serious national opera on the basis of the popular comic-opera style."[10]

The music Gay employed in his "gesture of revolt" was wonderfully accessible and singable: it had almost all been tested in the popular market, as it were. Although a thorough, scholarly discussion of the musical background of the *Opera* is still to be done, some generalizations may be made. The first is that Gay drew the music from wherever he found it around him. This means that he felt free to use music in the public domain, such as traditional ballad tunes circulating in rural Britain and Ireland, and the printed broadside ballad. As Claude Simpson has shown, "The broadside ballad was essentially an urban variety of subliterary expression, and London was its undisputed headquarters."[11] These two musical streams, which were sometimes interchangeable, the one rural, the other urban, thus reflected and complemented the dual sources of Gay's best work for the stage: that derived from his Devon boyhood and that coming from the streets and sights and sounds of London. He also borrowed music when he felt the need from the composers of his own time who were working in the London musical marketplace, some excellent composers such as Arcangelo Corelli, Richard Leveridge, and Francesco Geminiani, and one towering genius, Handel. All this music was in effect available for free employment; Gay could use what he chose to use. The expensive aspect of music was in having it transcribed and performed.

The variety of the music, the tunes that come from opera, concert hall, theatre, and streetsinger, that variety is echoed and reinforced by the variety of lyrical forms that Gay supplies for the tunes he has chosen. The ballad stanza as such he uses from time to time, but sparingly. The first act curtain song, Macheath and Polly's duet of parting, is in the ballad stanza, and is sung to a broadside ballad tune, "The Broom," of enormous popularity (Johann Christian Bach and Haydn each later adapted it):[12]

Macheath.   The Miser thus a Shilling sees,
                 Which he's oblig'd to pay,
                 With Sighs resigns it by degrees,
                 And fears 'tis gone for aye.
Polly.   The Boy, thus, when his Sparrow's flown,
                 The Bird in Silence eyes;
                 But soon as out of Sight 'tis gone,
                 Whines, whimpers, sobs and cries.
                                (I.xiii.70-77)

The broadside ballad presents the lament of a milkmaid who has been betrayed by her lover, so the tune would have an appropriate resonance in its own right for Polly, whose betrayal by Macheath is thus foreshadowed. This constitutes, then, one of those "critical instants" that Dianne Dugaw has noted in the songs of late seventeenth-century plays.[13]

An even better example of a "critical instant" and of Gay's lyrical skills is the duet at the beginning of the same scene, which brings the lovers Polly and Macheath together for the first time in the opera. The underlying song, "Pretty Parrot, say," was popular in London, sold separately in broadside form and collected in, among other collections, Thomas Durfey's *Wit and Mirth: or Pills to Purge Melancholy*. It, too, is a duet; between a parrot and its master, who has returned home and wants to find out what has been happening in the household while he was gone:[14]

> Pretty Parret, say when I was away,
> And in dull Absence pass'd the Day
> What at home was doing;
>   With Chat and Play,
>   We are Gay,
>   Night and Day,
>   Good Chear and Mirth renewing;
> *Singing, Laughing all, Singing Laughing all,*
>   *Like pretty, pretty* Poll.

Gay transfers the resonance of the suspicious master to Macheath, also suspicious of his Polly's fidelity, and transforms it into a love duet, the first of a series of love songs between the two. Gay's metrical virtuosity contrasts sharply with that of the parrot's anonymous chronicler:

> Macheath.   Pretty *Polly*, say,
>   When I was away,
>   Did your Fancy never stray
>   To some newer Lover?
> Polly.   Without Disguise,
>   Heaving Sighs,
>   Doating Eyes,
>   My constant Heart discover.
>   Fondly let me loll!
> Macheath.   O pretty, pretty *Poll*. (I.xiii.1-10)

Gay then employs two song tunes from Farquhar's enduringly popular *The Recruiting Officer*,[15] the first of which introduces that simile of "the *Bee*," which the Beggar had promised the Player in his Introduction.

> Macheath.   My Heart was so free,
>   It rov'd like the Bee,
>   'Till *Polly* my passion requited;
>   I sipt each Flower,
>   I chang'd every Hour,
>   But here ev'ry Flower is united.
>   (I.xiii.18-23)

The music, composed by Richard Leveridge, is memorable in its own right but undemanding, so undemanding that Robert Wilks could sing it as Captain Plume in the original production of *The Recruiting Officer*. Gay's lyric, with its anapestic beat, crystal clarity, and wit—deep critics of the twentieth century will point out the appropriate phallic symbolism—is a perfect match for Leveridge's music.

Polly then asks Macheath if he could leave her behind, if he were sentenced to transportation to the colonies. The line perhaps indicates Gay already had in mind his sequel to the *Opera, Polly,* where Macheath's transportation to the West Indies and Polly's search for him there provide the basis of the ballad opera's action. Macheath's reply aptly illustrates Gay's comic and satiric technique:

> Macheath.   Is there any Power, any Force that could tear me from thee? You might sooner tear a pension out of the Hands of a Courtier, a Fee from a Lawyer, a pretty Woman from a Looking-glass, or any Woman from *Quadrille.*—But to tear me from thee is impossible! (I.xiii.26-30)

The critic of comic technique flirts with the risk of becoming Wordsworth's botanist, who murders to dissect. Nevertheless, a commentator is bound to point out that the scene reflects the basic transvaluation of values of the *Opera* as a whole, with the underworld aping the ruling elite—and the ruling elite, by implied inversion, aping the underworld. Macheath, leader of the criminals, in speech and action resembles a member of the nobility or gentry. A leader of the elite—Robert Walpole, for example—by implied inversion, in action resembles and *is* a criminal. The satiric victims in Macheath's lines are members of the elite: courtiers, lawyers, coquettes, society wives, and finally Macheath himself, the faithless lover.

Macheath modulates smoothly into another love duet, to the familiar ballad tune of "Over the Hills and Far Away." This, too, had been employed by Farquhar in *The Recruiting Officer* but as a recruiting song. The recruits there are encouraged to take the Queen's shilling to get away from domesticity:

> We all shall lead more happy Lives,
> By getting rid of Brats and Wives,
> That scold and brawl both Night and Day;
> Over the Hills and far away—Over the Hills, &c.[16]

The echoes of Gay's love duet, as Ian Donaldson has pointed out,[17] are amusingly different, a dream of domestic bliss rather than domestic discord:

> *Macheath.*   And I would love you all the Day,
> *Polly.*   Every Night would kiss and play,
> *Macheath.*   If with me you'd fondly stray
> *Polly.*   Over the Hills and far away. (I.xiii. 39-43)

After another song by Polly, to a traditional ballad tune, the lovers have their parting duet discussed in the preceding chapter, and the act ends, very quietly.

Gay has employed five tunes in the brief scene, a traditional ballad tune, two broadside ballad tunes (one well-known as a popular street song), and two tunes identified with a familiar play. Each would have resonances for his audience, resonances that are of course denied us who do not know the tunes in their original contexts, but the pleasing melodic variety still results in an attractive theatrical moment at this point in the action. The love plot is set and Gay looks ahead dramatically to the re-entry of Macheath in the Act II, as the leader of the highwaymen.

Gay's use of a male singer for the principal role, instead of a castrato, is an assertion in its own way of the opera's English independence, as Yvonne Noble has pointed out.[18] Macheath, however, is an equivocal figure. In terms of the drama, it goes without saying, he is the focal male character. Gay knew his underworld lore well, much of it firsthand from his years as an apprentice, and he was aware that highwaymen (Macheath = Son of the Heath—where highwaymen plied their trade) had long been regarded as the aristocracy of the underworld, since they did their work as equestrians, rather than as footpads, nimmers, pickpockets, or other of the dismounted infantry. Mrs. Peachum observes of Macheath in the first act, "Sure there is not a finer Gentleman upon the Road than the Captain!" (I.iv.41-3), and Peachum later notes that "the Captain looks upon himself in the Military Capacity, as a Gentleman by his Profession" (I.vii.30-31). This hierarchy was reflected in the criminal biographies that had proliferated in the preceding half-century, as Lincoln Faller has recently shown: highwaymen were at the top of the ranking and footpads at the bottom.[19] The Introduction to *Harle-*

quin Sheppard, the pantomime to which Gay contributed his ballad, was a current example of the tendency among criminal biographies to portray the criminal as a gentleman, or at least a gentleman *manqué.*

Gay accepts this and turns the custom to his satiric uses. Macheath is a gentleman to his fingertips: in his expensive taste for gambling, wine, and women, in his aggressive and exploitative sexuality. The poet/beggar underlines the point in his final speech: "Through the whole Piece you may observe such a similitude of Manners in high and low Life, that it is difficult to determine whether (in the fashionable Vices) the fine Gentlemen imitate the Gentlemen of the Road, or the Gentlemen of the Road the fine Gentlemen" (III.xvi.18-22). The sinister aspects of Macheath's heroism are softened by the *Opera's* boisterous comicality; his sexual adventurism results only at the end in "Four Women more, Captain, with a Child a-peice!" (III.xv.23). In *Polly* Gay traces Macheath's character to its logical, ruthless conclusion, and kills him off.

The female characters are effectively sketched in, using the resources of both dialogue and music. As Handel's librettist Gay had learned the virtues of verbal economy. He has room enough to build the essential contrast between innocent Polly and worldly Lucy at length, to the attempted poisoning in the third act, but even a supporting character such as Jenny Diver is sufficiently differentiated to be memorable. Unlike the rest of the females, Jenny is not swept off balance by Macheath's pungent masculinity: she betrays him to the constables, just as Edgeworth Bess had betrayed Jack Sheppard. Before the betrayal she had evidenced her differentness. "I never go to the Tavern with a Man, but in the View of Business. I have other Hours, and other sort of Men for my Pleasure" (II.iv.75-7). What sort of men? we ask ourselves. And what sort of pleasure? Jenny then sings a song to the assembly, which includes Macheath, that satirizes both the hero and his admiring females (the tune is "All in a misty morning," a broadside ballad of the previous century):

> Before the Barn-door crowing,
> The Cock by Hens attended,

> His Eyes around him throwing,
> Stands for a while suspended.
> The One he singles from the Crew,
> And cheers the happy Hen;
> With how do you do, and how do you do,
> And how do you do again. (II.iv.84–91)

The enigmatic Jenny interested Gay: he uses her again in *Polly*. And she interested Berthold Brecht, so much so that he made her perhaps the most arresting character in *Die Drei-groschenopfer*, Die Hure Jenni, Whore Jenny, translated for tender American sensibilities as Pirate Jenny.

Gay's dramatic sympathies are clearly with the women— and children: Mrs. Peachum is a mother figure to the precocious apprentice Filch: "He hath as fine a Hand at picking a Pocket as a Woman, and is as nimble finger'd as a Juggler. If an unlucky Session does not cut the Rope of thy Life, I pronounce, Boy, thou wilt be a great Man in History" (I.vi.2-6). Mrs. Peachum's dialogue exemplifies one of Gay's typical glancing satiric blows: Filch may grow up to be a great man in history, that is a great pickpocket; Robert Walpole was being characterized in the Opposition press—especially from this time forth—as a "Great Man." Great politicians are great pickpockets; Henry Fielding, who was in London preparing a play for production, would work the equation out in detail in *Jonathan Wild*.[20]

At the play's opening Filch is a child, who has not learned how to tell lies in the proper adult manner. He has as his role model, however, the true Jonathan Wild figure in the *Opera*, Mr. Peachum. The genuine master criminal is not Macheath, the man on horseback, but Peachum, the bourgeois shop-keeper—this *is* an opera by a Tory, after all. Pat Rogers has argued that Peachum was modeled on the portrait of a businessman drawn in all seriousness by Daniel Defoe in *The Complete English Tradesman*.[21] The term "to peach," to inform on or give incriminating evidence against, had been in ordinary English usage for a long time: the earliest reference given by the *Oxford English Dictionary* being that of 1570, in Foxe's *Martyrs*.

Peachum's underworld empire is built on betrayal, deception, and denunciation. So is the great world of Town,
Court, and City. Gay endows this transvaluation with dramatic reality and comic verve in the opening scene of the opera proper, after the framing dialogue has taken place
between beggar/poet and player. Peachum is seen with his
ledger before him. A tradition as early as 1730 held that Swift
had a hand in writing the song Peachum sings; it is certainly
Swiftian in style and content.

> THROUGH all the Employments of Life
>   Each Neighbour abuses his Brother;
> Whore and Rogue they call Husband and Wife:
>   All Professions be-rogue one another.
> The Priest calls the Lawyer a Cheat,
>   The Lawyer be-knaves the Divine;
> And the Statesman because he's so great,
>   Thinks his Trade as honest as mine. (I.i.1–8)

To ensure that the audience grasps the transvaluation of the
song, Gay reinforces it with a monologue by Peachum: "A
Lawyer is an honest Employment, so is mine. Like me too he
acts in a double Capacity, both against Rogues and for 'em;
for 'tis but fitting that we should protect and encourage
Cheats, since we live by them." Peachum is a rich comic creation, one of Gay's masterstrokes: exuding false benevolence
and phony gentility. "I love to let Women scape. A good
Sportsman always lets the Hen Partridges fly, because the
breed of the Game depends upon them. Besides, here the Law
allows us no Reward; there is nothing to be got by the Death
of Women—except our Wives" (I.ii.19-24). It will be noted
that Gay's criminals speak impeccable standard English. He
chooses not to attempt dialect or, with few exceptions, to
employ criminal argot, other than in the choice of names:
Nimming Ned, Mrs. Slammekin, and so on. These are all ac-
curately chosen: to nim is to steal, and a slammekin is "a female sloven."[22] In name, appearance, and action these people
may be criminals, but when they speak, their diction is above

reproach. As, for example, Peachum directs Filch to be off to Newgate and "let my Friends know what I intend; for I love to make them easy one way or other."

> *Filch.*   When a Gentleman is long kept in suspence,
>   Penitence may break his Spirit ever after.
>   Besides, Certainty gives a Man a good Air upon his
>   Tryal, and makes him risque another without Fear
>   or Scruple. (I.ii.39–45)

Samuel Johnson could not have put it more elegantly, though he would certainly not have endorsed Filch's sentiments.

Lockit is Peachum's alter ego, scarcely to be distinguished from him, although it could be said, I suppose, that the one represents commercial and the other judicial corruption. Gay accents their similarity of outlook in Lockit's soliloquy and song in Act III—and draws also on his recent experience in writing beast fables:

> *Peachum* then intends to outwit me in this Affair; but I'll be even with him.—The Dog is leaky in his Liquor, so I'll ply him that way, get the Secret from him, and turn this Affair to my own Advantage.—Lions, Wolves, and Vulturs don't live together in Herds, Droves, or Flocks.—Of all Animals of Prey, Man is the only sociable one. Every one of us preys upon his Neighbour, and yet we herd together.—*Peachum* is my Companion, my Friend—According to the Custom of the World, indeed, he may quote thousands of Precedents for cheating me—And shall not I make use of the Privilege of Friendship to make him a Return?

Lockit's ensuing song is to the tune, "The Cut-Purse," or "Packington's Pound," which Gay had used for his ballad "Newgate's Garland" in *Harlequin Sheppard*. Whether Gay thought the audience would establish the association between the two ballads I do not know; Thurmond's pantomime had enjoyed only a brief run, and at Drury Lane, but as Roger Fiske has shown, the tune had ancient associations in the drama with criminality. Lockit extends the trope of man as beast:

Thus Gamesters united in Friendship are found,
Though they know that their Industry all is a Cheat;
They flock to their Prey at the Dice-Box's Sound,
And join to promote one another's Deceit.
  But if by mishap
  They fail of a Chap,
To keep in their Hands, they each other entrap.
Like Pikes, lank with Hunger, who miss of their Ends,
They bite their Companions, and prey on their Friends.
                              (III.ii.1-10, 12-20)

Gay's decision to avoid dialect and criminal argot is a significant one and represents a change from his practice in *The
Mohocks*, where the Constable's watchmen do some amusing
damage to the language. It is conceivable that his choice was
based on his observation of Frisky Moll's song in *Harlequin
Sheppard*, which, it will be remembered, required footnotes
when it was printed and must have been virtually unintelligible to the Drury Lane audience.

The Beggar's Opera, then, seemed new to the audiences at
Lincoln's Inn Fields in 1728, and its Englishness in language
and music made it an attractive alternative to the Italian productions at the King's Theatre in the Haymarket, but was it
an opera, as the *Daily Journal* had termed it? The statement,
often heard, that it was planned as a satire on Italian opera
must be rejected or severely qualified.

Gay was intimately familiar with the *opera seria* and with
the London theatrical scene. His education in both had been
from the inside, as it were. As with politics so with music: *The
Beggar's Opera* is a fabric of allusions to what has been happening on the musical stage. For example, the Beggar/Poet's
statement in the Introduction: "As to the Parts, I have ob-
serv.d such a nice Impartiality to our two Ladies, that it is
impossible for either of them to take Offence." Bertrand
Bronson has explained that the reference is to Lucy and Polly
but the allusion is to a famous quarrel the year before between the rival singers Faustina and Cuzzoni. "Matters came
to a hysterical climax when, in a performance of Buonon-
cini's *Astyanax*, in the spring of 1727, the rivals actually

resorted to mutual scratching and hair pulling on the stage."[23] Bronson notes how Lucy's lines in Act III, Scene vii are precise imitations of the recitatives in an *opera seria*, which establish the emotional mood for the aria they precede: "Jealousy, Rage, Love and Fear are at once tearing me to pieces," Lucy exclaims. " How I am weather-beaten and shatter'd with distresses!" The simile of the Ship that the Beggar/ Poet had promised follows:

> I'm like a Skiff on the Ocean tost,
> Now high, now low, with each Billow born,
> With her Rudder broke, and her Anchor lost,
>   Deserted and all forlorn.
> While thus I lye rolling and tossing all Night,
> That *Polly* lyes sporting on Seas of Delight!
>   Revenge, Revenge, Revenge,
> Shall appease my restless Sprite. (III.vii.1–11)

This is a richly comic application of what the composers of *opera seria* were doing at the time; it is scarcely a satire on Italian opera. Bronson points out that the parting between Polly and Macheath at the end of Act I, discussed above with respect to the variety of tunes employed there, resembles closely the scene in Handel's *Floridante* (1721) between Floridante and Elmira.[24]

The dramatic sequence that opens Act II is yet another example of Gay working creatively with his musical materials, in the operatic tradition. This is the point at which, according to Benjamin Victor, the first night's audience began showing its approbation by applauding. As well it might: it is a dynamic moment on the stage. Macheath's gang are assembled in their tavern, "with Wine, Brandy, and Tobacco," voicing satisfaction at their lot and themselves:

Crook-finger'd Jack. Where shall we find such another Set of practical Philosophers, who to a Man are above the Fear of Death?
Wat. Sound Men, and true!
Robin. Of try'd Courage, and indefatigable Industry!
Ned. Who is there here that would not dye for his Friend?

Harry. Who is there here that would betray him for his Interest?
Matt. Show me a Gang of Courtiers that can say as much.

Matt of the Mint then leads them in their drinking song, "Fill
Ev'ry Glass," the tune of which was already familiar to the
audience as a drinking song—and perhaps also as the French
Christmas carol in which it had an earlier manifestation:

> Fill ev'ry Glass, for Wine inspires us,
>   And fires us
> With Courage, Love and Joy.
> Women and Wine should Life employ.
> Is there ought else on Earth desirous?
> *Chorus.* Fill ev'ry Glass, &c.

This can be, and often is, sung as a round. The scene builds
with musical and dramatic excitement to the entrance of the
hero, Macheath. He instructs the band of highwaymen to
head for their place of business on the Western Road; they
exit singing, to the stirring—and very familiar—march from
Rinaldo, "with Drums and Trumpets." (Gay's stage direction
is enough in itself to refute the ridiculous story that he
planned the music to be sung without accompaniment.)[25]

> Let us take the Road.
>   Hark! I hear the sound of Coaches!
>   The hour of Attack approaches,
> To your Arms, brave Boys, and load.
>   See the Ball I hold!
> Let the Chymists toil like asses,
> Our Fire their Fire surpasses,
>   And turns all our Lead to Gold. (II.i&ii.1-29,1-52)

This sequence—chorus, entrance of a central figure, chorus—
is one that nineteenth-century composers would use again
and again—Verdi in *Il Trovatore* for example, focusing and en-
hancing the dramatic/musical impact. Gay's employment of
the march from the first *opera seria* that he knew well is fitting tribute to the great composer he had learned so much
from.

But Gay has a further, comic, variation in mind: Macheath does not march off with his band: he stays in the tavern for a rendezvous with "all the Ladies." "I must have Women," he soliloquizes. "There is nothing unbends the Mind like them. Money is not so strong a Cordial for the Time." When they enter Macheath lovingly takes inventory of his treasures: Mrs. Coaxer, Dolly Trull, Suky Tawdry, Jenny Diver, pronouncing on each one's qualities: *"Molly Brazen!* [*She kisses him.*] That's well done. I love a free-hearted Wench. Thou hast a most agreeable Assurance, Girl, and art as willing as a Turtle" (II.iv). A dance "a la ronde *in the* French *Manner"* follows. The lyrics of the accompanying cotillion are skillfully crafted for the occasion: the mixed trochaic and anapestic rhythms of the verse guide the dance, of course, and the theme of love's fleeting joys foreshadows with appropriate dramatic irony what is just ahead: Macheath's betrayal and seizure by the constables and Peachum.

> Youth's the Season made for Joys,
>   Love is then our Duty,
> She alone who that employs,
>   Well deserves her Beauty.
>   Let's be gay,
>   While we may,
> Beauty's a Flower, despis'd in decay.
> Youth's the Season &c.
>
> Let us drink and sport to-day,
>   Ours is not to-morrow.
> Love with Youth flies swift away,
>   Age is nought but Sorrow.
>   Dance and sing,
>   Time's on the Wing,
> Life never knows the return of Spring.
> *Chorus.* Let us drink &c. (II.iv. 28–43)

After Peachum pronounces his verdict ("Your Case, Mr. *Macheath*, is not particular. The greatest Heroes have been ruin'd by Women") and Macheath is led away by the constables, the remaining women *"Exeunt with great Ceremony."*

Gay wants the tavern sequence decorously rounded off. It has
been a powerful sequence, succeeding the quiet love scenes
between Polly and Macheath with an evolving tableau of
great musical and dramatic vivacity. A colleague, Michael
Marcuse, recently observed to me that he had never read a
discussion of the *Opera* that adequately conveyed its impact.
He is correct: its visual, verbal, and musical qualities can
only be fully appreciated in performance. It is, in a word,
an opera.

As if to emphasize the Englishness of this opera, Gay lav-
ishes English music on Macheath's prison scene (the Beggar/
Poet had told the Player that he had "a Prison Scene which
the Ladies always reckon charmingly pathetick.") In III.xiii,
Macheath and brandy bottle in the condemned hold, Gay
puts together nine familiar tunes—from Purcell, from Henry
Carey ("Sally in our Alley"), from the ballads, from popular
songsheets—followed by Greensleeves, which Macheath uses
to set forth the opinion Gay had voiced in his ballad for *Harlequin Sheppard:* that the Law has a double standard:

> Since Laws were made for ev'ry Degree,
> To curb Vice in others, as well as me,
> I wonder we han't better Company,
>   Upon *Tyburn Tree*!
> But Gold from Law can take out the Sting;
> And if rich Men like us were to swing,
> 'Twou'd thin the Land, such Numbers to string
>   Upon *Tyburn Tree*!

The interweaving effect of the ten melodies is charming and
illustrates the command Gay had over his materials, musical
as well as dramatic. Macheath's solitary bibulous medita-
tions are broken by the entrance of Lucy and Polly, and the
three lovers sing a trio, rare in opera at the time.[26] The triangle situation, as Bronson has demonstrated, burlesques
that of Handel's *Alessandro* (1726), which the composer had
constructed so that the feuding singers Faustina and Cuzzoni
would have equal roles and refrain from further hair pulling.

Arias were "shaped as by the hand of an expert *couturier* to display the special excellences of each voice," and each singer had a duet with Alessandro, but there was no trio.[27] It is a conjecture that Gay, who owed so much to Handel, may in his ballad operas' use of duets and trios, have returned the favor in some small way by stretching, if only minimally, the limits of the *opera seria* in this regard.

Gay's underlying song, "All You That Must Take a Leap," concerns the execution of two criminals, Lawson and Clark, as once again Gay establishes appropriate musical resonances for his audience.[28] His trio is comic rather than pathetic, however: Macheath is no longer able to give Polly and Lucy what they came for:

Lucy.	Would I might be hang'd!
Polly.	And I would so too!
Lucy.	To be hang'd with you.
Polly.	My Dear, with you.
Macheath.	O Leave me to Thought! I fear! I doubt!
Macheath.	I tremble! I droop!—See, my Courage is out.
	[*Turns up the empty Bottle.*]
Polly.	No token of Love?
Macheath.	See, my Courage is out.
	[*Turns up the empty Pot.*]
Lucy.	No token of Love?
Polly.	Adieu.
Lucy.	Farewell.
Macheath.	But hark! I hear the Toll of the Bell.
Chorus.	Tol de rol lol, &c. (III.xv.10-22)

The bell of St. Sepulcher's calls Macheath to his execution, which as all the world knows is averted by the Player's theoretical objection to the Beggar: "Why then, Friend, this is a down-right deep Tragedy. The Catastrophe is manifestly wrong, for an Opera must end happily." The Player is quite correct: *opera seria* did not countenance the death of the hero. Gay's opera ends with a dance of the prisoners, Macheath surrounded by his wives and children "like the *Turk*, with his Doxies around."

If *The Beggar's Opera* is, as the *Daily Journal* reported, a "new English Opera," then what in final terms is its relationship to the *opera seria*, often said to be a prime target of Gay's satire? Although the topic has never been systematically worked through, it is clear that there are many echoes, allusions, motifs in Gay's ballad opera that burlesque aspects of Italian opera. The presentation of the female principals in relation to the once notorious feud between Faustina and Cuzzoni is an excellent example. But as in the case of specific political satire, burlesque of *opera seria* is not central to Gay's artistic purposes; one's enjoyment of *The Beggar's Opera* does not depend on a knowledge of baroque opera, any more than our enjoyment of the satiric treatment of Great Men and their ambitions depends on knowing what Robert Walpole and the Opposition thought about each other. On the other hand, the more one understands opera, the more one admires Gay's exquisite skill at putting together his own work. Bronson, whose knowledge of music and literature was profound, puts the matter this way: "Everything considered, *The Beggar's Opera* may more properly be regarded as a testimonial to the strength of opera's appeal to John Gay's imagination than as a deliberate attempt to ridicule it out of existence."[29]

The morality of *The Beggar's Opera*, labored over by critics with such tedious care, is the morality of comedy, which is designed to laugh us out of our follies and vice.[30] Yvonne Noble has written well: the *Opera* "exists in the comic mode; . . . the satire, extensive and important as it is . . . is throughout finally encompassed by the values of comedy."[31] John Gay's ebullient masterpiece, "Mr. Gay's new English opera," lives comfortably alongside Handel's great operas, works of that master from whom Gay learned his craft.

NINE

Polly and the Censors

Gay may have had a sequel in mind even while he was writing *The Beggar's Opera*. In Act III Macheath, facing execution, offers his female consorts some considered advice: "My dear *Lucy*—My dear *Polly*—Whatsoever hath past between us is now at an end.—If you are fond of marrying again, the best Advice I can give you, is to Ship yourselves off for the *West-Indies*, where you'll have a fair chance of getting a Husband a-piece; or by good Luck, two or three, as you like best" (III.xv.1-6). The West Indies turn out to be the setting for Gay's next production, *Polly*.

Some kind of follow-on to the runaway success of *The Beggar's Opera* must have seemed indicated to Gay, whose literary ambitions had always centered in the drama. His next piece for the stage was certain to provoke controversy, whether he wished it to do so or not. He may have wished it to do so. He was by the summer of 1728 irretrievably identified with Pope and the political opposition, and Pope was putting the goad to his literary opponents—most of whom, not coincidentally, were supporters of Walpole's ministry. In March Pope had published the "last" volume of the *Miscellanies*, which included the Scriblerian collaboration *Peri Bathous, or The Art of Sinking in Poetry*, presenting low points of the poetic frenzy, with authors' names attached.[1] In May he published the first of what would be many versions of *The Dunciad*. In this one, the Dunces were identified by initials only. Ten days later, Edmund Curll obligingly vended *A Compleat Key to the Dunciad*, so that no

Dunce would go unrecognized.[2] The reply of one of them, Giles Jacob, demonstrates how closely Pope and Gay were identified in the minds of their opponents (and how right Pope was in his judgment of their literary skills):

I do not pretend to say how long Mr. *Pope* was writing of his *Dunciad;* but his great Malice against me, has been ten Years hatching and laying up, so as not to be brought to Light till the *Beggars Opera,* by Mr. *Gay* and Company, was acted in the Theatre; which low and licentious dramatical Piece, design'd for the Encouragement of Gentlemen on the Highway, and their female Associates, in *Drury-Lane,* by its extraordinary Novelty, happening to strike the giddy Humour of the Town, has introduc'd a new Species of the vilest Farce, and turn'd the Heads of both *Pope* and *Gay.*[3]

One would suspect that this was a Scriblerian writing in Dunce disguise, but it is the genuine article. Observe that Jacob attacks the *Opera* on moral and aesthetic grounds, which had been the standard technique of the Walpole press, but all the London world would have recognized, as Bertrand Goldgar has demonstrated, that "an astonishing number of the Dunces turn out to be government hacks or minor office-holders under Walpole."[4] The government had good reason to believe that Gay's next play would contain at least as much political satire as *The Beggar's Opera,* if not more. And they possessed retaliatory measures they had not yet used.

Gay was enjoying himself in Bath that summer of 1728, where a production of the *Opera* was being performed. He was of course lionized in Bath society, to Swift's disapproval, who wrote Pope: "I suppose Mr. Gay will return from Bath with twenty pounds more flesh, and two hundred less in money: Providence never design'd him to be above two and twenty, by his thoughtlessness and Cullibility."[5] Under that corpulent form, however, was a quick mind and perhaps more literary talent, of an eccentric, nonclassical kind, than Swift was prepared to recognize. While he was at Bath Gay may have been eating, drinking, and gambling but he was also writing, hard. He completed his new ballad opera there and at Amesbury (where the Duchess supplied an occasional rime for his songs, she later recollected),[6] and had it ready for rehearsal by November 1728. In somewhat more than two years' time he had finished the first volume of his *Fables* and two ballad operas.

Meanwhile change was stirring in the rather somnolent world of the patent theatres, inspired by the extraordinary simultaneous success of *The Provok'd Husband* and *The Beggar's Opera*. The two theatre companies, along with the patent opera company, had exercised a virtual monopoly—triopoly would be the term—in the London theatre world during the 1720s, until the momentous summer of 1728. Competition, occasionally strong as during the Coronation autumn of 1727, existed only among the three houses, and both actors and playwrights were at an extreme disadvantage vis-à-vis management. By formal arrangement, known as the "cartel agreement," the two theatre companies agreed in 1722 not to hire anyone working at the other theatre without prior consent of that theatre's management.[7] Stage personnel were therefore tied to their houses by an agreement that possessed legal standing. Similarly, playwrights were forced to vend their plays to houses with most conservative repertory policies. During the season 1726–27, as Robert D. Hume has recorded, Drury Lane and Lincoln's Inn Fields mounted a total of 115 plays, of which only five were new—four at Lincoln's Inn and a solitary new play at Drury Lane.[8] By an understanding that was apparently informal but that was maintained faithfully, new plays remained the property of the house that had first produced them, though the playwrights received no remuneration after the initial run. Thus playwrights, like stage personnel, were in effect bound to the theatres that originally used their work.

All these cozy arrangements were rudely shaken in the summer of 1728, when a "New Company" produced *The Beggar's Opera* in the theatre in the Haymarket known as the Little Haymarket (to differentiate it from Vanbrugh's opera house). The Little Haymarket had been constructed in 1720 and had served the needs, from time to time, of visiting foreign troupes.[9] In May 1728 the first imitation of *The Beggar's Opera*, Thomas Cooke and John Mottley's ballad opera *Penelope*, was staged there but ran only three nights. Then, on Monday 24 June, a production of *The Beggar's Opera* was launched, with "All the Songs and Dances set to Musick, as it is perform'd at the Theatre in Lincoln's-Inn-Fields," where the orginal production had closed for the season just five days earlier. Who the actors were and where they came from we do not know but, unless John Rich was getting part of the take, the performance marks, as Hume has noted, a major break in the informal agreement among the theatres that allowed the companies to retain exclusive rights to new plays.[10] In the autumn of 1728 the new company launched a repertory season of their own, staging, among other productions, *The Beggar's Opera* in competition with the original company at Lincoln's Inn Fields. Things were loosening up.

Gay would have possessed increased leverage with John Rich, then, if he had chosen to use it, but the wild success of the *Opera* no doubt provided leverage of its own, even if Rich had his worries because of the political turmoil that had followed the *Opera's* production. The worries proved to be fully justified. In his Preface to the first printed edition of *Polly* Gay describes the circumstances of its aborted production, from his point of view.

After Mr. *Rich* and I were agreed upon terms and conditions for bringing this Piece on the stage, and that every thing was ready for a Rehearsal; The Lord Chamberlain [the Duke of Grafton] sent an order from the country to prohibit Mr. *Rich* to suffer any Play to be rehears'd upon his stage till it had been first of all supervis'd by his Grace. As soon as Mr. *Rich* came from his Grace's secretary (who had sent for him to receive the before-mentioned order) he came to my lodgings, and acquainted me with the orders he had received.[11]

The office of the Lord Chamberlain in theory enjoyed powers to regulate the theatre companies that operated under the royal patent, but in practice exercised those powers sparingly.[12] During sunnier days at Court for John Gay, the Lord Chamberlain, as we have seen, had intervened to order *Dione* produced at Drury Lane.[13] Now Gay was identified as a member of the political opposition; no Lord Chamberlain was going to do him another favor any time soon. Gay must have known that there was trouble ahead. He wrote Swift on 2 December, telling of Grafton's order to Rich not to rehearse until the Lord Chamberlain had read the play and adding "what will become of it I know not, but I am sure I have written nothing that can be legally supprest, unless the setting vices in general in an odious light, and virtue in an amiable one may give offence."[14] As I have remarked elsewhere, in the context of Gay and Swift's friendship this remark amounts to a knowing wink.[15] Under the tutelage of *The Craftsman* and the rest of the opposition press, the British public over the preceding two years had learned how to read vices in particular into presentations of vices in general, and how to make the application to particular politicians in power.

Gay presented a copy of *Polly*, prepared from the prompt copy, to Grafton on 7 December and was told to await judgment. Precisely what happened next has never been ascertained. Did Walpole order suppression or was it the Lord Chamberlain acting on his own initiative? Lord Hervey recalled in his *Memoirs* that Walpole "resolved, rather than suffer himself to be produced for thirty nights together upon the stage in the person of a highwayman, to make use of his friend the Duke of Grafton's authority as Lord Chamberlain to put a stop to the representation of it."[16] But Lord Hervey was living in Italy from July 1728 until October 1729, and thus necessarily received his information at second hand. There is nothing to corroborate it and no scrap of documentary evidence has ever been found. Politicians dislike reducing their threats and promises to writing if they do not have to do so, and it may well be that Grafton's secretary simply materialized at Lincoln's Inn Fields and told Rich the eighteenth-century equivalent of "The Boss says don't do it." Gay received the news on Thursday, 12 December and later

wrote in the play's Preface that "This was told me in general
without any reasons assign'd, or any charge against me of my
having given any particular offence" (*Dramatic Works*, II, 70).

The opposition press joyfully picked up the suppression
as a stick with which to beat their arch-foe, the Great Man
himself. Two days after the suppression, on 14 December, *The
Craftsman* reported that "the Sequel to the Beggar's Opera,
which was going into Rehearsal at the Theatre in *Lincoln's-
in-Fields*, is suppressed by *Authority*, without any particular
Reasons being alleged." The similarity of *The Craftsman's*
phrasing to that of Gay's is interesting: "without any reasons
assign'd," "without any particular Reasons being alleged."
Who was echoing whom? In any case, the opposition took the
line that the government was overreacting, in paranoid fashion. Innocent poets had to be cautious because the censor was
watching and reading everything with an ear for innuendo.
This of course exactly reverses their strategy with *The Beggar's Opera,* under which opposition writers showed how
much political innuendo was present everywhere in that
work. Goldgar cites a song,[17] called "A Bob for the Court," in
The Craftsman of 28 December that warns against the use of
the very name "Macheath."

> If *Macheath* you should name in the midst of his *Gang, fa,la*
> They'll say 'tis an Hint you would *Somebody* hang: *fa la*
> For *Macheath* is a Word of such evil Report, *fa la.*
> *Application* cries out, *That's* a Bob *for the C---t, fa, la.*

Whether Gay participated in the Walpole-baiting or not—
and with Pope's coaching there is every reason to believe that
he did in this case—because of the commotion he certainly
stood to profit from sales of the printed play. Looking ahead,
he decided to retain the copyright himself, and so arranged to
have the play printed at his own expense. Gay contracted
with William Bowyer to undertake a huge printing, 10,500
copies or perhaps ten times the usual press run. Some of the
actual composition and presswork was done by John Wright,
who had recently printed the first volume of the Swift-Pope

Miscellanies.[18] The campaign for subscriptions went on, with subscription price a fashionable guinea (that is, twenty-one shillings); the play with music was to sell for six shillings. These subscriptions were in reality a vote of confidence for or a testimonial to Gay, who did not need the money to finance the printing. Gay reported to Swift that Henrietta, Duchess of Marlborough, Congreve's paramour and Gay's companion at Bath, "hath given me a hundred pound for one Copy."[19]

Subscription could also be interpreted as a vote of protest against Court and ministry policies. That is the way the King saw it when the Duchess of Queensberry approached other members of the Court, soliciting subscriptions. Lord Hervey reported in his subacid fashion what he had heard—he was still in Italy when it happened. "Her solicitations were so universal and so pressing that she came even into the Queen's apartment, went round the drawing-room, and made even the King's servants contribute to the printing of a thing which the King had forbid being recited."[20] The Duchess was extruded from the Court and her husband resigned his appointment as Vice-Admiral of Scotland as a gesture of support for her, and for Gay. She also sent a letter to the King of quite remarkable sauciness, asserting that she "is surprised and well-pleas'd that the King hath given her so agreeable a Command as to stay away from Court, where she never came for Diversion but to bestow a great Civility upon the King and Queen," and adding in a postscript that she had given the Vice Chamberlain "this answer in writing to read to His Majesty," with the implication that German George had difficulty reading his own letters in English.[21] These were indeed substantial evidences of friendship on the part of the Queensberrys, who had recently been experiencing some financial embarrassment—even dukes can be short of cash at times.[22]

When *Polly* was published on 5 April 1729 curiosity brought customers to the stall of one Heney, a fan-painter at Gay's Head in Tavistock Street, Gay's curious choice as vendor for his ballad opera.[23] Customers found a sumptuous quarto, printed on excellent paper, with a rubricated title page like that which James Watts had prepared for the 1720

Poems on Several Occasions. The price, as noted, was six shillings. Within a week pirate booksellers had imitation editions on the street, prepared by the simple expedient of purchasing one of Gay's copies and setting type from that one. These piracies, in octavo format, sold for one shilling or a shilling and sixpence, thus drastically undercutting Gay's market price. Gay took legal action and by June some twenty-one booksellers and printers had been enjoined from publishing unauthorized editions in violation of the 1710 Copyright Act.[24] By then, however, the damage to Gay's profit margins had been done; he was forced to lower the price of his quarto to two shillings sixpence as early as 11 April to meet the unauthorized competition.

Even so, Gay made a most handsome profit from *Polly*'s publication. Cibber, writing years afterwards, reported that some persons believed Gay "had been a greater Gainer, by Subscriptions to his Copy, than he could have been by a bare Theatrical Presentation."[25] They may well have been correct. First produced in 1777, and then in altered form, *Polly* had no popular success until the twentieth century and not much then. Gay apparently netted twelve hundred pounds from his subscription campaign, however, and Swift, writing to Pope in August 1729, expressed the hope that "Mr. Gay will keep his 3,000£ and live on the interest without decreasing the principal one penny."[26] A total profit of three thousand pounds from the printing, though high, is not inconceivable. It would have been decidedly the highest remuneration for the publication of a single play, anywhere, to that time. One should note in Robert Walpole's defense, also, that his supposed vendetta against Gay did not extend to removing him from his post as commissioner of the lottery.

Aside from the vexation at having his ballad opera suppressed, Gay could savor not only his financial rewards but also his continuing success as a dramatic author. In May 1729 *The Beggar's Opera* was produced twice by the company at the Little Haymarket; Rich countered with two performances at Lincoln's Inn Fields, the one there on 21 May being a performance "by Command of His Royal Highness," as if to show

that Court hard feelings did not extend to Gay's *Opera* (or perhaps that the Prince of Wales shared Gay's disagreement with
his father). *The What D'Ye Call It* played five times at Drury
Lane that month, too. Shakespeare was in second place to
Gay among dramatic authors in May, with a total of four performances of his plays.

Some of this newfound artistic confidence shows in *Polly.*
In both preface and play—for *Polly* is more of a play with music than an opera—Gay seizes the moral high ground. He has
been accused, he maintains, of writing "disaffected libels and
seditious pamphlets." "As it hath ever been my utmost ambition . . . to lead a quiet and inoffensive life, I thought my innocence in this particular would never have requir'd a
justification" (p. 70). *Honi soit qui mal y pense.* "I think myself call'd upon to declare my principles; and I do with the
strictest truth affirm, that I am as loyal a subject and as
firmly attach'd to the present happy establishment as any of
those who have the greatest places or pensions" (Preface,
p.iii). Gay is cheeky enough here: the clear implication is that
those enjoying great places and pensions are not so very
firmly attached to the happy establishment, after all. "I have
been inform'd too, that in the following Play, I have been
charg'd with writing immoralities; that it is fill'd with slander and calumny against particular great persons, and that
Majesty it-self is endeavour'd to be brought into ridicule and
contempt" (pp.iii-iv). This serves the obvious function of encouraging the reader to buy the play and scrutinize it *very*
carefully, so that he or she will not miss the delicious slander
and calumny against great persons.

On first reading today, it must be admitted, one is not
likely to pick up much in the way of slander and calumny,
but as Bertrand Goldgar has reminded us, readers in Gay's
London had been and were being tutored in the art of inter-
preting political innuendo. A knowing reader, say Walpole
himself, would have found *Polly* considerably more aggressive
politically than *The Beggar's Opera.*[27]

The framing Introduction between Poet and Player continues the argument of Gay's Preface. The Player opines that

the Poet's "Satyr here and there is too free." Not so, replies the Poet, "I aim at no particular persons . . . but if any men particularly vicious are hurt, I make no apology, but leave them to the cure of their flatterers" (p. v). The action then quickly refutes the Poet's contentions: the singer "Signora Crotchetta" enters complaining that she has a cold and can't go on. Now "Crotchetta" indisputably represents one of two very particular persons: either Faustina or Cuzzoni, and of course both: the temperamental, hair-pulling lead singers at the King's, Haymarket. Her exit *"in a fury"* allows a Player to offer (herself?): "Since the town was last year so good as to encourage an Opera without singers; the favour I was then shown obliges me to offer my-self once more, rather than the audience should be dismissed" (p. vii). This quasi-apology may have been inspired by Gay and Rich's apprehensions about the quality of Lincoln's Inn's singers, now that Lavinia Fenton had retired to the Duke of Bolton's bosom. The dig at the rival Haymarket Italians was standard; notice that it is directed at Italian singers rather than Italian opera.

Gay resumes the story in the West Indies, where Macheath has been transported and where he has assumed the identity of a black pirate, Morano, living bigamously with Jenny Diver. Mrs. Trapes is also in the Indies, acting as a supplier of females to the colonists. When Polly arrives, seeking Macheath, Mrs. Trapes undertakes to supply her to the settler Ducat, over the objections of Ducat's shrewish wife. Mrs. Ducat is happy enough to connive with Polly and get her out of the house, disguised as a young man.

Polly in her breeches encounters the pirates, and Jenny Diver makes a pass at the supposed young man—or do her quick eyes penetrate the disguise? The pirates under Morano's leadership are preparing to attack the settlement. Ducat and the settlers make common cause in defense with the Native Americans, a group of most noble noble savages, and the attack fails. Morano is captured, revealed to be Macheath in blackface disguise, and executed. At the curtain Polly is left to marry the Indian prince Cawwawkee when her grief subsides.

By displacing the action to the West Indies, Gay has given up much of the satiric point, the wealth of local references, with which *The Beggar's Opera* is enriched. On the other hand, perhaps particular references would have been illuminated for London audiences, or readers, without the highlife/lowlife transvaluation of the *Opera*. In the first scene, for example, Mrs. Trapes is encouraging the colonial Ducat to live up to British customs. "You are wealthy, very wealthy, Mr. *Ducat;* and I grant you the more you have, the taste of getting more should grow stronger upon you." What he needs is a kept mistress, which she can supply him.

Madam, in most of my expences I run into the polite taste. I have a fine library of books that I never read; I have a fine stables of horses that I never ride; I build, I buy plate, jewels, pictures, or any thing that is valuable and curious, as your great men do, merely out of ostentation. But indeed I must own, I do still cohabit with my wife; and she is very uneasy and vexatious upon account of my visits to you.

 Trapes. Indeed, indeed, Mr. *Ducat*, you shou'd break through all this usurpation at once, and keep—. (I.i.53-61)

As Goldgar has argued, "Gay can hardly have been ignorant of the similarity between this self-portrait and the ridicule by the opposition press of Walpole's display of rich vulgarity at Houghton; and Ducat's atttempts to be unfaithful to his wife would have added one more detail to the similarity."[28]

 Gay continues his attack on politicians (for politician read Walpole) a few scenes later in Trapes's soliloquy and song. There is an echo of the *Opera*'s transvaluations here: politicians are like me, Trapes declares; only their situation is different: "[W]ere they in my circumstances they would act like me; were I in theirs, I should be rewarded as a most profound penetrating politician." (She sings):

> In pimps and politicians
> The genius is the same;
> Both raise their own conditions
> On others guilt and shame:
> With a tongue well-tipt with lyes

> Each the want of parts supplies,
> And with a heart that's all disguise
> Keeps his schemes unknown. (I.iv.9-18)

Robert Walpole's alleged greed, secretiveness, and mendacity are displayed with a guiding fingerpost. This is strong stuff; much stronger than *The Beggar's Opera*: compare this scene with the similar opening scene there, Peachum's soliloquy and song "Through all the Employments of Life." Though the satiric note with respect to individuals is stronger, *Polly* lacks much of *The Beggar's Opera*'s comic buoyance and brilliance.

Still, there are many good things in *Polly*, which richly deserves careful study and a new edition that includes the music.[29] It is Polly's play. Polly herself is the starry-eyed ingenue of the *Opera*, set down in the West Indian plantations: Gay was not going to jettison that role, which had put Lavinia Fenton's face on Chinese fans and playing cards. In a scene worthy of Oscar Wilde, he has her confront Mrs. Ducat, a splendid shrew, who is repelled at first sight of Polly: "By that over-honest look, I guess her to be a horrid jade. A mere hypocrite, that is perfectly white-wash'd with innocence. My blood rises at the sight of all strumpets, for they are smuglers in love, that ruin us fair traders in matrimony" (I.xiv.2-6). Gay's wit had not abandoned him.

When Polly accepts Mrs. Ducat's help and makes her way in male disguise to the pirate band she finds the pirates are a self-indulgent, avaricious gang of thieves, but so are the colonists, as represented by Ducat. The colonists have more money than the pirates with which to disguise their thievery. Ducat tells his ally Pohetohee, the Indian chief, of his reluctance to do battle: "Sir, fighting is not our business; we pay others for fighting; and yet 'tis well known we had rather part with our lives than our money" (III.i.15-18). The Indian is appalled at the cynicism. When the Indians and colonists capture the pirates, Pohetohee sets up an interview with Morano/Macheath to pursue his interest in comparative sociology. What got you into piracy, he asks, "Would not your honest industry have been sufficient to have supported you?"

Morano. Honest industry! I have heard talk of it indeed among the common people, but all great genius's are above it.

Pohetohee. Have you no respect for virtue?

Morano. As a good phrase, Sir. But the practicers of it are so insignificant and poor, that they are seldom found in the best company.

Pohetohee. Is not wisdom esteem'd among you?

Morano. Yes, Sir: But only as a step to riches and power; a step that raises ourselves, and trips up our neighbours.

Pohetohee. Honour, and honesty, are not those distinguish'd?

Morano. As incapacities and follies. How ignorant are these *Indians!* (III.xi.38-51)

Gay here, like Swift in Book Four of *Gulliver's Travels*, is employing what Charles A. Knight in a recent theoretical essay has called "simple satiric nationalism," the use of supposed national characteristics to attack the shortcomings of one's own nation.[30] Pohetohee and his band of Native Americans are idealized characters, like Swift's Houyhnhnms, but the colonists and pirates are not Yahoos; they are recognizable English men and women. Jenny Diver makes the point when she proposes to Macheath that they betray their pirate colleagues and go back to England where money talks with an aristocratic accent: "You have a competence in your power. Rob the crew, and steal off to *England*. Believe me, Captain, you will be rich enough to be respected by your neighbours" (II.iii.50-52).

The Polly-Macheath-Jenny Diver triangle has resonances with that favorite artistic *topoi*, the choice of Hercules, as Joan Hildreth Owen has argued.[31] In an important recent study, Dianne Dugaw has shown how it echoes, and parodies, the situation in Dryden's Antony and Cleopatra play, *All for Love*. Polly in male disguise, she demonstrates, is an exemplar of the Female Warrior motif, familiar in popular ballads, and used here by Gay "to question the whole Western ideal of heroism as Love and Glory."[32] *Polly* is Polly's play because Gay wants it that way: to demonstrate the inadequacies of the heroic ideal.

Gay makes something, but not much, of Morano's blackness: the name echoes both Marrano, the christianized—and persecuted—Jews and Moors of Spain, and Maroon, fugitive slaves in the West Indies, some of whom were Marranos, who had escaped Spanish captivity. (The words may be related etymologically.) But Macheath uses his blackness only as a disguise. More significant is the confrontation between colonist and Indian, a confrontation in which the Indian is the total moral victor: Cawwawkee wins Polly, the only colonist with any virtue left, because he deserves her. As she tells him, "Those that know and feel virtue in themselves, must love it in others" (III.xv.43-44). The final dance and chorus, given to the Native Americans, is a celebration of justice, retributive justice:

1 *Indian.*	Justice long forbearing,
	Power or riches never fearing,
	Slow, yet persevering,
	Hunts the villain's pace.
Chorus.	*Justice long, &c.*
2 *Indian.*	What tongues then defend him?
	Or what hand will succour lend him?
	Even his friends attend him,
	To foment the chace.
Chorus.	*Justice long, &c.*
3 *Indian.*	Virtue, subduing,
	Humbles in ruin
	All the proud wicked race.
	Truth, never-failing,
	Must be prevailing,
	Falsehood shall find disgrace.
Chorus.	*Justice long forbearing, &c.*

The Indians are referring to Macheath; Gay voices through them another Scriblerian attack on the Great Man himself, Walpole, who had held, Swift told Gay, "the longest hand at hazard that ever fell to any Sharpers Share and keeps his run when the dice are changed."[33]

So much for the play's ideology, which accentuates Gay's problem from the dramaturgical point of view. The problem is that the Indians, father and son, are the attractive men in the action, while Polly is committed from the opening to finding her husband Macheath. Throwing off her male disguise, Polly asks Pohetohee's aid, "I detest his principles, tho' I am fond of his person to distraction. Could your commands for search and enquiry restore him to me, you reward me at once with all my wishes. For sure my love still might reclaim him" (III.xii.85-89). The audience is poised for a reformed-rake ending, like Cibber's famous closure of *The Careless Husband*. The handsome Prince Cawwawkee, smitten with Polly's charms, is standing by. Gay has painted himself into a dramaturgical corner: the point of the entire play is Polly's search for Macheath, who has already been put in embarrassing contrast with the high-minded Indians. How will the reunion take place and what will be its form?

It will not take place. The benevolent Indian king sends for Macheath but too late; he has already been executed. As an attempt to redirect the action of the piece, Gay provides Prince Cawwawkee and Polly with a duet, a proper aria that expresses their emotional state:

Cawwawkee.	Why that languish!
Polly.	Oh he's dead! O he's lost for ever!
Cawwawkee.	Cease your anguish, and forget your grief.
Polly.	Ah, never!
	What air, grace and stature!
Cawwawkee.	How false in his nature!
Polly.	To virtue my love might have won him.
Cawwawkee.	How base and deceiving!
Polly.	But love is believing.
Cawwawkee.	Vice, at length, as 'tis meet, hath undone him.

By your consent you might at the same time give me happiness, and procure your own. My titles, my treasures, are all at your command. (III.xv.25-37)

Polly agrees to think the proposal over, and asks for "a decent time to my sorrow." To end the play Gay presents the Indians with their dance and solemn chorus to justice already examined. This contrasts with the boisterous ending of the *Opera*, Macheath surrounded by his women, "Thus I stand like the *Turk*, with his Doxies around,"—the contrast is painful.

As has been observed earlier, *Polly* is rather a play with music than an opera; it has enough plot for two ballad operas. Yet it also, surprisingly, has more music than *The Beggar's Opera* if one counts the number of airs, seventy-one to sixty-nine. As in his earlier work, Gay borrowed his music from whatever sources interested him: British ballad tunes, popular street music, theatre music. He was still much attuned to opera, borrowing the Dead March from Attilio Ariosti's *Coriolanus*, which had premiered in 1723. The March from Handel's *Scipione* (1726), familiar today as the slow march of the Grenadier Guards, Gay converts into an amusing quartet in Act I (Air 17). The other two borrowings from Handel, Roger Fiske has demonstrated, are "based on minuets in *The Water Music* which had not then been published except in inaccurate song-arrangements."[34] Gay's musical taste was both catholic and current.

Though the musical techtonics of *Polly* are perhaps less sure than those of *The Beggar's Opera*—and it will not be possible to make a final judgment until we have genuine musical editions of both—Gay's skill as a lyricist had remained with him. Consider the duet between Ducat and Mrs. Trapes in the first act, for example, in which Trapes is trying to persuade Ducat to enliven his lot with a mistress whom she will supply. The lyric has a naughty metaphoric sparkle, and the metric contrast between the dispirited Ducat and the bright-eyed entrepeneur Di Trapes is perfect:

> *Ducat.*   What can wealth
>   When we're old?
>   Youth and health
>   Are not sold.
> *Trapes.* When love in the pulse beats low,
>   (As haply it may with you)
>   A girl can fresh youth bestow,
>   And kindle desire anew.

> Thus, numm'd in the brake,
> Without motion, the snake
>   Sleeps cold winter away;
> But in every vein
> Life quickens again
> On the bosom of *May*. (I.i.74–87)

Ducat agrees to give Polly a try, but like Peachum he believes marriage is something different. "I married [my wife]," he tells Trapes, "in a reasonable way, only for her money." His solo confirms his view:

> He that weds a beauty
>   Soon will find her cloy;
> When pleasure grows a duty,
>   Farewell love and joy:
> He that weds for treasure:
>   (Though he hath a wife)
> Hath chose one lasting pleasure
>   In a married life.

Polly was not produced in Gay's lifetime. Perhaps theatre managers continued to be nervous about the Lord Chamberlain's order, but certainly they would have been wary of getting into a production if they had a look at the script and assessed *Polly's* theatrical problems. Not until June 1777 was it produced, with alterations, by George Colman the Elder. It played for only seven nights but, appropriately, Catherine Hyde, Duchess of Queensberry was at the Little Haymarket for an early performance and loved it: This play, a diarist friend wrote, "cost the Duchess her death, She went constantly to See it, & would not be prevented by a very bad cold."[35] One of Gay's circle of friends, at any rate, lived to see his controversial play on the stage at last, half a century after he wrote it.

TEN

Last Plays

Gay's health had taken a turn for the worse in the winter of 1728–29. "I am but just recover'd," he wrote Swift in March, "from the severest fit of sickness that ever any body had who escap'd death."[1] The faithful Queensberrys nursed him at their house in Burlington Gardens and took him in their entourage to Edinburgh in the spring of 1729, after he had supervised the publication of *Polly*. There he met the poet Allan Ramsay, who would eventually write an elegy for Gay in tribute to his use of the ballad tradition:

> To him . . .
> We awe our thanks baith day & night
> Wha did frae dust and Rubish dight
> Blyth British tunes.[2]

Coming south again with the Queensberrys, he spent the summer at their Oxfordshire seat at Middleton Stoney. He was in the lap of ducal luxury, and he had made a comfortable small fortune, but he continued to labor on his plays. In the three short years that remained to him he would rewrite *The Wife of Bath* completely and see it performed, and would leave behind him at his death three other pieces for the theatre.

Gay was working on the new *Wife of Bath* in the autumn of 1729, for a production in early 1730. We can only conjecture when he wrote the other three, that is, *Achilles*, a ballad opera; *The Distress'd Wife*, a satiric London comedy; and *The*

Rehearsal at Goatham, a satiric afterpiece. Examined collectively, these four dramatic works reveal Gay to be moving in four different directions. It is as if he realized that new plays now had a chance again, as competitive pressures on the patent theatres increased, and that he hoped to take advantage of the favorable situation. Henry Fielding was just then finding his way to a successful career in the theatre, under exactly these circumstances.[3]

Gay was in a reflective mood in November 1729, telling Swift of his plans: "I have employ'd my time in new-writing a damnd play which I writ sever[al] Years ago call'd the Wife of Bathe, as 'tis approv'd or disapprov'd of by my friends when I come to town I shall either have it acted or let it alone, if we[ak] Brethren do not take offence at it. The ridicule turns upon Supe[rsti]tion, & I have avoided the very words Bribery & corruption."[4] Swift replied in his best dry style, "I have heard of the Wife of Bath, I think in Shakespear."[5]

Rich's house at Lincoln's Inn Fields was to have the play. In the Preface to *Polly* Gay had stipulated that "as far as a contract of this kind can be binding; I am engag'd to Mr. *Rich* to have [*Polly*] represented upon his Theatre."[6] He may have felt—or Rich may have argued that he should feel—some kind of residual obligation to Lincoln's Inn Fields. He may also have harbored lingering resentment toward Wilks, Cibber, and Drury Lane for turning down the *Opera.*

Unfortunately, the new *Wife of Bath*—for the second version is an entirely different play in every respect except the major plot structure—is precisely the sort of piece that the Drury Lane audience expected to see, that the Drury Lane company was prepared to do, and that the company at Lincoln's Inn Fields had little talent for: intrigue comedy.

The play went to rehearsal in December 1729 and opened on 19 January 1730, that is, the night before the Eve of St. Agnes, when the action of the play is set. *The Wife of Bath* made its way through three performances, grossing ninety-six pounds on opening night but falling ominously to thirty-seven pounds on the second night and scraping by house charges on Gay's benefit third night, with fifty-six pounds. He took home, that is, about six pounds after Rich had made his deductions.[7] Lintot, who was now spelling his name with one final t, gave him seventy-five pounds for the copyright or three times what he had paid him for the first *Wife*, a tribute, of course, to Gay's literary reputation.[8] The play was never revived.

The second *Wife of Bath* is a sad comedown from the earlier version. A clue to its decline may be Gay's remark to Swift that he intended to submit the manuscript to his friends for their approval or disapproval. This is a change: Gay usually wrote what he pleased, the way he thought best. He did not dedicate his plays to wealthy patrons, even though dedications were an accepted means by which a playwright could profit from his or her work, sometimes profit handsomely.[9] The mock-dedication of *The Mohocks* to John Dennis is the exception that proves the rule in Gay's case.

The second *Wife of Bath* is prettified, cleaned-up; made right for polite society. For example, Gay takes Chaucer, that robust, dominating character, right out of his play and replaces him with Sir Harry Gauntlet, a country squire in the spirit—but without the vividness—of Addison and Steele's Sir Roger de Coverley. The Franklyn becomes Mr. Plowdon, as if Gay feared his audience would not understand what a Franklyn did (he plowed on). The Franklyn's servants, Antony and William, who introduced rural dialect into the earlier play, are eliminated here. The farce scenes are cut and toned down. No one has been able to discern political satire in the second *Wife;* Gay maintained his pledge to avoid the very words bribery and corruption. The formal structure, it must be acknowledged, is improved; Gay had learned a great deal about dramaturgy in sixteen years. But in tightening the structure he squeezed the life out of the play.

Gay retains Doggrell the poetaster, descended as he likes to maintain from the aristocratic D'Ogrelles. His pretentious versifying and his final discomfiture when he is tricked into marrying Busy the chambermaid provide the best comic touches in the play, but they are not enough.

Most puzzling is the virtual exclusion of music. Here was an area in which Gay had become unchallenged master of the London stage, but in the second *Wife of Bath* he leaves out the songs of the 1713 version. It was not from want of singing talent, either: John Hippisley, who had created Peachum in *The Beggar's Opera*, was in the cast, as was Jane Egleton, who had played Lucy Lockit. They were both excellent vocalists, but they were not given songs to sing this time.

"My old vamp'd Play got me no money, for it had no success," the disappointed Gay wrote Swift in March 1730.[10] This was an exaggeration; as we have seen it made him better than eighty pounds, but it was the apathetic audience response that stung. Lack of success now hurt more than lack of money.

It is impossible to say precisely when Gay wrote *The Rehearsal at Goatham*, but because it concerns dramatic censorship, a reasonable guess is that it dates from about this time, 1730 or 1731, when Gay was still smarting from the silencing of *Polly*, and that it should find its place in the canon before *Achilles*. After his self-imposed abstinence from political satire in *The Wife of Bath*, Gay may simply have felt like getting the old lash out of the closet. As will be seen, there are other reasons for dating *The Rehearsal* 1730 or 1731. *The Rehearsal* is in form a satiric afterpiece of ten short scenes. As it happened, in the inscrutable manner of theatregoers, audiences were for some reason again demanding afterpieces about this time, after *The Beggar's Opera*'s triumph. "Having been threatened with near extinction," Leo Hughes writes, the afterpiece "now returned to its former flourishing state."[11] Hughes argues plausibly that the good theatrical fortunes of *The Beggar's Opera* and the expansion of the Little Haymarket's bills provided simultaneous encouragement for authors of afterpieces. Gay may have sensed this change and written *The Rehearsal* as his latest offering for the increasingly competitive London stage. Once again, as in his very first piece for that stage, *The Mohocks*, Gay deals with topical concerns. For many reasons, *The Rehearsal at Goatham*, like that earlier unproduced but interesting afterpiece, merits attention in some detail.

The subject matter of *The Rehearsal*, the staging of a puppet show, also provides some dating clues that point to the probable date of composition as being during the timespan of 1730 to 1731. In the spring of 1730 Henry Fielding had great success with *The Author's Farce* at the Little Haymarket. His satire on the London theatre establishment opened on 30 March and ran for forty-one performances in the first season, the best run since that of *The Beggar's Opera* itself. *The Author's Farce* is a performance play—a play about plays—and Colley Cibber comes in for full satiric treatment as Sir Farcical Comick (and as Mr. *Keyber,* as well).[12] I suggest that Gay may have composed *his* performance play after seeing Fielding's—Gay was living in London that spring of 1730. Perhaps he even hoped to have his afterpiece produced at the Little Haymarket, too. If young Henry Fielding in this case influenced John Gay—and there was at least one known connection: Fielding's friend Hogarth of course depicted *The Beggar's Opera* in performance—then this represents a fitting return, because Gay's ballad opera profoundly influenced Fielding, in general and specifically in *The Author's Farce*.

Another clue to dating *The Rehearsal* is its association with *Don Quixote*, and once more Fielding enters the performance, as it were. In the Advertisement prefixed to the printed play Gay states that he derived his story from the episode of Peter and his puppet show in *Don Quixote*, Part II, chapters 25-27. Interestingly, the year before the first production of *The Author's Farce*, in 1729, Henry Fielding was writing the first version of his *Don Quixote in England*, which was not however produced until 1734. In his use of songs there Fielding may have been influenced by Thomas Durfey's *Don Quixote* (in three parts 1694–96); he was certainly influenced by Gay's own example in *The Beggar's Opera*.[13] All three parts of Durfey's play were published together for the first time in 1729, and this publication perhaps coincidentally fueled the interest of both Fielding and Gay in Cervantes.[14]

Part II of Durfey's *Don Quixote* (which does not, however, contain the puppet-show sequence—that is in Part III) had been played from time to time at Lincoln's Inn Fields since 1717. In *The Beggar's Opera* spring of 1728, in April, Rich had produced it once with Lavinia Fenton and the *Opera* players, grossing a very respectable £167 for the single performance. The legend of Quixote, at least as presented by Durfey, was in the air. The translation by Peter Motteux, revised by Ozell, had also been re-published as recently as 1725.

Readers of Cervantes will recall that Peter the puppeteer stages a performance in a country inn, at the request of Don Quixote. The puppet play is the romance of Melisandra, Charlemagne's daughter, a prisoner of the Moors. Quixote becomes so engrossed by the puppet drama that when Melisandra is portrayed as escaping from captivity he rises from the audience, draws his sword and slashes the puppet theatre to aid her escape. Quixote, the innocent idealist, does not recognize Peter, a former galley slave turned confidence man whom he had formerly assisted.

The innocent in Gay's afterpiece is not, however, Quixote but Peter the puppeteer, more or less Gay himself, who has come to Goatham hoping to stage his puppet show about Melisandra (Gay spells it Melisendra) in the hall of Broach's tavern. Gay's Advertisement, read in the context of the late 1720s and early 1730s, is revealing. It is a piece of Opposition rhetoric, which encourages the seeker of political innuendo by denying that any such innuendo exists. The puppet show, he writes, is

recorded to have happen'd in the Town which liv'd in perpetual Broils with the braying Aldermen. In the following Piece I have related the Story in a Dramatic Way; I have too taken the Liberty to make it conformable to our own Customs, and made *England* the Scene of the Farce: But (knowing the Captiousness of Guilt) to prevent particular Persons from claiming general Satire, I have chose to place the Adventure in a fictitious Country Town, suppos'd to be remote from the great Scenes of Life. Whoever will be at the Pains to compare it with the *Spanish*, will find that (excepting these Particulars) I have, in every material Circumstance, faithfully follow'd the Original. (*Dramatic Works*, II, 348)

Whoever will be at pains to make the comparison will find no such thing. Gay does not follow the original in any respect, except in the brief description of what takes place among the puppets. His play concerns the efforts of Jack Oaf and Will Gosling to prevent the production of Peter's puppet show by telling Goatham's aldermen and their wives that the show will "turn the whole Corporation of *Goatham* into Ridicule," as Oaf puts it. Oaf certainly represents Cibber, John Fuller has argued persuasively,[15] and I take it that Gosling represents Cibber's partner at Drury Lane, Robert Wilks. Oaf/Cibber, it transpires, is a dramatic author himself and concerned, he says, about his own productions and the Town's taste:

> *Oaf.* The Town, you know, is capricious,—and one would not have it follow a low, dull, vulgar, spiteful, bitter, satirical Thing. I am concern'd for the Credit of our Town, that's all. I would have it encourage only Things of Taste; and in that View, I own, it would be a mighty mortifying Thing to me, to see this Fellow draw an Audience. (i. 82-87)

That Cibber had a hand in the suppression of *Polly* seems doubtful to me—the Drury Lane management, though basically Whigs, were notoriously cautious about involving themselves and their theatre in politics. But Gay may have *thought* that he did, and Pope certainly believed Cibber capable of almost anything. After Steele's accession to the governorship, furthermore, the Drury Lane management had expressed its concern for the "Credit of our Town" on more than one occasion, implying as Jack Oaf does that genuine reformed drama was to be found only at Drury Lane. As recently as 1724 Cibber and his partners had written a joint letter to Steele with respect to the pantomimes at Lincoln's Inn Fields, complaining that "those low Entertainments which you & we so heartily despise, draw the Numbers."[16] Note the similarity of their complaint to Oaf's: the vulgarians on the other side are drawing the numbers/audience.

In *The Rehearsal* Gay dramatizes those qualities of vanity, malice, and ignorance that the Scriblerians believed Cibber exemplified in final form and that of course supplied the basis of Pope's portrayal in the ultimate *Dunciad*. As if to confirm their very worst fears he was named poet laureate in 1730 (another clue to the dating of *The Rehearsal*). Innkeeper Broach asks Oaf if he has actually seen or read Peter's puppet show.

> *Oaf.* I cannot say that.
> *Gosling.* But we know enough of the Thing in general.
> *Oaf.* There are Things quoted.
> *Gosling.* Passages, very obnoxious Passages.
> *Broach.* Why then, Gentlemen, I must acquaint you that I have heard it repeated; and I could find out none of those dreadful obnoxious Passages. I heard nothing that possibly could give Offence.
> *Oaf.* As they are not levell'd at you, you might very easily overlook them. (ii.56-65)

Betty Broach opines that the "Splutter *Jack Oaf* makes, is the Envy and Rancour of an Author; that's all," but her mother replies that "Poor Master *Peter* little thinks how many formidable Enemies he hath already."

When Peter asks Broach who his (Peter's) enemies are, Broach replies, "Those who are afraid you have Merit; and if ever you make it appear, you at once make all Fools your Enemies. It hath ever been so in all Times, and all Countries" (iv.52-54). This is a Swiftian comment, resonating with one of that author's "Thoughts on Various Subjects": "When a true Genius appears in the World, you may know him by this infallible Sign, that the Dunces are all in Confederacy against him."[17]

Jack Oaf fails to gain the support of the town's ladies in his attempt to have the puppet show suppressed: they are all eager to hear the alleged satire on the Aldermen. Harriet Noddipole asks Oaf, "what signifies a Joke or two upon the Aldermen, supposing the Puppets are so impertinent? Don't we, who are their Wives and Daughters, love now and then to laugh at them among ourselves[?]" (vi.23-26). Here, as he usually does, Gay reveals himself to be sympathetic to the plight of women in this emphatically patriarchal society. One of the few recourses women—or authors—have left to them in such a society is laughter. "Pox take 'em," exclaims Will Gosling, "the Women, you see, *Jack*, will not bite."

The patriarchs themselves are in a different sort of biting mood, as Gosling and Oaf know. Pickle, Peter's assistant, gets no further than the first two lines of the prologue when he is interrupted by the Aldermen, who have been warned to expect slander by an anonymous letter—written by Jack Oaf, of course.

> *Pickle.* Courteous Spectators, see with your own Eyes,
> Hear with your Ears; and there's an end of Lies.
> *Braywell.* Hold! Stop, not a Word more, I charge you. Cast your
> Eye upon that Letter, Sir *Headstrong*—
> [*They all rise, some read and shake their Heads;*
> *all in Commotion.*]

The anonymous letter convinces them that the play *must* be damaging and has to be stopped before anyone sees it. "To what End," asks Sir Headstrong Bustle, the Walpole figure, "hath a Man Riches and Power, if he cannot crush the Wretches who have the Insolence to expose the Ways by which he got them" (ix.2-5, 14-16).

Gay's bleak view of Walpole, by 1730, is that he enjoys crushing wretches who oppose and expose him, Opposition writers like himself. Mr. Pother, one of Sir Headstrong's confederates, seconds his sentiment: "We must keep these Wretches down. 'Tis right to keep Mankind in Dependance." In a much-quoted pamphlet of 1731 William Pulteney of the Opposition accused Walpole of having all the "most eminent Authors of the *Dunciad*," that is, the Dunces, on his payroll.[18] It is precisely the independence of Peter and his kind that Headstrong/Walpole is represented as finding intolerable: "'Tis the Rascals who live by their Industry," Headstrong complains, "who are so impertinent to us. We should suffer no body in Town to get Money but by our Licence, and then we should never be treated with Disrespect" (x.31-34). Did Gay foresee Walpole's Licensing Act of 1737, which brought precensorship to the London stage, or does this merely reflect his irritation at the silencing of *Polly*? It is impossible to say: sentiment for dramatic censorship of one kind or another had been in the air for many years.[19]

In the end Headstrong has his way. When Pickle describes the action of the play, in which Marsilius, the Moorish King causes his kinsman to be whipped "without . . . the Shadow of legal Proceeding," Headstrong decides that the "*Moor Marsilius* is meant at me. Beyond all Dispute, I am the *Moor.*" The reference to Gay's complaint in the Preface to *Polly* that the suppression had been "without any reason assign'd, or any charge against me of my having given any particular offence," is reinforced by the association of Macheath as Morano, a negro or blackamoor, in the ballad opera.

Gay gives Peter the last words on the matter even though his play is shut down. "I hate private Slander," he tells the assembly. "As for general Satire; the Satirist is not to be accus'd of Calumny; he that takes it to himself is the Proclaimer and Publisher of his own Folly and Guilt." Headstrong/Walpole has convicted himself. It is precisely the situation described in Lockit's famous song from *The Beggar's Opera:*

> When you censure the Age,
> Be cautious and sage,
> Lest the Courtiers offended should be:
> If you mention Vice or Bribe,
> 'Tis so pat to all the Tribe;
> Each crys—That was levell'd at me.

The Rehearsal at Goatham is an allegory of Lockit's song, born of Gay's, and the Scriblerians', experience with Walpole's government. Any reasonably sophisticated Londoner in 1731 would have read it instantly as such.

In dramatic terms, the afterpiece has its problems. There are too many characters for most professional productions, twenty-nine speaking parts, and as in *The Mohocks* doubling is impossible: all of the characters are on stage in the final scene. The dramatic action rises to that curtain scene and then goes flat: the blocking characters have blocked, leaving the principals nowhere to turn. As Peter says, "There is nothing to be done here; they have the Power, and we must submit." That is not what occurred in real rather than stage life at the suppression of *Polly:* Gay pulled a propaganda victory and a small fortune out of that episode of censorship, thwarting power and refusing to submit. In *The Rehearsal,* however, Gay is not able to provide Peter with the dramatic equivalency of his own earlier success.

And yet *The Rehearsal at Goatham* has many good qualities. The dialogue is excellent. Several rich comic parts, male and female, beckon to the capable actor. An enthusiastic amateur group—a local theatre organization or a university drama club that was experiencing differences with the authorities—could make a lively production of it without fretting over the historical allegory. It is a play about censorship of the arts, an activity that has scarcely disappeared from the horizon in our enlightened age. It is also a saucy piece of satire, in the Scriblerian mode. Perhaps Gay intended it for circulation among his friends, with an amateur production at the Queensberrys'. Neither Swift, nor Pope, nor Arbuthnot would have disagreed with Peter's curtain lines:

This Adventure of ours hath indeed answer'd the main End of a good Play. For

> The Drift of Plays, by *Aristotle*'s Rules,
> Is, what you've seen—Exposing Knaves and Fools.

If *The Rehearsal at Goatham* was a creation of late 1730 or early 1731, as I have argued, Gay was especially busy in the last two years of his life. He had also essentially completed both *Achilles* and *The Distress'd Wife* before his death in December 1732. It is impossible to determine the order of their composition from the evidence available now; unlike *The Rehearsal at Goatham*, neither dramatic piece contains sufficient topical or political references to assist in the dating. He was also working on the *Fables: Second Series* during this period, a work that was highly political, much more so than the earlier series.[20] It is entirely possible that he was writing all three, the fables and the two stage pieces, at the same time, in 1731 and 1732. It must have been the ballad opera *Achilles*, however, to which he referred in a letter to Swift of May 1732: "I have also a sort of a Scheme to raise my finances by doing something for the Stage."[21]

Ballad operas were still viable. Fielding's *The Grub-Street Opera*, had, it is true, vanished mysteriously into silence just before production in the summer of 1731, for reasons that have never been clarified.[22] Charles Coffey's *The Devil to Pay*, at first full-length but reduced to an afterpiece, was produced in 1731 and became a staple of the Drury Lane repertory: the ballad opera second only to *The Beggar's Opera* in popularity during the century. Jane Austen was "highly amused" by it.[23] Allan Ramsay's *The Gentle Shepherd*, based on Scottish melodies, had its premiere in Edinburgh in 1729, as Gay must have known from his many Scottish connections if not from Ramsay himself. Roger Fiske has identified forty-one ballad operas published with music during the first eight seasons after *The Beggar's Opera;* "at least as many more were published without music."[24] In the competitive situation of the London stage in the early 1730s ballad opera appeared to offer a scheme of raising Gay's finances.

He did not live to see his last ballad opera performed. His health, which had been uncertain for years, was beginning its final failure. In October 1732 he went back to the west of England where he had come from, to try sea air and exercise as a cure at Orchard Wyndham in Somersetshire, the seat of his friend Sir William Wyndham. Neither air nor exercise seemed to help, but he continued to work, writing Swift in November that "I have not been [idle] while I was in the Country."[25] It was the last correspondence between the old friends; Gay died on 4 December 1732 and was buried in Westminster Abbey on 23 December.

Pope wrote his friend Caryll on 14 December, "Poor Gay is gone before and has not left an honester man behind him; he had just put a play into the house, which the D. of Queensbury will take care of, and turn to the benefit of his relations. I have read it, and think it of his very best manner, a true original. He has left some other pieces fit for the press."[26] Gay had thus submitted *Achilles* to Rich before his death; the "other pieces" presumably included *The Distress'd Wife*.

Rich was in an expansive mood: his plans for a new theatre had reached fruition with the opening of a large new house in Covent Garden, and in the holiday season of 1732–33 he had performances running at *both* theatres.[27] Profits were cascading in, and he could afford an expensive production at Covent Garden of Gay's new ballad opera, without developing the migraines of 1728.[28]

The prologue to *Achilles* bore the note "Written by Mr. *Gay*" when the play was first published by James Watts in 1733 but a commentator of that year contended that Pope had written it, and Norman Ault has argued, I believe cogently, for his authorship.[29] The prologue emphasizes the play's daring originality, comparing Gay to a tightrope dancer "that tries at all,/In each unpractis'd Caper risques a Fall." Other dramatists repeat what they have done successfully before:

> Why is this Man so obstinate an Elf?
> Will he, alone, not imitate himself?[30]

Whether this represents Gay's defense of his own practice or, as seems more likely, Pope's compliment to his friend's work, "a true original," the prologue prepares the audience for something different.

Audiences liked it. They came in large numbers to Rich's capacious new theatre at Covent Garden when it opened on Saturday, 10 February 1733. Drury Lane was worried enough to run a production of *The Beggar's Opera* against it but Rich's receipts came to more than two hundred pounds for the premiere performance. *Achilles* made its way against fierce competition: on the fifth performance, Saturday 17 February, for example, it faced Fielding's new play *The Miser*, opening at Drury Lane, Farquhar's perennial favorite *The Constant Couple* at Goodman's Fields, and Handel's *Orlando* at the King's,

Haymarket. Gay's sisters received lucrative benefit nights on the third, sixth, and ninth performances, and the ballad opera ran more or less continuously through the middle of March because audiences kept coming.

What they saw was, at least superficially, a comic ballad opera on a classical theme. This in itself represented a change. John Mottley's *Penelope*, which played three performances at the Little Haymarket in May 1728, also has a classical theme as its title indicates, but the setting is displaced from Ithaca to London during Queen Anne's War, where Penelope keeps a tavern and waits for her soldier husband's return.

Gay's ballad opera is set in Greece, just before the outbreak of the Trojan War. Achilles, disguised as "Princess Pyrrha," is placed by his mother, Thetis, in the court of Lycomedes at Scyros so that he will escape the war that the goddess knows is coming. "I can't bear the Thoughts of your going," she tells the warrior, "for I know that odious Siege of *Troy* wou'd be the Death of thee." As her diction indicates, Thetis and the other Greek ladies are actually English aristocrats.[31] Knowing her son, who would be a polo player if the sport had been invented, Thetis has doubts about her scheme: "What I am most afraid of is, that when you are among the Ladies you shou'd be so little Master of your Passions as to find your self a Man" (I.i.85-87).

Her fears are well-grounded; sexuality flourishes like a weed in the steamy court of Lycomedes. Lycomedes himself lusts after the charming "princess," much to the displeasure of his consort, Theaspe. As Claire Pettengill has pointed out, this interestingly mirrors the situation in *Polly*, where Polly is the object of Ducat's sexual advances (and where, disguised as a man, she must fend off Jenny Diver).[32] Achilles meanwhile, as his mother had feared, is falling in love with and impregnating their daughter, Deidamia. Lycomedes makes his approach to Pyrrha in a duet; notice his rising astonishment that the princess would dare resist him. The verbal exchange—though not the situation!—with its lilt and feminine rimes reminds one irresistibly of Gilbert and Sullivan:

Lycomedes.	Why such Affectation?
Achilles.	Why this Provocation?
Lycomedes.	Must I bear Resistance still!
Achilles	Check your Inclination.
Lycomedes.	Dare you then deny me?
Achilles.	You too far may try me.
Lycomedes.	Must I then against your Will!
Achilles.	Force shall never ply me. (II.iv.80-88)

When Lycomedes attempts to overcome resistance and rape
Pyrrha then and there, the sturdy princess throws him and
holds him down until the guards come.

In the third and final act Ulysses, Agyrtes, and Diomedes
come through Scyros, disguised as clothing and armor merchants. Gay, who had once sold clothing himself to the gentry,
adroitly sets up the comic situation. The court ladies are all
aflutter at the prospect of what new clothes, or new men, can
bring them. The dialogue is Gay's raciest since *Three Hours
After Marriage:*

Philoe. I shall be horridly disappointed if they don't shew us
something charming.
Lesbia. Shou'd any Woman alive get Sight of their things before
us—
Philoe. I cou'd not bear it.—To appear in what another Woman
had refus'd wou'd make the Creature so intolerably vain! (III.ix.15-21)

Diomedes and Ulysses as the handsome haberdashers make
it known that they are well able to cater to the ladies, in
any way they may desire. Ulysses addresses Lesbia and
her friends:

Ulysses. Our Experience, Madam, must have profited very little
by the Honour of dealing with Ladies, if we cou'd imagine they cou'd
possibly be pleas'd twice with the same thing.
Diomedes. You might as well offer 'em the same Lover.
Ulysses. We have learnt the good Manners, Madam, to distinguish our Customers.—To produce any thing that had ever been
seen before wou'd be a downright Insult upon the Genius of a Lady
of Quality.

Diomedes. Novelty is the very Spirit of Dress.
Lesbia. Let me die, if the Fellows don't talk charmingly.
Philoe. Sensibly, Sister.
Lesbia. 'Tis evident they must have had Dealings with Ladies of
Condition. (III.x.4-17)

The court ladies admire the merchants and the materials
they have brought, but Pyrrha-Achilles hefts a sword, which
feels just right to the hand. Ulysses sees through the disguise
at once; he can tell a soldier in drag from a court lady, even if
Lycomedes cannot: "Son of *Thetis,* I know thee, *Greece* demands thee, and now, *Achilles,* the House of *Priam* shakes"
(III.x.89-90). Achilles is eager to join the forces and does so after making an honest woman of Deidamia. Ajax, a bluff captain who lacks the grace of Diomedes and Ulysses, cracks a
final joke that would be a natural for Farquhar's *The Recruiting Officer:* "This is the old Soldier's Play; for we seldom leave
Quarters but the Landlord's Daughter is the better for us.—
Hah!" A final dance and three songs to music by Arcangelo
Corelli end the ballad opera.

The music of *Achilles* is notably more sophisticated than
that of *The Beggar's Opera.* It, like that of *Polly,* demands thorough unraveling by musicologists. There are the usual ballad
tunes, for example "John Anderson my Jo," from the Scottish
tradition and more generally known since Robert Burns.
Broadside tunes, as in the *Opera* and *Polly,* are borrowed from
the general popular stock, but there are also present a number of interesting musical anomalies. For example, Gay employs a total of four tunes, including the three at the final
curtain, adapted from the concerti grossi and trio sonatas of
Arcangelo Corelli. "It is unexpected," writes Roger Fiske,
"that Gay should have known this music." The title of Air 37,
"The Clarinette," antedates by half a century the earliest usage found by the *OED;* was the instrument used as accompaniment in *Achilles?*[33]

Fiske further notes that a stage direction in Act III has
Agyrtes (one of Ulysses' companions) sound a trumpet, preceding a quartet (to Air 47) by Ulysses, Diomedes, Achilles,

and himself. "The probability is that the introduction to this quartet consisted of the first half of the tune played as a trumpet solo."[34] A vocal solo by Achilles follows the quartet, in which he sings of Deidamia's charms, drops his sword and shield symbolically, but picks them up when the trumpet sounds again. The melody he sings to is from a minuet by Francesco Geminiani, who was becoming established in the musical worlds of Dublin and London. After the solo by Achilles, the quartet returns to the first air "Sung in Four Parts as a Catch" (III.x.101-15). All this presents a sequence on the musical stage of considerable sophistication: a quartet with a solo trumpet introduction, a solo to a tune by a composer of "serious" music, rounded off with a catch. Since everything is spelled out in the stage directions the sequence unquestionably represents Gay's own musico/dramatic intentions.

The sequence underlines as well the increasing musical competence of the London stage. The same company that had boggled at playing the first ballad opera only five years earlier could bring off *Achilles* without missing stride. A number were in fact veterans of the *Opera:* Thomas Chapman, who had played the Beggar, had the key role of Ulysses; John Hall was the original Lockit and in *Achilles* created the role of Ajax. Their oafish characters are similar, and Gay clearly envisioned Hall as Ajax when he wrote the part. Thomas Walker, almost everyone's favorite as Macheath, surprisingly took the somewhat peripheral role of the courtier Periphas. Jane Egleton, the original Lucy Lockit, created Artemona. James Quin, who had supposedly turned down the role of Macheath in the original production, and who was now at the crest of his popularity as Falstaff in *The Merry Wives of Windsor,*[35] accepted the important but unattractive role of Lycomedes. Thomas Salway created the crucial title character, which, with its cross-dressing, must not have been the easiest of acting roles.

Salway, unlike Thomas Walker, was primarily a singing actor, and Gay had given him a great deal of singing to do: of the fifty-four airs, Achilles sings in sixteen, or seventeen if he joined the chorus in the next to last air as he must have done. Gay evidently felt confident about the vocal abilities of the Covent Garden cast because he gave them duets, trios, and quartets as he pleased, concentrating these, however, in the last act, which thus exerted a sort of musical dynamic to the ballad opera, building to Achilles's departure for the Trojan War.

Gay's skill as a lyricist, polished since *The Mohocks*, had remained with him over the years. The lyrics are, one may grant, not up to the overall quality of those of *The Beggar's Opera*, but most are good and some are excellent. Like those in the *Opera* and *Polly*, they embellish or extend the satirical thrust of the action. Achilles/Pyrrha's musical complaint about the court pimp Diphilus, for example, has satiric bite, which would have been appreciated in 1733:

> How unhappy are the Great,
>   Thus begirt with servile Slaves!
> Such with Praise your Reason cheat.
>   Flatt'rers are the meanest Knaves.
> They, in Friendship's Guise accost you;
>   False in all they say or do.
> When these Wretches have ingross'd you,
>   Who's the Slave, Sir, they or you? (II.iv.49-56)

This reminds one of Pope's well-known inscription for the collar of the Prince of Wales's dog: "I am his Highness' Dog at Kew, / Pray tell me, Sir, whose Dog are you?"[36] In a similar disillusioned vein is Theaspe's comment on her nephew Periphas's plan to marry before he goes to war:

> Soldier, think before you marry;
>   If your Wife the Camp attends,
> You but a Convenience carry,
>   For (perhaps) a hundred Friends.
> If at home she's left in Sorrow,
>   Absence is convenient too;
> Neighbors now and then may borrow
>   What is of no Use to you. (III.i.66-74)

As in *The Beggar's Opera*, Gay does not often employ the ballad stanza for his ballad operas but in Theaspe's advice to Periphas he uses a modified ballad stanza, strictly a 4/4 hymn stanza, for this most un-hymnlike sentiment.

To the jealous and cynical Theaspe, who with Lycomedes for a husband has justification for jealousy and cynicism, Gay gives some of the most arresting lyrics, such as her meditation in Act I on women's weakness. She is discussing with Artemona whether or not her husband has yet succeeded in debauching the visiting princess Pyrrha.

> All Hearts are a little frail
>   When Temptation is rightly apply'd.
> What can Shame or Fear avail
>   When we sooth both Ambition and Pride?
> All Women have Power in view;
>   Then there's Pleasure to tempt her too.
> Such a sure Attack there's no defying,
> No denying;
> Since complying
> Gives her another's Due. (I.vii.59-68)

It is conceivable that audiences in 1733 would have seen the unhappy domestic situation at the court of Lycomedes as having parallels to the relationship of George II and Queen Caroline. Fielding had daringly satirized the unhappy royal family in *The Welsh Opera* of April 1731,[37] and Gay's sources for Court gossip were better than Fielding's, but as far as I am aware no contemporary viewers made the application.

Gay's *Achilles* has enjoyed little attention since its initial run. The pamphlet *Achilles Dissected* (1733), perhaps by Thomas Burnet, examined it for political satire but could not find enough to make a case. *The Daily Courant* of 16 February 1733 complained of the ballad opera's dullness and ascribed that quality to the efforts of his friends, including the Queensberrys, to complete the work after his death. As we have seen, however, *Achilles* was apparently ready for production in December 1732 when Gay died. A version altered by George Colman the Elder, with new music by Thomas Arne, *Achilles in*

Petticoats, was produced at Covent Garden in December 1773 and ran occasionally until March 1774. Colman's alteration involved producing it as an afterpiece in two acts by virtually eliminating the first act of Gay's original and thus washing out most of the sexuality, which in 1773 may have been judged too gamy for audience tastes.[38] In our own time Roger Fiske also has pronounced Gay's *Achilles* "a dull piece."[39] Great scholar though he is, Fiske has no special affection for ballad operas; "the ballad opera craze," as he refers to the genre (p. 114). Were the audiences who paid their way into Covent Garden—a new, large theatre—for nineteen performances in 1733 simply responding to ballad-opera mania? Or were they drawn by the social satire, the sophisticated music and lyrics, the comic sexuality?

In an important recent study Yvonne Noble has shown how Gay has taken the familiar legend of the disguised Achilles, found in Statius, Bion, Ovid, and elsewhere, and typically made it his own. Gay, she argues, charges a farcical situation with meaning, focusing on the attempted rape of Achilles. If Achilles had indeed been a woman, the rape would have taken place—as we have seen, Lycomedes had every confidence that it *would* take place, if necessary. The "predicament of women represents one mode of the wider condition of dependency, the dynamics and abuses of which Gay knew all too well in his own life."[40] As I have argued elsewhere, audiences in the eighteenth century were choosing plays that focused on the "predicament of women," perhaps because solutions to the predicament were not available.[41] Noble convincingly blends Gay's biography with his dramaturgy in her essay on Gay's last successful dramatic work.

Because his very last work, and I shall argue that *The Distress'd Wife* is his last work, was not a success. Performed in the season following the one in which *Achilles* received its premiere, *Wife* opened at Rich's Covent Garden theatre on 5 May 1734 and played there three more times, then closed. The play was not published until 1743. Rich gave it a fair trial, from all evidence, warming up the audience, as it were, with a production of *Achilles* in late March (*Achilles* had also been produced once in the previous November "at the Desire of several Persons of Quality"—Gay's name was not entirely forgotten). The cast for *The Distress'd Wife* included his best actors: James Quin, Thomas Salway, Tony Aston, though it is not clear who played what because the printed version did not include a dramatis personae and newspaper accounts are lacking.[42] There was a third-night benefit for Gay's sisters, but a sparse house on Saturday, 16 May, the fourth night, must have signaled the end.

Aside from its own defects, there were important forces working against the success of Gay's last play. For one, competition had not been more severe for a very long time, if ever. Because of internal disagreements there were now two opera companies playing simultaneously: one conducted by Handel at the King's, Haymarket, and another under the composer Nicola Porpora at Lincoln's Inn Fields. Four houses were presenting plays at the same time: Covent Garden, Drury Lane, Little Haymarket, and Goodman's Fields. Of course the proliferation of theatres implied what was also true: that the drama's patrons, audiences, were out there, too, but in stiff competition the weak go to the wall. And stage comedy, for another consideration, was weak.

Although theatrical competition encouraged the production of new plays, new stage comedy was not prospering in London theatres after *The Beggar's Opera*.[43] Ballad opera itself flourished for a number of seasons after 1728 and its influence never disappeared, with music moving from mainpieces to musical afterpieces. Pantomime, which of course also included music, continued to draw crowds at all the theatres. Serious drama could get produced, even if audiences showed little enthusiasm for seeing serious plays a second time.[44] But writers of stage comedy continued to shoulder the burden of the past: the "perennial favorites" were there for managers to draw on, without having to bother about permission or author's benefit, year after year. Drury Lane, under the "Triumvirate" of Cibber, Booth, and Wilks, had been for more than fifteen years the house for stage comedy. In the summer of 1732 the management had changed, but there was no reason to think that the new managers, Sir John High-more, John Ellys, and Theophilus Cibber would alter the the-atre's essential character, and it was at Drury Lane, I would argue, that Gay hoped to see *The Distress'd Wife* produced.

Competition had forced the three veteran managers to produce some new plays. In the summer of 1731 Henry Field-ing, the most successful playwright in London, had made up his differences with the three and moved back to Drury Lane, which had produced his *Love in Several Masques* in 1728, playing against *The Beggar's Opera*. During the season of 1731–32 Drury Lane staged Fielding's *The Modern Husband*, an outstanding success at the box office,[45] and James Miller's controversial *The Modish Couple*, for which Fielding wrote the epilogue.[46] Both these new plays were satiric marriage-problem comedies, set in London. Gay's *The Distress'd Wife* is precisely in the same category.

This represents a new direction for Gay—*Three Hours After Marriage* presented plenty of marriage problems, but it was a satiric farce. An even more surprising new direction is the author's altered ideological stance: Gay's raisonneur, Barter, uncle and advisor to the principal male character Sir Thomas Willit, is a London merchant who extolls the virtues of trade and commerce almost as if he were Steele's Sir Andrew Freeport in *The Spectator*. It is not a coincidence, I believe, that Lillo's *The London Merchant* had begun its long stage life with a most successful run at Drury Lane in the summer and autumn of 1731. If the London stage was becoming more sympathetic in its depiction of men of trade and finance, as John Loftis has demonstrated,[47] then Gay re-flects the trend. *The Distress'd Wife* was written for the Drury Lane audience.

Part of that audience, an important part, included the London *bon ton*, who are in fact the satiric victims of Gay's play. The distress comes to the wife in question, Lady Willit, when her older husband, Sir Thomas Willit, proposes that they quit London and return to their country estate, to relieve their financial problems. Lady Willit has learned to gamble, drink, and flirt fashionably under the tutelage of her friend

Lady Frankair. Sir Thomas's uncle and confidant, Barter, the London merchant, appears at intervals, counseling prudence and retrenchment.

Two marriageable young kinswomen, Miss Sprightly and Miss Friendless, are in the care of the Willits. Miss Sprightly, an heiress, receives but rebuffs the attentions of old Lord Courtlove, who has offered to get a place at Court for Sir Thomas in return for Miss Sprightly's hand. The place that Sir Thomas has come to London seeking does not materialize. In the last act Lady Willit has agreed to return to the country, in spite of the scornful noises made by her companions of the Town, when Miss Sprightly reveals that she has been married all along to her cousin Harry, now at Oxford. Miss Friendly somewhat implausibly accepts Lord Courtlove's offer of his hand. Barter pronounces final judgment at the curtain: "The Man hath recover'd his Reason; and the Woman, when she hath no more fashionable Fools to keep her in countenance, must return to herself" (V.xiii.51-54).

Barter and Sir Thomas represent English virtue, as exemplified by the man of business and the country squire. They are contrasted with Lady Willit's foppish London admirers Pert, Forward, and Flutter, and especially with Lord Courtlove, who pursues his fortune, as his name suggests, by associating with the rich and powerful.

These are familiar materials with which Gay is working; the reformed rake of many a stage comedy is here a reformed—what is the feminine equivalent? Pope would say that "every Woman is at heart a Rake."[48] Miss Friendless, the poor relation, is humiliated by Lady Willit, who has the servants search her pockets for letters. Friendless's character as the poor but honest relation is in some respects the most interesting in the play; once again Gay displays his sympathy for the female in a dangerous or humiliating situation. But the overall effect of *The Distress'd Wife* is strangely flat. Of the satiric victims only Lady Willit is characterized with sufficient fullness for comic effect; Lady Frankair and her brother Lord Courtlove are faintly sinister but not at all comic, and in truth not very menacing either. Barter confronts them both in Act IV and reads them their resonsibilities: "'Tis you, my Lord, and such as you, that influence the Manners of Mankind.—Common Charity obliges those of your Rank to show clear and conspicuous Proofs of Honour and Disinterestedness; for whenever you are mean and mercenary, the Vulgar are hang'd for following your Example" (IV.xvi.69-73). Courtlove is won over immediately to Barter's way of thinking by this address and decides to marry the worthy Miss Friendless. Excellent sentiments, but as expressed not very dramatic, and certainly not comic, ones.

As Howard Erskine-Hill has noted, *The Distress'd Wife* is the only play in which Gay attempted comedy of manners.[49] The world of realistic comedy was not his world. *The Distress'd Wife* seems to have been crafted for a specific theatre and a specific time: Drury Lane in 1732, but Gay's heart was not in the enterprise. It is just as well he did not live to see the play's early end in 1734. The end was a note in a minor key for the creator of the century's most popular stage entertainment.

Epilogue

Gay witnessed the great triumph of his *Beggar's Opera* and saw it alter dramatic practice, but he was not content simply to savor his winnings. From the beginning of his literary career to the end of his life, the theatre fascinated him. Experiment came naturally to him, but experiment was viewed suspiciously in his theatre, and many of his experiments went on the rocks.

A play about street gangs, with music? Too controversial by half in 1712. Bernstein and Sondheim would do one later. Film might have been his salvation; he was grasping for its equivalent in *Acis and Galatea* and *The What D'Ye Call It*. It is almost as if he imagined that revolutionary medium.

With the medium he possessed, stage comedy, he did well enough. He wrote a number of pieces for his theatre that deserve another look in ours, and he wrote one that has never dropped out of the world dramatic tradition. The phenomenal success of *The Beggar's Opera* in the eighteenth century, when it was played just about everywhere in the English-speaking world where room could be found to put up a stage, might be and has been explained as another age's different politics, another age's different taste. In our time, however, in the second half of the twentieth century, the *Opera* has found new audiences all over the globe. That great variation on the *Opera's* theme, the Brecht/Weill *Threepenny Opera*, exists comfortably with its original; both are very much alive. As this book is written, Vaclav Havel's version of *The Beggar's Opera* is being filmed in Prague; the president of

Czechoslovakia composed this while he was in and out of political prison. The politics and taste of our age seem to welcome Gay's creation, too. But, as Tristram Shandy said, that is another story—and a good one.

APPENDIX A

"Were the Mohocks Ever Anything More than a Hairstyle?"

In spite of my contention in this chapter that the Mohocks were largely the creation of Gay and Steele as publicity for Gay's play, I realize that (a) street depradations ascribed by some to "Mohocks" did occur in London at this time and (b) the visit of the Indian Kings has had effects on the transatlantic imagination, and transatlantic hair styles, which persist to the present day. Some of these effects I traced in a paper with the above title at the Second De Bartolo Conference on Eighteenth-Century Literature in Tampa, 1988. My objection to the use of the term "Mohock" as applied to an organized group or club is that—*pace* Robert J. Allen and the *OED*—there is little or no evidence that one existed. This judgment is not new. In the middle years of the eighteenth century William Maitland in his massive *History and Survey of London* remarked that the rumor of street offences gained "universal credit," and "many durst not stir abroad, for Fear of being *mohock'd*." (Note the verb. Defoe in his *Review* replying to the anonymous broadside was apparently the first to use it.) Maitland continues, "However, it does not appear that ever any Person was detected of any of the said Crimes, and notwithstanding I made all the Inquiry imaginable, in those Places where the Offences were said to have been chiefly committed, I never could learn of any one Person having received the least Hurt upon that account."[1]

The Government was sufficiently concerned to frame a Royal Proclamation issued on 15 March 1712—note the date: three days after Steele's "Philanthropos" letter in *Spectator* No. 324 and exactly the time the anonymous broadside attacking Defoe appeared (and perhaps the publication date of Gay's own undated broadside on

"Mohocks and Hawkubites"), to which Defoe replied in the *Review* of 20 March that he had been "mohock'd." The Proclamation cited "the great and unusual Riots and Barbarities which have lately been committed in the Night times," by "numbers of Evil disposed Persons . . . [who] have had the Boldness to insult the Constables and Watchmen in the Execution of their Office." This of course describes precisely the action of Gay's play. The Proclamation called on the authorities to see that "said Offenders be Prosecuted with the utmost Severity and Rigour of the Law," and offered one hundred pounds reward, a very substantial sum.

In spite of the authorities' best efforts, spurred by a hundred-pound bounty, almost everyone slipped through the net. Only two names, to my knowledge, have ever been cited—and they are constantly cited and recited—as having been arrested (excepting of course the purely fictional "Sir" Richard Tonson and Father Nery, the Irish priest, of the broadside). They are one Sir Mark Cole and, as Allen spells the name, Richard Lord Hinchinbroke. Their presence in the controversy, it should be noted, derives from the fact that their names appeared on a list of those arrested printed in another Grub Street broadside, which Swift himself characterized as "all a Lye."[2] No one, apparently, was ever convicted of anything under the Proclamation.

I am not sure who Sir Mark Cole was, but if Lord Hinching-brooke, as the *Complete Peerage* spells it, was rioting, his actions at least make for an amusing historical footnote, with Gay associations. In 1712 he was a captain in the Earl of Essex's regiment of dragoons. His son, the fourth Earl of Sandwich, later became a member of a real club, the notorious Hell Fire Club of Medmenham Abbey. When Sandwich denounced his Hell Fire colleague John Wilkes on the floor of the House of Lords for writing the obscene poem, *An Essay on Woman*, he was tagged for his betrayal with the name "Jemmy Twicher," the faithless character in *The Beggar's Opera* who betrays Macheath.

But one drunken army officer does not a club make, even if his son turned out to be a Monk of Medmenham. Mohocks were hard to catch. "Scowrers," drunken rioters who beat up the watch and broke windows, had of course been around London for generations, as Gay's Justice Scruple pointed out, and as scholars have also carefully noted, seeking to give the Mohocks reality.

Matthew Prior probably had it right when he got around to publishing his *Alma* in 1718 (which had largely been written earlier).[3] In the poetic dialogue, the spokesman Richard argues for the importance of diet in human conduct. The youngster who drinks milk and tea, comes home early and gets to bed at ten o'clock:

> But give him Port, and potent Sack;
> From *Milk-sop* He starts up *Mohack:*
> Holds that the Happy know no Hours;
> So thro' the Streets at Midnight scow'rs;
> Breaks *Watch-men*'s Heads and *Chair-men*'s glasses;
> And then proceeds to nicking Sashes:
> Till by some tougher Hand o'ercome,
> And first knock'd down, and then led Home;
> He damns the Foot-man, strikes the Maid,
> And decently reels up to Bed.[4]

The Mohocks and the Mohock Club were, I would argue, effectively given their existence by Richard Steele and John Gay, who believed in them as devoutly as we adults believe in Santa Claus. Fiction in this case has effectively superseded fact. As distinguished a historian as Edward Gregg in his recent biography of Queen Anne accepts the existence of the Mohocks as genuine, even while he recognizes the highly-charged political atmosphere of the time. "The appearance of 'Mohawks,' a group of aristocratic young bloods who nightly molested pedestrians in the streets of London, added credence to the government's continuing anti-allied, anti-Whig campaign that a conspiracy was afoot to kidnap the queen."[5] Mr. Gregg has been reading Allen and the *OED*.

APPENDIX B

Gay's Payment for the *Opera*

The figure of £693 13s 6d., which is quoted so confidently by Fuller, Irving, and others, derives from an article by "Dramaticus" in *Notes and Queries* I (1850): 178-79. Dramaticus had access to Rich's accounts now in the Harvard Theatre Collection (see p. 192). Dramaticus gets his sum by simply taking the gross receipts for the third, sixth, ninth, and fifteenth nights and adding them up, commenting that this was to Gay "all clear profit." Now, the third night is not indicated as a benefit night in the accounts, but we will not quarrel with that.

However, every student knows that the patent companies deducted the house charges—by this time about fifty pounds—from *every* benefit performance: Dramaticus's total should be some two hundred pounds less. By the fifteenth night Gay was watching the take carefully—that was the night of his comment to Swift on benefit nights quoted above—and he may well have worked out an agreement with Rich that is not reflected in the accounts. Notice that Gay in the March letter to Swift specifies that Rich was "deducting the whole charges of the House." One of the leading lawyers of England, William Fortescue, was Gay's friend, and Fortescue had recently assisted Pope in some of his dealings with the publishers. Although the accounts give no indication of it that I can distinguish, some kind of arrangement may have been struck between Gay and Rich that would have secured him additional remuneration, bringing his take to "between seven & eight hundred pounds," as he told Swift. But the famous £693 13s. 6d. is moonshine and nothing else, no matter how many times it is cited. It does not gain accuracy by reiteration. It should be put to rest.

Reference Abbreviations

Battestin, *Fielding*	Martin C. Battestin, with Ruthe R. Battestin, *Henry Fielding: A Life* (London: Routledge, 1989).
Biographical Dictionary	Philip H. Highfill, Jr., Kalman A. Burnim, and Edward A. Langhans, *A Biographical Dictionary of Actors, Actresses, Musicians, Dancers, Managers and Other Stage Personnel in London, 1660–1800*, 16 vols. (in progress) (Carbondale: Southern Illinois Univ. Press, 1973–).
Bowyer Ledgers	Keith Maslen and John Lancaster, eds., *The Bowyer Ledgers: The Printing Accounts of William Bowyer Father and Son, with a Checklist of Bowyer Printing 1699–1777, a Commentary, Indexes, and Appendixes* (London: Oxford Univ. Press, 1991).
Cibber, *Apology*	*An Apology for the Life of Colley Cibber*, ed. B. R. S. Fone (Ann Arbor: Univ. of Michigan Press, 1968).
Complete Peerage	G. E. C[okayne]., *Complete Peerage England, Scotland, Ireland . . .* , rev. ed., 12 vols., by V. Gibbs, H. A. Doubleday, G. H. White, and R. S. Lea (London: St. Catherine Press, 1910–59).
Deutsch	Otto Erich Deutsch, *Handel: A Documentary Biography* (New York: Norton, 1955).
Dramatic Works	John Gay, *Dramatic Works*, ed. John Fuller, 2 vols. (Oxford: Clarendon, 1983).
Fiske	Roger Fiske, *English Theatre Music in the Eighteenth Century*, 2nd ed. (Oxford: Oxford Univ. Press, 1986).

Goldgar

Bertrand A. Goldgar, *Walpole and the Wits* (Lincoln: Univ. of Nebraska Press, 1976).

Hume, *Henry Fielding*

Robert D. Hume, *Henry Fielding and the London Theatre 1728–1737* (Oxford: Clarendon, 1988).

Irving

William Henry Irving, *John Gay Favorite of the Wits* (Durham: Duke Univ. Press, 1940).

Letters

The Letters of John Gay, ed. C. F. Burgess (Oxford: Clarendon, 1966).

Literary Anecdotes

John Nichols, *Literary Anecdotes of the Eighteenth Century,* 8 (London: for the Author, 1814).

London Stage

The London Stage, 1660–1800. Part 1, 1660–1700, ed. William Van Lennep, Emmett L. Avery, and Arthur H. Scouten (Carbondale: Southern Illinois Univ. Press, 1965). Part 2, 1700–1729, ed. Emmett L. Avery, 2 vols (1960). Part 3, 1729–1747, ed. Arthur H. Scouten, 2 vols. (1961). Part 4, 1747–1776, ed. George Winchester Stone, Jr., 3 vols. (1962). Part 5, 1776–1800, ed. Charles Beecher Hogan, 3 vols. (1968).

London Theatre World

The London Theatre World, 1660–1800, ed. Robert D. Hume (Carbondale: Southern Illinois Univ. Press, 1980).

Memoirs

Memoirs of the Extraordinary Life, Works, and Discoveries of Martinus Scriblerus, ed. Charles Kerby-Miller (1950; rpt., New York: Oxford Univ. Press, 1988).

Noble, *Interpretations*

Twentieth-Century Interpretations of The Beggar's Opera, ed. Yvonne Noble (Englewood Cliffs, N.J.: Prentice Hall, 1975).

Poetry and Prose

John Gay, *Poetry and Prose,* ed. Vinton A. Dearing, 2 vols. (Oxford: Clarendon, 1974).

Pope, *Correspondence*

The Correspondence of Alexander Pope, ed. George Sherburn, 5 vols. (Oxford: Clarendon, 1956).

Spacks

Patricia M. Spacks, *John Gay* (New York: Twayne, 1965).

Spectator

The Spectator, ed. Donald F. Bond, 5 vols. (Oxford: Clarendon, 1965).

Spence, *Anecdotes*	Joseph Spence, *Observations, Anecdotes, and Characters of Books and Men*, ed. James M. Osborn, 2 vols. (Oxford: Clarendon, 1966).
Simpson	Claude M. Simpson, *The British Broadside Ballad and Its Music* (New Brunswick: Rutgers Univ. Press, 1966).
Victor	Benjamin Victor, *The History of the Theatres of London and Dublin*, 3 vols. (London: T. Davies, 1761–71).

Notes

1. See the account of the lamentable regress by Yvonne Noble, "John Gay's Monument," in *John Gay and the Scriblerians*, ed. Nigel Wood and Peter Lewis (London: Vision Press, 1988), 216-218.

1. APPRENTICESHIP—A PRELUDE

1. Significantly, Pope excised any mention of Willet or of Gay's apprenticeship from Thomas Birch's early (1736) biography of Gay. See E. L. Ruhe, "Pope's Hand in Thomas Birch's Account of Gay," *Review of English Studies* n.s.5 (1954): 171-74, a brief but very important article, which is the source of the name of Gay's employer.

2. *Poetry and Prose*, 145.

3. Indenture of 1705 quoted in Peter Laslett, *The World We Have Lost Further Explored* (New York: Scribner's Sons, 1984), 3.

4. James Boswell, *Boswell's Life of Johnson*, ed. George B. Hill, rev. ed. L. F. Powell (Oxford: Clarendon, 1934–50), 2:337 (entry for 2 April 1775).

5. The earliest reference to his apprenticeship is in a letter of 1705. See *Letters*, 1.

6. See Shirley Strum Kenny, "Perennial Favorites: Congreve, Vanbrugh, Cibber, Farquhar, and Steele," *Modern Philology* 73, no. 4, Part 2 [Friedman *Festschrift*] (1976): S4-S11.

7. For documents and information about this troubled playhouse, see Robert D. Hume and Judith Milhous, eds., *Vice-Chamberlain Coke's Theatrical Papers, 1706–1715* (Carbondale: Southern Illinois Univ. Press, l982), xviii, passim.

8. Scottish Record Office, G.D. 124/15/259/3, letter of William Cleland dated 6 December 1705: "Eccles [has] another [opera]

the words by Congreve." This dating corrects Winton Dean, *Handel's Dramatic Oratorios and Masques* (London: Oxford Univ. Press, 1959), 366.

9. The fairs appear to have been relatively more profitable for the actors than the patent theatres: see Sybil Rosenfeld, *The Theatre of the London Fairs in the Eighteenth Century* (Cambridge: Cambridge Univ. Press, 1960), 10, quoting Ned Ward in 1699: the actors concluded "that it was equally reputable to Play the Fool in the *Fair,* for Fifteen or Twenty Shillings a Day as 'twas to Please Fools in the *Playhouse,* at so much *per* Week." Recently analyzed documentary evidence emphatically confirms Ward's judgment: see Cheryl Wanko, "Mary Morein (*fl.* 1707): Drury Lane Actress and Fair Performer," *Theatre Survey* 32 (1991): 22-30. For hard information on managers' profits at a slightly later period, see Judith Milhous and Robert D. Hume, "Profits at Drury Lane, 1713–1716," *Theatre Research International* 14 (1989): 253: "the [Drury Lane] managers had a good probability of making £3,000 to £4,000 each season, competition notwithstanding."

10. See Shirley Strum Kenny, "The Publication of Plays," in *London Theatre World,* 309-36.

11. See my edition of *The Tender Husband* (Lincoln: Univ. of Nebraska Press, 1967), xiv. Steele felt, probably correctly, that he had been defrauded of his second (sixth night's) benefit by the theatre manager, Christopher Rich.

12. "Company Management," in *London Theatre World,* 1-34. This is an accurate and succinct discussion, on which I rely here. Quotation is at p. 2.

13. *Defoe's Review,* ed Arthur W. Secord (New York: Columbia Univ. Press, 1938), II, No. 26, for Thursday, May 3, 1705. Site described in *Survey of London,* vol. 30: The Parish of St. James Westminster, Part One (London: Athlone, 1960), 224.

14. Quoted in my "The London Stage Embattled: 1695–1710," *Tennessee Studies in Literature* 19 (1974): 15.

15. *Ibid,* 16.

16. "Mr. Steele's Apology," in *Tracts and Pamphlets by Richard Steele,* edited by Rae Blanchard (Baltimore: Johns Hopkins Press, 1944), 339.

17. See my introduction to *The Plays of Aaron Hill* (New York: Garland, 1981) and the good recent essay on Hill by Sophia B. Blaydes, "Aaron Hill," in *Dictionary of Literary Biography,* vol. 84, ed. Paula Backscheider (Detroit: Gale Research, 1989), 200–218.

18. Papers of William, Sixth Lord Paget in London, Public Record Office, SP 97/21/53.

19. Levant Company papers, Public Record Office, SP 105/178/234. The total for a full round of vests "to maintain the Priviledges of the English Nation" is given, with meticulous exactitude, as £4,236 and one shilling.

20. *British Apollo*, No. 10 (12 to 17 March 1708). Question in italics in original.

21. *Poetry and Prose*, 474. See also Richmond P. Bond, "The Pirate and the *Tatler*," *The Library* 5th. ser., 18 (1963): 257-74.

22. See their article, on which I rely here, "The Haymarket Opera in 1711," *Early Music* 17 (1989): 523-37.

23. See Leo Hughes, *A Century of English Farce* (Princeton: Princeton Univ. Press, 1956), 41, 86; and Philip K. Jason, "The Afterpiece: Origins and Early Development," *Restoration and 18th Century Theatre Research* 2nd. ser., 1 (1986): 53-63.

24. Gay's possible hand in *The Walking Statue* has not, I think, been previously suggested. Leo Hughes points out that the afterpiece was derived from the Italian *commedia dell'arte* tradition and that the second episode, that of the walking statue itself, may have been taken directly from the Italian. See *A Century of English Farce*, 245-48.

25. *Vice Chamberlain Coke's Theatrical Papers, 1706–1715* (n. 7 above), 120.

26. See Milhous and Hume's summary in "The Haymarket Opera in 1711," (n. 22 above), 525.

27. *Rinaldo, An Opera. As it is Perform'd At the Queen's Theatre in London* (London: Howlett, 1711).

28. Hill's complaint to Chancery, quoted for the first time in Milhous and Hume, "The Haymarket Opera in 1711," 526.

29. Winton Dean and John Merrill Knapp, *Handel's Operas, 1704–1726* (Oxford: Clarendon, 1987), 183. Dean and Knapp tend to agree with Rossi's estimate of the time Handel took to compose *Rinaldo*, pointing to signs of haste in the composition: p. 173.

30. Permission to photograph and reproduce this was kindly granted by Her Majesty's Ambassador, Sir Peter Laurence. The painting, by an unknown artist, probably Venetian, represents the reception of Edward Wortley-Montagu as ambassador in 1718.

31. See *A Full and Just Account of the Present State of the Ottoman Empire In all its Branches*, 2nd ed. (London: J. Mayo, 1710), 286.

32. See Curtis A. Price, "The Critical Decade for English Music Drama, 1700–1719," *Harvard Library Bulletin* 26 (1978): 38.

33. Deutsch, 299.

34. See *Poetry and Prose*, 605. Dearing dates these by guess at about 1720, but they could have been done earlier.

2. *The Mohocks*

1. For literacy, see David Cressy, *Literacy and the Social Order: Reading and Writing in Tudor and Stuart England* (Cambridge: Cambridge Univ. Press, 1980); for spread of journalism, see Michael Harris, *London Newspapers in the Age of Walpole* (London: Associated Univ. Press, 1987), Chapter 1: "The Shaping of the London Newspaper," esp. notes pp. 198-201.

2. *Poetry and Prose*, 454.

3. *Poetry and Prose*, 40.

4. *Correspondence*, I, 138.

5. Here and elsewhere I follow the discrimination of David Foxon among printer, bookseller, and publisher, with the latter term being applied to those such as James Roberts, who purveyed pamphlets and other brief works ordinarily printed by others. See Foxon, *Pope and the Early Eighteenth-Century Book Trade* (Oxford: Clarendon, 1991).

6. Strictly speaking, he had already bought his way in, since this transaction involved trading the managership at the Haymarket with Owen Swiney, who had been one of the Drury Lane partners. See Milhous and Hume, *Vice Chamberlain Coke's Theatrical Papers*, 178.

7. Spacks, *John Gay* (New York: Twayne, 1965), 130.

8. Peter E. Lewis, "Another Look at John Gay's *The Mohocks*," *Modern Language Review* 63 (1968): 790-93.

9. *Dramatic Works*, 81. References to the plays hereafter will ordinarily be inserted in the text parenthetically.

10. *Poetry and Prose*, 21.

11. *The Works of George Farquhar*, ed. Shirley Strum Kenny (Oxford: Clarendon, 1988), 2:7, 65, 551.

12. Original in italics.

13. Lewis, n. 8 above.

14. *Dramatic Works*, 7. They are named in the Prologue: "And heard in *Cloudy* honest *Dicky* talk,/Seen *Pinkethman* in strutting *Prig* appear" (p. [79], italics reversed).

15. Allen, *Clubs* (Cambridge: Harvard Univ. Press, 1933). Spacks, following Allen, assumes their existence; Fuller is more cautious, but uses the same "sources" as Allen (*Dramatic Works*, 3-5).

16. Richmond P. Bond, *Queen Anne's American Kings* (Oxford: Clarendon, 1952). The reference was *Tatler* No. 171 of 13 May 1710.

17. *Journal to Stella*, ed. Harold Williams (Oxford; Clarendon, 1948), 2:509.

18. *Spectator*, ed. Bond, 3:187-88.

19. J. H. Plumb, *Sir Robert Walpole: The Making of a Statesman* (London: Cresset, 1956), 178.

20. See Centlivre's Preface to *The Perplex'd Lovers* (London: for Owen Lloyd and others, 1712), sig. [A3r + v].

21. Swift, *Journal to Stella*, ed. Harold Williams (Oxford: Clarendon, 1948), 2:509; and *The History of the Four Last Years of the Queen*, ed. Harold Williams (Oxford: Basil Blackwell, 1951), 26-27.

22. *Remarks and Collections of Thomas Hearne*, vol. 3, ed. C.E. Doble (Oxford: Clarendon, 1889), 326. Hearne's description of their barbarities dated 30 March is patently derived directly from Steele's *Spectator* No. 324.

23. *Defoe's Review*, intro. Arthur W. Secord, 22 vols. (New York: Columbia Univ. Press, 1938), issue of 4 March 1712: vol. 21, p. 594. Later quotations are from this facsimile edition. Defoe was particularly active on behalf of Harley's government during this period: see Alan Downie, *Robert Harley and the Press* (Cambridge: Cambridge Univ. Press, 1979), 147-53.

24. Broadside, apparently unique, in Folger Shakespeare Library, Washington, shelf mark 156127. Printed by Charles King in Holborn, no date.

25. This has been ascribed to Gay by Dearing in *Poetry and Prose*, 646–47, on evidence "not very strong," but the piece's inclusion by Pope and Swift in the 1727-32 *Miscellanies* and its obvious connection with the play would seem to argue for Gay's authorship. The association of Mohocks and Hawkubites, in the broadside and in Gay's play, also supports the argument for Gay's hand in the broadside.

26. See Ronald A. Knox, *Enthusiasm* (Oxford: Clarendon, 1950), 366-69.

27. *Poetry and Prose*, 457. These references to the Junto were omitted in 1727, presumably as being anachronistic, when the broadside was reprinted in the Pope-Swift *Miscellanies*.

28. (London: Printed for J. Baker at the Black Boy in Pater-Noster Row, 1712), Folger shelfmark PR/3291/G4/1712/Cage. The note is apparently contemporaneous.

29. For evidence of an apparent political attack on the management precisely at this time, see Judith Milhous and Robert D. Hume, "*A Letter to Sir John Stanley:* A New Theatrical Document of 1712," *Theatre Notebook* 43 (1989): 71-80.

30. Lintott's accounts printed in Nichols, *Literary Anecdotes* 8:296. At this period, Lintott spelled his name with a final double t.

31. See *The Critical Works of John Dennis*, ed. Edward N. Hooker, 2 vols. (Baltimore: Johns Hopkins Press, 1939–1943), 1:396-419.

32. *Poetry and Prose*, [79], italics in original.

3. Chaucer in Augustan England

1. Lintott's account book in Nichols, *Literary Anecdotes*, 8:296: "Sld the Mohocks to him again."

2. This is the conjecture of Irving, p. 30, but he does not supply dates. A pedigree in the G. A. Aitken papers at the University of Texas, was apparently prepared by a descendant of Gay's nephew, the Rev. Joseph Baller, who inherited much of Gay's property. This gives brother Jonathan's birthdate as 25 November 1679 and notes "Captain in the Army, d[ied] unmarried 1709." The pedigree is correct in other details which can be verified. Aitken Collection, Ransom Research Center, Miscellaneous Autograph Notes *re* pedigree of John Gay.

3. Here and elsewhere, unless otherwise noted, biographical information on the nobility derives from G. E. C[okayne], *Complete Peerage England, Scotland, Ireland...* rev. ed., 12 vols., by V. Gibbs, H. A. Doubleday, G. H. White and R. S. Lea (London: St. Catherine Press, 1910–59); and *Handbook of British Chronology*, 3rd ed., ed. E. B. Fryde, D. E. Greenway, S. Porter, and I. Roy (London: Royal Historical Society, 1986).

4. As quoted in E. L.Ruhe, "Pope's Hand in Thomas Birch's Account of Gay," *Review of English Studies* n.s.5 (1954): 171.

5. "The significance of Gay's drama," in *English Drama: Forms and Development*, ed. Marie Axton and Raymond Williams (Cambridge: Cambridge Univ. Press, 1977), 146.

6. See William L. Alderson and Arnold C. Henders, *Chaucer and Augustan Scholarship*, Univ. of California Publications, English Studies No. 35 (Berkeley: Univ. of California Press, 1970).

7. Pope used a 1687 reprint of Speght. Urry's 1721 edition was the first published in roman type. See *The Rape of the Lock and Other Poems*, ed. Geoffrey Tillotson, 2nd ed. (London: Methuen; New Haven: Yale Univ. Press, 1954), 4n: "Modern readers are apt to underestimate the difficulty which eighteenth-century readers found in the language of earlier English literature."

8. See Tillotson (n. 7), 236.

9. For a recent discussion of the *Fables*, which is not however primarily concerned with the language, see Cedric D. Reverand, *Dryden's Final Poetic Mode: The "Fables"* (Philadelphia: Univ. of Pennsylvania Press, 1988).

10. *The Poems of John Dryden*, ed. James Kinsley, 4 vols. (Oxford: Clarendon, 1958), 4:1458.

11. Pope, *Pastoral Poetry and an Essay on Criticism*, ed. E. Audra and Aubrey Williams (London: Methuen, 1961), 293 (lines 482-83).

12. *Advertisement* to his *Works* (1736), as quoted in Tillotson (n. 7), 5.

13. Damrosch, *The Imaginative World of Alexander Pope* (Berkeley: Univ. of California Press, 1987), 231.

14. Spence, *Anecdotes*, 1:62.

15. *Dramatic Works*, 1:109 (ll. 81-82). As with *The Mohocks*, references to the play will hereafter ordinarily be given in parentheses by act/scene/line.

16. *Spectator*, 3:395.

17. Victor, 2:57.

18. Victor, 2:64.

19. *Poetry and Prose*, 249. Dearing does not discuss the legend, but see the discussion under her entry in *Biographical Dictionary*.

20. The earliest entry in the *OED* for the flower is 1891.

21. *Letters*, 3. Addressee is Maurice Johnson, Jr.

22. Nichols, *Literary Anecdotes*, 8:296. I use the term bookseller as holder of the copyright here, following the discrimination among bookseller, publisher, and printer established by David Foxon in his recent *Pope and the Early Eighteenth-Century Book Trade* (Oxford: Clarendon, 1991).

23. Shirley Strum Kenny, *The Works of George Farquhar*, 2 vols. (Oxford: Clarendon, 1988), 2:18.

24. *The Guardian*, No. 50, for Friday, 8 May 1713. Steele is writing as Nestor Ironside, the editor.

25. Thomas A. Knott, "A Bit of Chaucer Mythology," *Modern Philology* 8 (1910), 135-39. Knott points out that editors since have followed Urry's reading of the Host's remarks.

26. *Poetry and Prose*, 1:198-99.

27. Steele invited contributors to his *Miscellany* in *Guardian* No. 50, the same issue in which Ironside reports on Margaret Bicknell. As James May has recently demonstrated, Gay answered that call with an episode from the *Week* that was subsequently cancelled: "Cancellanda in the First Edition of Steele's *Poetical Miscellanies*," *The Papers of the Bibliographical Society of America* 82 (1988): [71]-82.

28. Steele refers to Margaret Bicknell's snatching a "little Ruff" from the Lizard family collection of antique clothing, for her costume. Whether or not Margaret Bicknell wore period costume is an interesting point. Gay's friend Aaron Hill campaigned for costuming appropriate to the place and period depicted in drama but in 1713 this was a minority view, largely ignored by the patent companies.

29. See *Dramatic Works*, 1:412, 416; and Fiske, *English Theatre Music*, 100.

30. See Fuller's argument in *Dramatic Works*, 1:412-14, which seems to me convincing.

31. This assessment of Arbuthnot's primacy is admittedly not a majority view. Pat Rogers, however, also argues that Arbuthnot "took a leading part in the *Memoirs*," in *The Augustan Vision* (New York: Barnes and Noble, 1974), 227. A thorough reassessment of the Scriblerian association is in order, now that the Oxford University Press has reissued the essential edition by Charles Kerby-Miller.

32. Just *how* much has been the subject of extended debate. Spacks (28-33) summarizes the controversy.

33. *Letters*, 12.

34. John Hervey, *Some Materials Towards Memoirs of the Reign of King George II*, ed. Romney Sedgwick (London: Eyre and Spottis-woode, 1931), 40, 42.

4. WORDS AND MUSIC

1. Cibber, *Apology*, 270.

2. As Judith Milhous and Robert D. Hume have recently shown, their distress should not be exaggerated, as it has been. The managers were making excellent money at Drury Lane: "Profits at Drury Lane, 1713–1716," *Theatre Research International* 14 (1989): 241-55.

3. *Dramatic Works*, 177.

4. Sig. C2v, italics reversed. Quotations in this case are from the so-called third edition of 1716, which was altered significantly by Gay, as will be discussed below, and should serve as copytext for future editions.

5. Leo Hughes, *A Century of English Farce*, 121.

6. *A Complete Key To the last New Farce The What D'Ye Call It* (London: for James Roberts, 1715). The question of the authorship of this slim pamphlet has engendered an extraordinary amount of con-troversy, summarized in Fuller, 1:418-19. The theory espoused by Kerby-Miller in his edition of the *Memoirs* (43) that it was "largely, if not wholly, the work of Pope and Gay," has been given an, in my judgment, unfortunate new lease on life by Fuller. Although Pope and Gay were of course capable of doing a parody of their own work, the *Key* is different in tone and spirit from anything they would have undertaken in 1715. Gay himself wrote of the pamphlet, "There's a Sixpenny Criticism lately published upon the Tragedy of the What dye call it, wherein he with much judgment & learning calls me a Blockhead, & Mr Pope a knave" (*Letters*, 23). Would he have charac-terized it so if he and Pope had written it? Pope later declared, in his collected *Letters* of 1735, that the pamphlet was by "one *Griffin* a Player, assisted by *Lewis Theobald*." That is, presumably, Benjamin

Griffin, an actor and playwright at Lincoln's Inn Fields and Theobald, the scholarly author and editor who would be Pope's first Prince of Dullness in the *Dunciad.* J.V. Guerinot in *Pamphlet Attacks on Alexander Pope 1711–1744* (London: Methuen, 1969), 29, rejects Kerby-Miller's argument and adds, "It may be pointed out that very few of Pope's attributions of Popiana can be proved wrong."

7. *The Works of Thomas Otway,* ed. J. C. Ghosh, 2 vols. (Oxford: Clarendon, 1932), 2:284.

8. *Complete Key,* 24.

9. Pp. 33-34. Claude Simpson, *The British Broadside Ballad,* 719-20, records several political songs that imitated Gay's ballad, such as one of c. 1716, "When Faction loud was Roaring."

10. Burgess, "Gay's 'Twas When the Seas Were Roaring' and Chaucer's 'Franklin's Tale': A Borrowing," *Notes and Queries* (Dec. 1962): 454-55.

11. Dugaw, "The Popular Marketing of 'Old Ballads': The Ballad Revival and Eighteenth-Century Antiquarianism Reconsidered," *Eighteenth-Century Studies* 21 (1987): 71-90.

12. *Dramatic Works,* 434. The fact that Gay's lyrics were joined to Handel's music from the beginning settles an uncertain point among Handelians and demonstrates another instance of early association between the two.

13. *Dramatic Works,* 19.

14. Pope, *Correspondence,* 1:283.

15. Nichols, *Literary Anecdotes,* 8:296. This odd sum is the same that he paid Farquhar for *The Recruiting Officer:* ibid (Lintott's accounts).

16. Penkethman was a pioneer in exploiting these theatrical booths: see Sybil Rosenfeld, *The Theatre of the London Fairs in the 18th Century* (Cambridge: Cambridge Univ. Press, 1960), 9, 78, and, for attendance figures, James E. May and Calhoun Winton, "The 'Prodigal Son' at Bartholomew Fair: A New Document," *Theatre Survey* 21 (1980): 64: "a great number that is to say to the number of Two hundred persons then and there being present" (from an information prepared by the office of the Attorney General).

17. Cf. *Dramatic Works,* 1:434.

18. Foxon and McLaverty, *Pope and the Early Eighteenth-Century Book Trade* (Oxford: Clarendon, 1991), 184-85. Since the 1716 edition therefore represents Gay's intentions I have quoted from it, rather than Fuller, who follows the 1715.

19. See Spence, *Anecdotes,* 1:103. The manuscript of the play, once in the fabulous collection of Sir Thomas Phillipps, was sold at Sotheby's on 20 June 1893 and presumably still exists, somewhere.

20. *Letters*, 18.

21. Pope, *Correspondence*, 1:332.

22. "Menalcas' Song: The Meaning of Art and Artifice in Gay's *Trivia*," *Journal of English and Germanic Philology* 65 (1966): 662-79.

23. *Poetry and Prose*, 153.

24. Kerby-Miller dates the "Double Mistress" episode from this period: *Memoirs*, 45-46.

25. *Dramatic Works*, [208]. George Sherburn details the reactions to the play in "The Fortunes and Misfortunes of *Three Hours After Marriage*," *Modern Philology* 24 (1926): 97-99.

26. *A Century of English Farce*, 249-50.

27. See note 25 above.

28. John Woodward, *Select Cases, and Consultations in Physick* (London: for Dr. P. Templeman, 1757).

29. *Memoirs*, 363. Much interesting scholarship on Woodward and the controversy has appeared in recent years, beginning with Joseph M. Levine's *Dr. Woodward's Shield: History, Science, and Satire in Augustan England* (Berkeley: Univ. of California Press, 1977) and his subsequent articles on the subject. See also Christopher Fox, *Locke and the Scriblerians* (Berkeley: Univ. of California Press, 1988). A recent theoretical article traces the dividing line between Scriblerians and scholars to a split in Renaissance humanism itself: see John F. Tinkler, "The Splitting of Humanism: Bentley, Swift, and the English Battle of the Books," *Journal of the History of Ideas* 49 (1988): 453-72.

30. (London: J. Roberts, 1717), 8.

31. Steele reprints the patent in *Town Talk*, No.6. See *Richard Steele's Periodical Journalism, 1714–16*, ed. Rae Blanchard (Oxford: Clarendon, 1959), 229-32.

32. Pope, *Correspondence*, 1:388.

33. *Dramatic Works*, 1:28-29.

34. Nichols, *Literary Anecdotes*, 8:296. Lintot had by this time dropped the final t in printing his name. Nichols entry (1716) is corrected in Bowyer's ledger. Bowyer printed a very large run of 2,500 copies for Lintot, who apparently sold them. See *The Bowyer Ledgers*, No. 369.

35. *Letter*, fo. A2r-A2v.

36. Brydges quoted in C. H. Collins Baker and Muriel I. Baker, *The Life and Circumstances of James Brydges First Duke of Chandos* (Oxford: Clarendon, 1949), 125.

37. Fiske, 95.

38. "The True Proportions of Gay's Acis and Galatea," in *Facets of the Enlightenment* (Berkeley: Univ. of California Press, 1968), 59.

5. FALSE STARTS

1. *Letters*, 34. Pope in his 1737 edition of his *Letters* ascribes this letter to Gay, but Pope may have written it himself.

2. This is the version quoted in Pope's first letter on the subject, in Pope, *Correspondence*, 1:481. Compare Lady Mary Wortley Montagu's delightful reply, ibid., 523.

3. *Letters*, 36.

4. The order is addressed to Wilks, Cibber, and Booth (Steele being temporarily excluded from management): Public Record Office, LC 5/157, fo. 148 verso.

5. *Dramatic Works*, 1:[278].

6. *Poetry and Prose*, 214.

7. See "The Tragic Muse in Enlightened England," in *Greene & Centennial Studies: Essays Presented to Donald Greene*, ed. Robert R. Allen and Paul J. Korshin (Charlottesville: Univ. Press of Virginia, 1984), 125-42.

8. *The Lives of the Poets*, ed. G. B. Hill, 3 vols. (Oxford: Clarendon, 1905), 2:284-85.

9. *Poetry and Prose*, pp. 201-3, with notes 579-81.

10. "Life of Gay," (see n. 8 above), 274.

11. *Poetry and Prose*, 281.

12. See Linda S. Merians, *The Courtier's Maze: Matthew Prior and the Business of Poetry* (forthcoming). I am grateful to Professor Merians for allowing me to consult this book in manuscript.

13. *Letters*, 45.

14. Victor, 2:155-57.

15. *The Briton*, for 22 January 1724, quoted in *Dramatic Works*, 74. I have not been able to consult the original.

16. *Dramatic Works*, 1:[345], original in italics.

17. Fielding, *The Tragedy of Tragedies*, ed. James T. Hillhouse (New Haven: Yale Univ. Press, 1918), 93.

18. See my essay, n. 7 above.

19. Fuller, 1:31, states flatly that Gay rewrote the *Vertuoso's* "intending to expose Cibber's plagiarism from the same play in his *The Refusal.*" There is a tissue of improbabilities spun out here, which should be disentangled at greater length elsewhere, beginning with the fact that Cibber's play opened a month *after* the production of *No Fools Like Wits* in January 1721. Are we to suppose that Cibber generously supplied Gay with the promptbook in advance, so that he could write his attack?

20. Victor, 2:4.

21. Financial figures from *London Stage*, citing Rich's accounts. There were of course no benefits for the author, Farquhar being dead.

22. Pope, *Correspondence*, 2:216. Sherburn, the editor, writes that Fenton "is pretty certainly wrong," but the rumor seems plausible to me: if the managers closed the play after the fourth night they would not have to pay Gay for a second benefit.

23. Pope, *Correspondence*, 2:215.

24. Fuller, *Dramatic Works*, 1:39-40, discusses these sources and influences.

25. Fuller, in *Dramatic Works*, 1:40-41. One may be tolerably certain that the Drury Lane managers would have perceived, and excised, any inflammatory political references.

26. *The Complete Letters of Lady Mary Wortley Montagu*, ed. Robert Halsband, 3 vols. (Oxford: Clarendon, 1965-67), 2:35.

27. Receipts for Drury Lane at this period are not available, but since its capacity was probably about half that of Lincoln's Inn Fields and since a good night at LIF grossed between one hundred and two hundred pounds, it seems probable that the author's benefit would turn out to be less than a hundred a night at Drury Lane, after house charges.

28. *Dramatic Works*, [346], original in italics.

6. THE BEGGAR AND HIS *Opera*

1. And tactfully avoiding Henrietta Howard: he afterwards said, in his pungent manner, that he took the right sow by the ear. See J. H. Plumb, *Sir Robert Walpole: The King's Minister* (London: Cresset, 1960), 163.

2. Pope, *Correspondence*, 2:311.

3. Pope, *Correspondence*, 2:294. See also Maynard Mack, *The Garden and the City* (Toronto: Univ. of Toronto Press, 1969), 51-76.

4. *Letters*, 49.

5. *Poetry and Prose*, 287ff.

6. See Gerald Howson, *Thief-Taker General: The Rise and Fall of Jonathan Wild* (London: Hutchinson, 1970), 5-6, 215. Howson is inclined to doubt the story of Gay's meeting Wild, which first appeared in *The Flying-Post, or The Weekly Medley* for 11 January 1729. The reference there was first noted in modern times by James Sutherland, "The Beggar's Opera," *Times Literary Supplement*, No. 1734 (25 April 1935), 272. Sutherland admits that no one familiar with eighteenth-century journalism "would claim very much for this anecdote."

7. *English Theatre Music,* 67.

8. See Viola Papetti, *Arlecchino a Londra [:] La Pantomima Inglese* (Naples: Istituto Universitario Orientale, 1977), 45.

9. See the discussion of edition priorities in *Poetry and Prose,* 613-14. Dearing does not, however, discuss the possibility that Gay gave or sold the ballad to Thurmond for use at Drury Lane.

10. Papetti (n. 8) assumes that he did, since he had danced the lead in his own successful *Harlequin Dr. Faustus* in 1723.

11. Printed and sold by J. Roberts and A. Dodd, 1724. Price: sixpence.

12. John Weaver, historian of the dance, cites this pantomime and *Harlequin Dr. Faustus* as examples of grotesque characterization in the dance, "where, in lieu of regulated Gesture, you meet with distorted and ridiculous *Actions,* and Grin and Grimace take up entirely that Countenance where the *Passions* and *Affections* of the Mind should be expressed." See his *The History of the Mimes and Pantomimes* (London: for J. Roberts and A. Dodd, 1728), 56. Weaver clearly does not approve of what Thurmond was doing with the pantomime.

13. Fiske, 90.

14. See John Richetti, *Popular Fiction before Richardson: Narrative Patterns, 1700–1739* (Oxford: Clarendon, 1969), 23-59; and Michael McKeon, *The Origins of the English Novel, 1600–1740* (Baltimore: Johns Hopkins Univ. Press, 1987), 90-96.

15. See Claude M. Simpson, *The British Broadside Ballad and Its Music* (New Brunswick: Rutgers Univ. Press, 1966), 564-70.

16. Fiske, 96.

17. Dianne Dugaw, " 'Critical Instants': Theatre Songs in the Age of Dryden and Purcell," *Eighteenth-Century Studies* 23 (1989): 157-81.

18. David L. Vander Meulen, *Pope's Dunciad of 1728: A History and Facsimile* (Charlottesville: Univ. Press of Virginia, 1991), 152.

19. *Weekly Journal or Saturday's Post* for 5 December, quoted in *London Stage* under date of Saturday, 28 November 1724.

20. Dearing in *Poetry and Prose* notes that it was published in *The Weekly Journal: or, British Gazetteer* of 5 December 1724, and as a broadside at least twice, before inclusion in the so-called "last" volume of the Pope-Swift *Miscellanies.*

21. Battestin, *Henry Fielding,* 46.

22. *Letters,* 52.

23. *Correspondence,* 2:332.

24. Pope, *Correspondence,* 2:325.

25. Maynard Mack, "The Happy Houyhnhnm: A Letter from John Gay to the Blount Sisters," *The Scriblerian* 11 (1978), 1-3.

26. Edition used is the facsimile of the first (1727 and 1738) (Menston, Yorkshire, and London: Scolar, 1969), 78.

27. *Fables*, 170-71.

28. *Letters*, 65.

29. *Correspondence*, 2:426.

30. *Correspondence*, 2:437.

31. *Correspondence*, 2:446-47.

32. *Letters*, 68-69.

7. *The Beggar's Opera* in Theatre History

1. Pope edited the letter extensively before publishing it: see Pope, *Correspondence*, 2:454-56.

2. Pope, *Correspondence*, 1:360.

3. See Rosamond McGuiness, "*The British Apollo* and Music," in *Journal of Newspaper and Periodical History* 2 (1987): 9-19. I am indebted to Yvonne Noble for this reference.

4. This has been an especially frustrating inquiry. Both Fiske and Irving assume it as fact, without providing documentation. I have no quarrel with the assumption but would feel more secure if I knew of a contemporary reference to Gay's playing the flute.

5. See Fiske, *English Theatre Music*, 105.

6. See Shirley Strum Kenny, "The Publication of Plays," in *London Theatre World*, 309-36; and John Feather, *The Provincial Book Trade in Eighteenth-Century England* (Cambridge: Cambridge Univ. Press, 1985), 44-68.

7. Irving, 236.

8. J. H. Plumb, *Sir Robert Walpole The King's Minister* (London: Cresset, 1960), 157-61.

9. Goldgar, 51: "from the beginning [*Gulliver's Travels'*] political allusions were obviously understood."

10. Public Record Office [of Great Britain], T. 29/25, p. 26: "200£ to Mr. Pope as his Mat Encouragemt to his translacion of Homers Odyssey and to the Subscripcons making for the same." Other Treasury documents having to do with this gift are in T. 60/12, p. 391; and T. 52/52/33, p. 324.

11. Goldgar, 67.

12. In addition to Goldgar, see Maynard Mack, *The Garden and the City* (Toronto: Univ. of Toronto Press, 1969), 116-28.

13. Spence, *Anecdotes*, 107.

14. To appreciate just how tough, see Robert D. Hume's tables in *Henry Fielding*, 15, 105.

15. Goldgar, 64-86.

16. Irving, 238.

17. Hughes, *The Drama's Patrons* (Austin: Univ. of Texas Press, 1971), 102.

18. [Benjamin Victor], *Memoirs of the Life of Barton Booth, Esq;* (London: John Watts, 1733), 13. "Pompous" was of course a term of praise with Victor.

19. Figures are based on Rich's accounts in the Harvard Theatre Collection, shelfmark fMS Thr 22, from which the *London Stage* statistics are drawn. This account book includes much information not published in *LS* and there are discrepancies between the information it contains and the published figures.

20. Not seen. Here as quoted in *London Stage.*

21. The Rich accounts (n. 19) show that after the first night the bill with the pantomime made the house charges only once.

22. Biographical information from the *Complete Peerage* and personal observation.

23. Schultz, 2, accepts the eighteenth-century legend much too uncritically, and he has been followed by scholars, including Fuller, since. Cooke's *Memoirs of . . . Macklin* (pub. 1804), on which this story and other *Opera* legends are based, is shot through with demonstrable error and must be used with great caution. See the article on Macklin in *Biographical Dictionary.*

24. Hume, *Henry Fielding*, 21.

25. Victor, 2:153.

26. This, too, is part of that tangle of theatrical gossip which surrounds the *Opera*, but it does seem likely that Quin could have had the role if he wanted it. He took it in a 1730 revival.

27. Here and elsewhere shillings and pence are eliminated in totals from Rich's accounts (which record them to the halfpenny).

28. Pope, *Correspondence*, 2:469.

29. *Daily Journal*, issue of 1 February.

30. *Anecdotes*, 107-8.

31. Victor, 2:154.

32. *The Country Journal: Or, The Craftsman;* copy used here and hereafter in the microfilm series of Early English Newspapers.

33. *Letters*, 70-71.

34. Including the most recent editor, John Fuller, who adopts the novel technique of discussing "some of the significant variants" (*Dramatic Works*, 374) without, however, specifying which some. This, it goes without saying, is worse than discussing *none* of the significant variants, because it presents the unwary user a bibliographical minefield: that undiscussed significant variant may be of the highest significance. P. E. Lewis, *The Beggar's Opera* (Edinburgh: Ol-

iver and Boyd, 1973), strives valiantly but does not succeed in discriminating among the differing states of the first editions and declines to introduce the music into his edition, saying (42) that "is a task for a musicologist." A critical edition of the *Opera*, with music, is a prime desideratum. Dr. Yvonne Noble has one in preparation.

35. There is no other apparent correlation with, say, day of the week, for the mysterious fluctuations in receipts. Common sense suggests that Rich was packing every possible body into every performance, and this is corroborated by the *Daily Journal*'s statement.

36. I accept the *London Stage* totals here, though they do not seem to add up correctly for the box and stage attendance when one divides the reported cash totals by the admission price. The fragile condition of the account book, which has so far made any kind of duplication impossible, inhibits detailed study.

37. Fuller, 1:46, following Irving, 254. See Appendix B.

38. The places of the Royal Family and entourage are all carried as "orders" in Rich's accounts, a puzzling category omitted from the *London Stage* calculations. Free seats?

39. Hume, *Henry Fielding*, 26-33.

40. Pope, *Correspondence*, 2:475.

41. Schultz, 368, cites the Book List for March in the *Monthly Chronicle*, which I have not seen, as authority for the publication date of 14 March. The play itself appears to be a reissue of the 1715 edition with new prelims and, of course, the appended anti-Walpole material.

42. Swift, *Irish Tracts, 1728–1733*, ed. Herbert Davis (Oxford: Basil Blackwell, 1955), 34.

43. Goldgar, 70.

44. *Letters*, 72.

45. Pope, *Correspondence*, 2:482.

46. *Second Thoughts Are Best* (1729), quoted in Paula Backscheider, *Daniel Defoe His Life* (Baltimore: Johns Hopkins Univ. Press, 1989), 518. It is interesting that Defoe associates Sheppard with Macheath, in view of Gay's ballad on Sheppard.

47. *The Lives of the Poets*, ed. G.B. Hill (Oxford: Clarendon, 1905), 2:278.

48. James Plumptre, "Life of John Gay," Cambridge University Library, Manuscript Add. 5829. Plumptre dates his summary comment September 19, 1821.

49. From Rich's account book, which sometimes names ticket holders.

50. *Letters*, 76.

51. Pope, *Correspondence*, 2:479.

8. THE *Opera* AS WORK OF ART

1. Dugaw, " 'Critical Instants': Theatre Songs in the Age of Dryden and Purcell," *Eighteenth-Century Studies* 23 (1989–90): 175.

2. See Curtis Price, "Music as Drama," in Hume, *London Theatre World*, 231-35.

3. Fuller, *Dramatic Works*, 45, who does not, however, point out that Gay could have seen these on his trips to Paris.

4. Price, n. 2 above, 225-30.

5. See Curtis A. Price, "The Critical Decade for English Musical Drama, 1700–1710," *Harvard Library Bulletin* 26 (1978): 38-76.

6. Lindgren, "*Camilla* and *The Beggar's Opera*," *Philological Quarterly* 59 (1980): 44-61.

7. Cibber, *Apology*, 76.

8. See Robert D. Hume, "The Sponsorship of Opera in London, 1704–1720," *Modern Philology* 85 (1988): 420-32.

9. Quoted in Deutsch, 299, and referred to in chapter 1 above.

10. Donald Grout, *A Short History of Opera*, 2nd ed. (New York: Columbia Univ. Press, 1965), 263.

11. Simpson, x.

12. Simpson, 69.

13. Ibid., n. 1.

14. Quoted from a Folger Library copy, shelfmark M 1738 D8 Cage, with the title page *Songs Compleat, Pleasant and Diverting*, 5 vols. (London: by W. Pearson for J. Tonson, 1719), 5:280. This was reissued the same year as *Wit and Mirth*. Cf. Cyrus L. Day, "*Pills to Purge Melancholy*," *Review of English Studies* 8 (1932): 177-84.

15. See *The Works of George Farquhar*, ed. Shirley Strum Kenny (Oxford: Clarendon, 1988), 2:28, 65-66.

16. *Works of George Farquhar*, ed. Kenny, 2:59. Italics in original.

17. Donaldson, *The World Upside-Down: Comedy from Jonson to Fielding* (Oxford: Clarendon, 1970), 172.

18. Noble, *Interpretations*, 14.

19. Lincoln B. Faller, *Turned to Account* (Cambridge: Cambridge Univ. Press, 1987), 179.

20. See Battestin, *Henry Fielding*, 280-82.

21. Rogers, *Eighteenth-Century Encounters* (Brighton, Sussex: Harvester, and New York: Barnes and Noble, 1985), 100.

22. See [Francis Grose and others], *Lexicon Balatronicum. A Dictionary of Buckish Slang, University Wit, and Pickpocket Eloquence* (London: for C. Chappel, 1811, repr. Northfield, Ill., 1971).

23. Bertrand H.Bronson, "The Beggar's Opera," in *Facets of the Enlightenment* (Berkeley: Univ. of California Press, 1968), 69.

24. Bronson, 74-75.

25. Schultz, 126, gave this preposterous legend new life, drawing on William Cooke's *Memoirs of Charles Macklin*, published in 1804 and notoriously unreliable. Fuller, 1:45, has most unfortunately accepted it. The decision to use accompaniment was supposedly taken at the next-to-last rehearsal. We are to assume, then, that the overture was composed and all the music scored and rehearsed in two days' time? In Hollywood during the 1930s, perhaps, but not in 1728 London. This is another one of those bits of gossip about the *Opera*, this one transparently false, that need to be put to rest.

26. Fiske, 63: "There was always a 'chorus' of principals at the end, and perhaps one or two duets and ensembles, but arias predominated overwhelmingly over other musical forms" [in the *opera seria*]. Gay appears to be working consciously to expand the range of musical possibilities available to opera: he certainly was doing so in his two later ballad operas, as will be seen. This is a matter for careful musicological investigation.

27. Bronson, 70-71.

28. Quoted in Schultz, 340. Peter Tasch has pointed out that the sequence also has a dramatic analogue in Thomas Shadwell's popular *The Libertine*, which presents the title character confronted by six "wives." See "*The Beggar's Opera* and *The Libertine*," *Notes and Queries* 36 (Mar. 1989): 52.

29. Bronson, 77.

30. Criticism that treats *The Beggar's Opera* purely as a work of literature seems reductive to me, focusing as it generally does on some aspect of the *Opera* as "satire," satire of the Walpole government, satire of Italian opera, satire of men or women or dogs, and so on. *The Beggar's Opera* is one of the great documents in the history of literary satire, true enough, but its satiric power lies in the opera's combination of literary, musical, and dramaturgical effects.

A critic whose stature demands recognition, however, has written a literary analysis that some have felt defines the *Opera*'s nature sufficiently well. I refer to William Empson's discussion in *Some Versions of Pastoral* (New York: New Directions, 1950), which John Fuller (I, 52) calls "the best criticism the play has had." Although displaying in attractive detail what Empson does best, close reading and imaginative literary association—intertextuality is the jargon word—the chapter seems to me, again, finally reductive in its equation of Macheath with Walpole. As I have attempted to show, there are of course satiric thrusts aimed in Walpole's direction, but the *Opera* is not principally, or even importantly, a satire directed at Walpole *as* Walpole, the historic figure. This was a creation of the

Opposition writers, well after the fact, with the compliance, one supposes, of Gay himself.

31. Noble, *Interpretations,* 12.

9. *Polly* and the Censors

1. *Memoirs,* 54-55. Another volume of the *Miscellanies* appeared in 1732.

2. For details, see David L. Vander Meulen, *Pope's Dunciad of 1728: A History and Facsimile* (Charlottesville: Univ. Press of Virginia, 1991), 16-23.

3. Letter to John Dennis, in *The Critical Works of John Dennis,* ed. Edward N. Hooker (Baltimore: Johns Hopkins Press, 1939–43), II, 373.

4. Goldgar, 75.

5. Pope, *Correspondence,* 2:505.

6. See his Preface: "the very copy I delivered to Mr. *Rich* was written in my own hand some months before at the Bath" (*Dramatic Works,* 2:69, italics reversed). For the Duchess's contributions, see L. W. Conolly, "Anna Margaretta Larpent, the Duchess of Queensberry and Gay's *Polly* in 1777," *Philological Quarterly* 51 (1972): 955-57.

7. See Judith Milhous and Robert D. Hume, "The London Theatre Cartel of the 1720s: British Library Additional Charters 9306 and 9308," *Theatre Survey* 26 (1985): 21-37.

8. *Henry Fielding,* 15-16.

9. For important corrections to *London Stage,* see William J. Burling and Robert D. Hume, "Theatrical Companies at the Little Haymarket, 1720–1737," *Essays in Theatre* 4 (1986): 98-118.

10. *Henry Fielding,* 37-39.

11. London: Printed for the Author, 1729. Italics reversed in original.

12. The murky legal basis of the theatres' regulation before 1737 is set forth by Judith Milhous in "Company Management," *London Theatre World,* 2-6.

13. See above, ch. 5.

14. *Letters,* 78.

15. See my essay "John Gay: Censoring the Censors," in *Writing and Censorship,* ed. Paul Hyland and Neil Sammells (London: Routledge, forthcoming).

16. John, Lord Hervey, *Some Materials Towards Memoirs of the Reign of King George II,* ed. Romney Sedgwick (London: Eyre and Spottiswoode, 1931), 98.

17. P. 83.

18. The relationship of Bowyer and Wright in the enterprise was my conjecture, agreeably confirmed by the appearance of *The Bowyer Ledgers*. The precise circumstances are complex: I plan to set forth the information at greater length in an article, which will supplement the standard work: James Sutherland, " 'Polly' Among the Pirates," *Modern Language Review* 37 (1942): 291-303. See also James McLaverty, *Pope's Printer, John Wright*, Oxford Bibliographical Society, Occasional Publications No. 11 (Oxford: Oxf. Bib. Soc., 1976).

19. *Letters*, 80.

20. Hervey (n. 16 above), 99.

21. Letter quoted in C. F. Burgess, "John Gay and *Polly* and a Letter to the King," *Philological Quarterly* 47 (1968): 596-98. Burgess makes the plausible suggestion that Gay may have assisted the Duchess in composing the letter.

22. See the letters from his agents, Alex Bourne and Thomas Goldie, counseling extreme economy in household matters, in papers of Duke of Buccleuch, Drumlanrig Castle, Queensberry Papers, Vol. 125.

23. Sutherland (n. 18 above), 293. Presumably James Roberts, the publisher, also sold it because he registered Gay's copyright at the Stationers Company: see David Foxon and James McLaverty, *Pope and the Early Eighteenth-Century Book Trade* (Oxford: Clarendon, 1991), 242.

24. Sutherland, 291.

25. Cibber, *Apology*, 136.

26. Pope, *Correspondence*, 3:43.

27. Goldgar, 81-83.

28. P. 82.

29. The only study of the music, which is nothing but a start in that direction, is A. E. H. Swaen, "The Airs and Tunes of John Gay's *Polly*," *Anglia* 60 (1936): 403-22. Fuller did no original research on the music in his edition; everything he has is derived from Swaen. Fiske, 110–11, discusses *Polly* briefly.

30. "The Images of Nations in Eighteenth-Century Satire," *Eighteenth-Century Studies* 22 (1989): 489-511.

31. "*Polly* and the Choice of Virtue," *Bulletin of the New York Public Library* 77 (1974): 383-406.

32. *Warrior Women and Popular Balladry 1650–1850* (Cambridge: Cambridge Univ. Press, 1989), 196.

33. Pope, *Correspondence*, 2:475; quoted above.

34. Fiske, 111.

35. Anna Margaretta Larpent quoted in L. W. Conolly, "Anna Margaretta Larpent, the Duchess of Queensberry and Gay's *Polly* in 1777," *Philological Quarterly* 51 (1972): 955-57.

10. Last Plays

1. *Letters*, 79.
2. "Kate and Susan, A Pastoral to the Memory of John Gay, Esqr.," in *The Works of Allan Ramsay*, ed. Alexander M. Kinghorn and Alexander Law, 7 vols. (Edinburgh: Blackwood, 1945–1974), 3:226.
3. Hume, *Henry Fielding*, 35-52.
4. *Letters*, 86.
5. Pope, *Correspondence*, 3:72.
6. *Dramatic Works*, 2:70.
7. Receipts, here and elsewhere, are rounded off to the pound. Fuller is of course mistaken when he writes that Gay received fifty-six pounds sixpence (*Dramatic Works*, 57): this is the gross *before* house charges.
8. Nichols, *Literary Anecdotes*, 8:296 (Lintot ledgers).
9. See Shirley Strum Kenny, "The Publication of Plays," in *London Theatre World*, 3ll: "at times [dedications] were considerably more profitable than the selling of copyright to a publisher."
10. *Letters*, 88.
11. *A Century of English Farce*, 90.
12. Hume, *Fielding*, 63-68.
13. Hume, 46-48.
14. Cited in Fuller, *Dramatic Works*, 2:394. I have not seen this edition.
15. *Dramatic Works*, 1:68-70.
16. *The Correspondence of Richard Steele*, ed. Rae Blanchard (Oxford: Clarendon, 1941), 185.
17. Swift, *A Tale of a Tub With Other Early Works*, ed. Herbert Davis (Oxford: Basil Blackwell, 1957), 242.
18. Goldgar, 78-79.
19. See my essay, "Dramatic Censorship," in *London Theatre World*, 300-305; and Vincent J. Liesenfeld, *The Licensing Act of 1737* (Madison: Univ. of Wisconsin Press, 1984), passim.
20. *Poetry and Prose*, 631-32; Goldgar, 165-66.
21. *Letters*, 122.
22. See Hume's discussion of the problems in *Henry Fielding*, 103-4.
23. Fiske, 112.
24. Fiske, 104, 111 (Ramsay).
25. *Letters*, 132.
26. Pope, *Correspondence*, 3:337.
27. Leo Hughes and Arthur H. Scouten, "John Rich and the Holiday Seasons of 1732–3," *Review of English Studies* 21 (1945): 45-56.

28. Hume, *Fielding*, 144-46, and Hughes and Scouten (n. 27), 46.

29. *New Light on Pope* (London: Methuen, 1949), 215-21.

30. *Dramatic Works*, 2:[222], original in italic font.

31. F. W. Bateson makes this point in *English Comic Drama 1700–1750* (Oxford: Clarendon, 1929), 98: Gay treats the Greeks "as if they had been his own contemporaries."

32. " 'A Misfortune Not to be Remedied': The Rhetoric of Sexual Politics in Gay's *Polly* and *Achilles*," paper presented at the annual meeting of the East Central/American Society for Eighteenth-Century Studies, Oct. 1991.

33. Fiske, 113-14.

34. Fiske, 118.

35. See Nancy A. Mace, "Falstaff, Quin, and the Popularity of *The Merry Wives of Windsor* in the Eighteenth Century," *Theatre Survey* 31 (1990): 55-66.

36. Maynard Mack relates the circumstances in *Alexander Pope: A Life* (New York: Norton, 1985), 676-80.

37. Hume, *Henry Fielding*, 93-96; and John Loftis, *The Politics of Drama in Augustan England* (Oxford: Clarendon, 1963), 105.

38. The Bell edition presents omissions within quotation marks and additions in italics: *Achilles. As written by John Gay* (London: for John Bell and C. Etherington at York, 1777).

39. Fiske, 113.

40. "Sex and Gender in Gay's *Achilles*," in *John Gay and the Scriblerians*, ed. Nigel Wood and Peter Lewis (London: Vision Press, 1988), 207-8.

41. "The Tragic Muse in Enlightened England," in *Greene Centennial Studies: Essays Presented to Donald Greene in the Centennial Year of the University of Southern California*, ed. Paul J. Korshin and Robert R. Allen (Charlottesville: Univ. Press of Virginia, 1984), 141-42.

42. The circumstances of publication of *The Distress'd Wife* are complex and have never been properly elucidated. The publisher, surely an odd choice, was Thomas Astley, who had been involved in the piracy of *Polly*. Michael Harris has included him in what he calls "the alternative book trade." See his "Paper pirates: the alternative book trade in mid-18th Century London," in *Fakes and Frauds: Varieties of Deception in Print and Manuscript*, ed. Robin Myers and Michael Harris (Winchester, [Hampshire]: St. Paul's Bibliographies, 1989), 47-69.

43. See Hume, *Fielding*, 109: "comedy was not flourishing."

44. Winton, "The Tragic Muse," (n. 41), 127-28.

45. Hume, 124-25.

46. Traditionally ascribed to Charles Bodens or Boadens, this play has recently been shown to be by Miller: see my article, "Benjamin Victor, James Miller, and the Authorship of *The Modish Couple,*" *Philological Quarterly* 64 (1985): 121-30.

47. *Comedy and Society from Congreve to Fielding* (Stanford: Stanford Univ. Press, 1959), 122: "the dramatic treatment of the rich merchant, is, in the comedies produced after 1728, nearly always sympathetic."

48. *Epistle to a Lady,* line 216.

49. Erskine-Hill, "The Significance of Gay's Drama," in *English Drama: Forms and Development,* ed. Marie Axton and Raymond Williams (Cambridge: Cambridge Univ. Press, 1977), 142.

Appendix A

1. Maitland, *The History and Survey of London From its Foundation to the Present Time,* 3rd. ed. (London: for T. Osborne, 1760), 1:510.

2. *Journal to Stella,* ed. Williams, 2:511, entry for 12 March.

3. See Linda Merians, *The Courtier's Maze: Matthew Prior and the Business of Poetry* (forthcoming). I am indebted to Professor Merians for allowing me to read this book in manuscript.

4. H. Bunker Wright and Monroe K. Spears, eds., *The Literary Works of Matthew Prior,* 2nd. ed. (Oxford: Clarendon, 1971), 1:506.

5. Edward Gregg, *Queen Anne* (London: Routledge and Kegan Paul, 1980), 354.

Index